*Canadian praise for*
## SILENT CRUISE

"There can be little doubt that Taylor is one of Canada's best short-story writers. He shows us the world completely absorbed and possessed by the human mind."

—*Quill & Quire* (starred review)

"Taylor's stories are intelligent and immensely readable—no, enthralling—[and] some are about as perfectly gemlike as they come. . . . Almost every one is a marvel of conception and construction. Ingenious, is what they are."

—*The Globe and Mail*

"Gripping . . . Brilliant . . . Taylor is in an entirely different class of writers than many of his contemporaries . . . His skills are so outsized, the unfolding of his fiction so seemingly effortless, [his creations so] smart, generous."

—*The Toronto Star*

"Fans of Taylor's previous book, *Stanley Park*, will expect the intelligence and rich polish on display in *Silent Cruise*. . . . The collection ends with a novella . . . a work of baroque elegance and inventiveness . . . [that] encapsulates the many occupations and preoccupations—food, art, technology, and the glories of a great con—that make Timothy Taylor a writer to seek and savor."

—*The National Post* (Toronto)

"Taylor is never happy repeating himself, and these stories range from Vancouver to Rome to Edmonton to Chicago, from cheese farms to art galleries to race tracks, without a hesitation or a fumble. . . . Few writers demonstrate the density, intellectual range and originality that Timothy Taylor does. This is a dazzling collection."

—*The Ottawa Citizen*

# SILENT

A NOVELLA AND STORIES

TIMOTHY TAYLOR

# CRUISE

COUNTERPOINT
BERKELEY

*For Jane and for my brothers and sisters,*
*Felicia, Dylan, Conan and Shelagh*

First U.S. edition published in 2002 by Counterpoint

Originally published in 2002 by Vintage Canada,
a division of Random House Canada Limited, Toronto

Library of Congress Cataloging-in-Publication Data

Taylor, Timothy L., 1963–
Silent Cruise: a novella and stories / Timothy Taylor.
p. cm
Contents: Doves of Townsend — Francisco's watch — Smoke's fortune
— Pope's Own — Prayers to Buxtehude — The resurrection plant — The
Boar's Head Easter — Silent Cruise — NewStart 2.0™.
ISBN 1-58243-216-3
1.Canada — Social life and customs — Fiction.  I. Title: Silent Cruise:
a novella and stories. II. Title.

PR9199.4.T39 S45 2002
813'.6—dc21                            2002022796

Printed in the United States of America

Counterpoint
2560 Ninth Street, Suite 318
Berkeley, CA 94710

ISBN: 978-1-58243-216-8

# CONTENTS

Doves of Townsend     1

Francisco's Watch     37

Smoke's Fortune     69

Pope's Own     83

Prayers to Buxtehude     115

The Resurrection Plant     149

The Boar's Head Easter     171

Silent Cruise     215

NewStart 2.0™     251

*Acknowledgments*     *403*

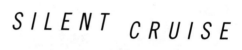

*SILENT CRUISE*

# DOVES OF TOWNSEND

"Doves of Townsend, good morning."

This is me, answering the phone at the shop. After which I frequently end up explaining the inherited family name. Sometimes (I admit), tired of telling the real story, I'll make something up. "There's a flock of doves found in Townsend, my dad's hometown," I'll start. Then I finish the story by saying the birds hunt as a pack and kill cats, or that they bring good luck if you catch one and pull out a tail feather. The mood of the story rides up and down on the sine wave of my menstrual cycle.

The truth is plain. My father came from Townsend and he was a fanatical collector. Knives, as it happens, but it could have been anything. Magpie, hoarder, pack rat, whatever you want to call him, I had long understood him to be obsessive-compulsive within certain categories. His suicide note read, *I fear I have covered the full length of this blade*. But at auctions, where he lived the happy parts of his life, he held up his wooden paddle and said his last name so the auctioneer would know who was bidding. "Dove," he'd say, eyes never leaving whatever dagger, cleaver, oiseau or machete had captivated him. And then—in case there was another Dove in the room—he'd say it again, louder: "Doves of Townsend."

So, here I am: "Doves of Townsend?"

It was two months ago, Alexander Galbraithe calling. He wanted a set of chrome 1940s ashtrays, the ones with the DC-3 doing the fly-past over the cigar butts. I've known Mr. Galbraithe since I was a child. When my father started Doves of Townsend as an extension of his own collecting (a very bad idea, I came to think), Mr. Galbraithe was one of his first steady buyers. I assume he stayed with me out of allegiance or sympathy, since after Dad's death I sold off the knife collection quickly and resolved never to replace it.

"Clare?" he said. "Are you familiar with the aeroplane ones?"

I knew he was talking about the famous deco ashtray since none of the other things he collects—coach clocks, cigar cutters, Iranian block-print textiles, even knives as far as I know—come in an airplane model.

"Pedestal or tabletop?" I asked him. "Illuminated?"

We began to work out the specs.

"Real?" I asked, breathing a little into the phone. "Or fake?"

Mr. Galbraithe didn't laugh often, although he found many things funny. What he did, instead, was roll his massive balding head back an inch or two, squint slightly and crinkle his cheeks. When he was done, he'd roll his head back to its normal position and resume where he left off.

This is what he did now. I could tell over the phone. And when he had returned he said, "Clare. My dear. Really."

IT PAYS TO BE STRAIGHT on this real-fake question. There's no point looking for something real, something authentic and old and possibly rare, if the client has no preference. My former-sometimes-boyfriend Tiko used to send art directors my way from time to time, and all they cared about was that an object look good on camera. Some collectors, on the other hand, collect fakes. So go figure.

What's bad, clearly, is to get fake when you're after real. Most dealers will learn this the hard way even if they resist being obsessive collectors themselves. Me, for example. I was just starting out. Dad had been gone a year, and I overcame all the good sense I had and bought a set of Les Frères locking steak knives. I literally saw them in a shop window, stopped on the sidewalk—reconsidering everything I had resolved after my father slipped somewhere beyond reach, after he did what he did—then went in and bought them. Of course, I knew the famous French maker produced knives that were rare and beautiful, knives with a four-inch hand-forged blade folding into black pearwood handle with silver inlay and locking in place with a tiny gold clasp in the shape of a dove. I knew the Les Frères dove had meant something special to my father, among all his knives. These were the first I had seen since his death and, for that instant, I was host to a perfectly synchronous collector's impulse.

What this lapse taught me was never to buy a thing merely because it is rare and beautiful and you are able to construe some tangled family significance. What I didn't know then was the number of counterfeit Les Frères steak knives that had been made over the years by Spanish, Korean and other manufacturers. When I learned this, which was soon enough, I sold my Taiwanese fakes for about one-twentieth what I paid for them. To Mr. Galbraithe, in fact, who rescued me. Tried to pay much more than they were worth, but I wouldn't let him.

"You see the clasp here, Clare?" he explained very kindly. "The reproduction clasps are stamped flat from stainless steel, then gold-plated. A real Les Frères has a hammered dove figurine, sculpted in three dimensions, in 18-carat gold."

"Fake," I said, shaking my head. "I should have known."

"But now you have seen it," he said, putting a large hand weightlessly on my shoulder. "I am quite sure you won't miss it again."

He was a huge presence, six and a half feet tall; God knows how many pounds. In his other hand, the knife looked like an antique folding toothpick I'd once seen at auction. Mr. Galbraithe always leaned a little forward when we spoke, canted just so, careful to hear and understand everything that I said. He wore dark, heavy double-breasted suits and two-tone black-and-white shoes. Tiko met him once and referred to him thereafter as Sydney Greenstreet, although he looked nothing like that. He brought to mind the force of gravity, yes, but not the crushing pressure of it. Instead, he made me think of the way some large things elegantly defy it. I've looked at suspension bridges the way I looked at Mr. Galbraithe.

He folded the fake Les Frères into his palm, first popping the gold-plated clasp with his thumb, then clicking shut the blade with his fingers. Then he wrote me a cheque using a large black fountain pen. In the nineteenth century, I thought on occasion, with my father gone and no family remaining, I would have married the widowed Mr. Galbraithe, friend of my father and lifelong presence. The thirty-year age difference would have seemed, I think, to be much less.

"You have an eye for the fine line," Mr. Galbraithe said to me another time, admiring a more successful purchase. I thought the words left unsaid were something like, *But be careful, so did your father.*

HE WANTED THE ASHTRAYS for his office, he explained.

"Of course," I said. He'd been a pilot at one time. During the war, the Second I suppose. He kept a suite of offices out near the airport, and when we talked on the phone I could hear the jets taking off and landing.

I began a fairly typical search: local, then national dealers. Then American. Surprisingly, I turned up only a few singles, none in fine condition and none illuminated. I searched the Internet and found a few more, but I couldn't tell what condition they were in and I didn't know the dealer.

I phoned Mr. Galbraithe back.

"Where are they?" he asked.

I told him it was Los Angeles. It wouldn't have been the first time he'd sent me off to inspect something. He flew me to Boston once to look over a case lot of clocks. He expressed deep trust in my judgement and reacted with gratitude, but not much surprise, when I produced exactly what he was looking for, time after time.

This didn't seem worth it, frankly. "Let's leave it for a while," I said. "Something will turn up."

He asked about local dealers, and I told him I'd long exhausted those options.

"Yes, yes. Of course you have . . ." A jet was coming in for a landing just then. "What about the flea markets and what have you?"

It was an unusual suggestion, from him. Everything in the entire flea market might be worth as much as one of his coach clocks on a good Saturday. It was, in my view (which I kept to myself), a vast sea of junk.

I phoned Tiko on Saturday, got him in bed. He said, "Baby . . . what time is it?"

I told him, and then described my plans for the day. "Chances of success are very slim, but it might be fun."

"What's Greenstreet want in a flea market?" he said, yawning and stretching. I could hear the sheets sliding over him, slipping off his chest, down his stomach. But when I asked him again, he said only, "I can't, I'm going skiing."

Work is work. I went down without him.

The flea market was held every weekend in a massive wooden warehouse in the industrial part of the city near the railway tracks. It's the kind of neighbourhood where the streets collude to form gigantic shallow ponds during the rainy season, and where an unlikely number of shopping carts spend their final days.

I paid my sixty-five-cent cover charge, took a big breath and went into the main hall. I didn't go there often enough for its vastness and futility not to strike me again. Here there were hundreds of independent dealers set up at folding tables, which stretched in their rows far back into the gloom, the warehouse air smelling of boiled hot dogs and vinegar, body odour, cat litter. The aisles sluggish with people. The vendors pessimistic.

I let myself drift with the currents of this sea, eyes down as I passed the tables, trolling through cheap, newish merchandise that would be of no interest to any collector now or in the foreseeable future. Acres of airport novels, CDs suspiciously unboxed, video games, socket wrench sets, Ren and Stimpy T-shirts and boxes of paper clips or batteries or ballpoint pens that presumably fell off the back of a truck somewhere. And scattered among these tables the personal collections, which for their madness and desperation held an increment more promise of delivering the unexpected. These were the tables heaped with costume jewellery, constellations of twinkling, unwearable rhinestone earrings, pendants, tiaras. Tables with shallow glass cases stuffed full of coins, or stamps, military medals, old wristwatches, brazenly ugly cuff links and spent cigarette lighters. Tables stacked dangerously high, any item on top of any other, a collection of large-format Japanese glamour magazines balancing on a pyramid of teak salad bowls, fondue sets and a condiment tray in the shape of a dachshund. A glass fishing float, purple. A collection of faded teacups, none Royal Doulton, most chipped, none worth any more than the fifty cents marked on masking tape and stuck to each handle.

I imagined Mr. Galbraithe here, however unlikely that was. He would hover at each table, just briefly, I thought. He would ask questions with respect, his eye scanning, sorting and cataloguing in an instant the incomprehensible rubble pulled together by these other collectors.

I was getting on towards the back of the warehouse by this point, having seen nothing of real interest. Here the black creosote-soaked timbers rose to a distant roof, netted under with sheets of small mesh to keep the pigeons from roosting there. It had only worked to keep them in, judging from the six or seven mummified birds lying suspended in the net. But it made me think of one of the Doves of Townsend stories I used to tell, the one about the doves living in the rafters of the Townsend railway station. And that thought brought me back to where I was, what I was supposed to be doing. I closed my mouth and looked down.

I was standing near a group of tables, a personal collection although no person was apparent. The mounds of junk on some of the tables had been covered over in orange tarps. A sign read "The Shickey Shack," scrawled in crayon on a piece of two-by-four nailed to an upright. There were stacks of magazines—years' worth of something called *American Rifleman*—which I leafed through, not curious about the content but about the person who would buy such a collection. Who might collect it in the first place.

There were other books, adhering to a military theme. Many dozen drinking glasses, no two the same. A large quartz polar bear with zirconium eyes, and a stack of room-service silverware from the Hotel Vancouver. I picked some of these up, wondering if the dull clang of the worn plate cover against the warped plate would call forward someone from behind one of these piles.

Under the plate cover, in the middle of the service platter, there was a butterfly.

It startled me enough that I took a step back from the table before I realized that it was dead, entombed in a clear plastic silver-dollar-sized coin case. I put the plate cover aside and picked up the butterfly, forced to smile.

It was fixed neatly to a square of Styrofoam cut to fit the box. The front wings were burnt orange, darkening to coffee-brown at the tips. The back wings were white, covered with a lacy grey pattern, impossibly complex. The two brittle antennae curled away to tiny club-like tips. It was an exquisite thing, quivering on its pin as I rolled the box in my fingers.

Looking around the table with renewed interest, I saw there were several more. A few were strewn among the hotel silverware, others dropped carelessly through the boxes of magazines and among the books. I pulled together a small pile of cases, a dozen or fifteen specimens, each one different. And before I even looked at them closely I began to sift through the junk on the rest of the table. In a beer mug marked "Oktoberfest 1988" I found another six. There was an old naval officer's cap sitting upside down at the very back of the table. I leaned as far as I could, got it by the brim and felt immediately that it was heavy with many more.

Large and small. Of more colours than I knew. None of the boxes labelled, although the names wouldn't have meant much to me. A tiny one with rounded dark khaki wings. One with notched brown wings and a pronounced nose. Another lacy pattern, this one brown and orange, fading to light brown on white like a melting snowbank.

A large, regal yellow one with black trailing pieces like counterweights on each wing. And a dull grey moth-like creature, which up close was not grey at all but a shimmering, luminescent blue. I stacked and restacked the boxes in small piles as I browsed, at first by size but then by wing shape and colour, arranging the boxes in a spectrum from the blacks and dark browns to the palest gold and shining white.

There was still nobody around, nobody to answer the questions that were forming. Where from? Significance of? Even, how much? It didn't occur to me then that I had no buyer in mind for these. That I had no personal need for what appeared to be dozens of dead butterflies that were probably worth nothing in the first place. Still, I had become curious and interested, imagining that if I didn't buy them somebody else might, if only for the delicate, colourful improbability of their being there.

"Very strange," I said aloud, shaking my head and picking up a case that held a black butterfly with blood-red stains in the centre of each forward wing.

At which point a small, rusty voice from nowhere said, "The purpose of butterflies will not be found . . ."

I was startled a second time. In fact I think I yelped.

The voice started again: "The purpose of butterflies will not be found . . . in the few flowers they may inadvertently pollinate." And then the man got up from where he had been sitting on a milk crate, and stepped out from behind one of the tables tented in orange tarp.

"I'm sorry?" I said, hand on my throat.

He stood looking down at his own merchandise without curiosity. "From a book," he said. "A butterfly book. William Howe."

"Oh, yes?" I said.

"Nor in the numbers of parasitic wasps they may support," he carried on, his voice building up to an insistent scrape. "And to peer beneath a microscope at their dissected fragments will in no way elucidate the reason for their being."

He stopped and thought.

"Where are they from?" I asked, but he didn't hear me. He had grizzled sideburns that tapered to points and wore a chocolate-milk-coloured thigh-length leather jacket, green gabardine flood pants with two-inch cuffs. His blue wool socks collapsed casually to the top of the arch of his chisel-toed black loafers. If it weren't for the missing front teeth and his age, I thought, he could have stepped from a Prada ad. Past hip though, not knowingly funky. Just poor.

He was reciting the last line again, to himself. *". . . their dissected fragments will in no way elucidate the reason for their being . . ."* Then his voice rose to full volume again as he remembered the remaining lines. "Their purpose is their beauty and the beauty they bring into the lives of those of us who have paused long enough from the cares of the world to listen to their fascinating story."

He nodded once, satisfied with his recitation, then returned behind the table and produced a heavy, crumbling encyclopaedia of a book. "*Our Butterflies and Moths.* William H. Howe."

It crossed my mind that the book was probably worth something. It was full of colour plates that could be removed and sold individually. I took the book in my hands, ignoring the fact that I didn't deal prints, that I didn't know them or their buyers particularly well.

"Twenty dollars," the man said, looking away, across the warehouse. Adhering to flea market convention by communicating a dry certainty that I would not buy.

"It's beautiful," I said, my hand drifting across the brocade pattern on the binding. And then I heard myself ask, "And the collection?"

"This is a tiger swallowtail," he said, not answering, but picking up the large yellow butterfly with black tails on its wings. I took it from him and admired it. "And this," he said, tapping another box on the table. "Ringlet. Here's a pearly eye. Pine white here. This guy's a little wood satyr."

"A what?" I asked, incredulous. He repeated himself, handing me a case holding a tiny butterfly, less than an inch across, with dark green-brown wings, spots like eyes, each rimmed in ghostly white.

"You like them?" he asked. "There's a collector's log here too . . ." And reaching again into a box behind the table, he took out a spiral-bound notebook, the precise journal kept by the original collector. On its pages, in achingly tidy rows and columns, had been recorded the capture data for each butterfly: date, place (latitude, longitude and altitude), time, prevailing weather, vegetation and topography of the habitat, full species name. And so I read that the butterfly known as the postman was to lepidopterists the *Heliconius melpomene* of the family Nymphalidae. And that the postman in this collection had been found in a tangle of brush at the edge of a tropical forest not far from the Orinoco River, some days' drive south of San Tomé in Venezuela. When netted, the notes went on, this particular postman had been feeding near passion vines.

I had never thought about butterflies before. Not the species, nor the thing that might be collected. Although for a few seconds I imagined them wall-mounted, a dozen in a frame. And the loose ones, this postman included, scattered in their little clear boxes across my desk for me to pick up and handle, to admire from time to time while working.

"Buck apiece," the man said, jarring me from my thoughts. "There's sixty-two of them. Seventy bucks and I'll throw in the book, the collector's log and this too."

He brought out the killing jar and held it up for me to admire. But I was already coming out of it. The price had startled me awake, having the reverse effect of the hydro-cyanic acid gas that (the man was explaining to me) emanated from the plaster of Paris at the bottom of the killing jar and put a butterfly painlessly, permanently to sleep. In an instant, by being so affordable, so not-exorbitant, the seventy-dollar price tag reminded me that this was exactly the kind of thing you can spend an unhappy lifetime picking up at auctions and flea markets, dollar by dollar, day by day, without purpose or analysis, until you need a bigger warehouse, a bigger line of credit. Until you wake up one morning—as this butterfly collector undoubtedly had—riding alone across the vast and lonely landscape to which you have been driven, the only place wide enough, unpeopled enough, to accommodate the obsession you have allowed to spread tangled within you.

"They're very pretty," I said, clearing my throat.

"Not what you're looking for though," he said, shaking his head, just short of disgust.

"No," I said, although it wasn't clear even to me whether I was disagreeing or agreeing with him.

"Didn't think so," he said. "A gift maybe?" And he hoisted the quartz polar bear with effort. It appeared to weigh twenty or thirty pounds.

I remembered then what I had come looking for, and blurted it out in one ragged breath, as if eager to convince him that I did have a purpose. When I was finished, he laughed out loud.

"Airplane ashtrays?" he said, the immensity of the world's foolishness revealed to him in full. "Those shiny things like from the movies?

"I suppose," I said.

"Little whirly bits and lights?"

"Yes," I said, weakly.

Nineteen-forties chrome-and-slag-glass DC-3 pedestal ashtrays. He pulled back the orange tarp on one of the covered tables and there they were. Filthy, but they cleaned up well. Back at the shop a week later, after I'd had the wiring fixed, the propellers turned and all the little windows on the airplanes lit up. One in this condition would have been rare. A matching set of four from something called the Long Island Flying Club was without question a very good find.

I delivered them to Alexander Galbraithe's office myself. I couldn't remember the last time I had been so excited about finding something exactly right. But there I was, heart beating lightly, quickly. I had the ashtrays on a flatbed mover's dolly, covered in a white sheet. He would know immediately what they were; he would react with his usual low-key appreciation, but he would know they were perfect.

His secretary let me into his office with an expectant smile. He came out from behind his broad mahogany desk, glided across the room-sized Tabriz to take my hand, gently raised it to his lips as he had so many times before, always somewhere between chivalry and self-deprecation.

"Clare. My dear."

I was grinning like an idiot. "Check this out," I said, as I sometimes do, becoming a teenager around him. I was pointing at the dolly, the sheet tented across the four objects underneath. His eyes went round. His eyebrows lifted high. When he pulled back the sheet, he actually drew in a breath, theatrically, and stared at them for several seconds, touching one lightly with his fingertips in disbelief. "Incredible," he said, finally. "Did you . . ." And here he spun very slowly on one foot to face me. "Did you go to Los Angeles?"

He knew I hadn't; it had been his suggestion I go to the flea market in the first place. And with this thought I registered Mr. Galbraithe's unusual surprise at my having performed just as I always did.

"No," I said. "I didn't."

"Well, where then, my dear girl?" He asked. Which was about when I decided he was faking it.

"Um . . ." I said, stumbling over my answer, because now not only was I transfixed by the thought that he had set the whole thing up, my mind was also sweeping across the history of his patronage. After my father's suicide he had never pressed, just stayed nearby. I knew where to find him, and I confess I looked from time to time. Not only to find for him his various objects of desire: I talked boys to him once. I told him a sad story, early-Tiko no doubt, before I had come to accept the limits of what that relationship was all about. Mr. Galbraithe had taken me out for a drink at the Wedgwood. I was talking between sips of a crantini. He was holding a gimlet judiciously between his index finger and his thumb, sitting forward in the wingback lounge chair that was too small for his full frame, listening, listening always. I think he said, "Well. Clare. It may be no reassurance . . . but let me say this. There are certain types of unkindness that will bleed out of a young man as he matures."

"The flea market," I said, finally answering his question. "I found them at the flea market, just as you suggested."

Sure enough, his face flattened with recognition. And his eyes did squint, and his cheeks did crinkle, and his bald head did roll back in silent recognition. But I wasn't seeing the humour in any of this.

I didn't say anything else. It felt impossible. I worried a range of things at once. Mutually assured embarrassment. That it was too late to unwind anything that had been done. That unwanted favours can't be graciously accepted or easily rejected. That I didn't know what I thought of the favour anyway. He defied gravity, Mr. Galbraithe did. He hovered without effort, a teacup in his hand now. He listened as I mechanically told of the flea market. He laughed silently at my description of the place, its strange topography and population, the very terrain over which he had walked himself to plant something in my path.

I charged him what I'd paid the Shickey Shack, claiming that I paid much less. He objected and used the opportunity to counsel me on profit margins until his secretary removed my teacup from my hand. I had my coat on again and was actually in the elevator, the doors sliding shut.

TIKO TOOK ME TO DINNER, a surprise. He was back from a shoot in Whistler that had taken much longer than expected and he took me to the Alibi Room. New, hip, sexy, full of film types.

I told him about the flea market, at least most of the story. I left out the butterflies, not sure why. But I told him about finding the ashtrays. I told him about the strange feeling I had that Mr. Galbraithe must have known they were there. Must have put them there for me to find.

Tiko didn't understand. I told the story three ways before he finally said, "You mean he goes to the flea market, gives the guy these ashtrays, then sends you there to find them?"

From a nearby table a woman's indignant words wafted over: *If he thinks I'm coming back from New York for a ten-minute short . . . well. . . .*

"It's an incredible coincidence," I said. "These things are hard to find. Impossible to find at a flea market."

"Why, though?" Tiko said, frowning.

"Because they're rare," I said.

"Not that." He was angry. "Why do it? Is it, like, a test?"

I hadn't really thought of that.

"Is he making fun of you? Having some kind of sport?"

I hadn't thought of that either.

"They're all total nutcases," Tiko said then, his nose wrinkling with distaste for my clientele. "Greenstreet's no different, just fatter."

Our peach consommé arrived just then, and Tiko ordered decaf espressos from a waiter who was almost embarrassingly eager to please. From the corner of my eye,

I could see the woman with the indignant voice looking in our direction.

Tiko looked somewhere beyond beautiful, as always. There were times I thought the only descriptor of his good looks was the word *ridiculous*. His eyes were brilliant green, his hair dark, thick, perfectly unkempt. His jawline descended like an executive order from his cheekbones.

He had work in Montreal, he told me. A perfume ad.

"Will you miss acting?" I asked him, when the espressos arrived.

"It's still acting," he said. "I wouldn't actually wear Yves Saint Laurent."

We kissed in the elevator going up to my place. I liked to touch his face, to trace it with my fingers. In the apartment, the blinds were up and the mercury glow from the street lights was awash over everything. He undressed me in the living room, led me by the hand to the bedroom, pushed me down onto the bed before taking his own clothes off. He stood over me, stripped off his jacket, then his shirt, unbuckled his belt very slowly. It was borderline Chippendales, but still sexy. I would have liked him to sleep there, wake up with me. But the fact that he had to leave, had to catch a flight in the morning, the fact of his rough kiss, the wool of his sweater brushing my breasts and his scarf falling to the pillow beside my head . . . all this stayed somehow romantic.

He said, just before he left, "Lying there . . . you are so beautiful."

WEEKS PASSED. MR. GALBRAITHE LEFT a message, which he had never done before. He said, "Clare. I am very fond of them. Thank you again."

"Doves of Townsend?"

The caller identified himself as an art director.

"Tiko says . . .," the art director spoke like he was waiting to hear an echo, ". . . that no *matter* . . . how obscure the item . . . and no *matter* . . . how much craziness you have to wade through in its pursuit . . . you, Clare, always find the Object of Desire."

"When did you talk to Tiko?" I asked him.

"He told me about your airplane things," the art director said.

"Oh yes," I said, but I have to admit I was distracted, thinking about where Tiko was at the moment. Montreal? Or back in Whistler?

"You know, women . . ." The art director seemed to be holding the phone away from his head. "Women are *made* . . . to find *things*. I believe."

"What?" I said.

"Well, certainly you are." And here I imagined that the art director leaned back in his ergonomic chair and kicked his feet up on a glass desk mounted on the backs of two giant black ceramic elephants. Cracked the micro-blinds with the tips of his fingers to peer into the parking lot. "You see, in old times . . . very old times . . . Jurassic Park–type old times . . . women found the thing . . . and then men *killed* the thing. There was this . . . division of labour."

I agreed to go down and see him anyway. He had a film on the go, an unhappy director. They had a character, he explained. "He needs a little *je ne sais quoi.*"

And no, he didn't know where Tiko was.

The art director's office turned out to be brightly lit, swatches and tile samples lying around. I was right about the blinds and the chair, but the resting place for the art director's pink-bunny-slipper-clad feet was actually a massive ball-and-claw partner's desk.

"Come in," he called across the room. The art director had flowing black hair, a large, thin nose and contacts the colour of a Bombay Sapphire gin bottle. He brought to mind a bust of one of the bad Caesars. "Coffee?"

"Sure, thanks." I took in his room, then his slippers as they disappeared off the desk and reappeared on the parquet hardwood, padding across to the espresso machine in the kitchenette.

"Cappuccino, espresso, flavouring?"

"Black," I said.

"Americano, is it?" The art director answered, delighted with whatever this revealed, humming now as he burped out the espresso into old Wedgwood cups. A discontinued pattern. Kimono, I thought.

"So?" he said, handing me the cup. It was Kimono.

"So," I answered. "Tell me about this character."

He nodded, then lifted the coffee cup to his lips, pinky quivering erect. "All business," he observed, as if he found women a bit useless to work with normally. "Male. Thirties. A loser I'm afraid. Tight for money."

They needed something for his apartment, it seemed. Something that would make a subconscious comment on the character's head, his heart and history. "We tried boxing posters, to emphasize his physicality," the art director said. "But in the rushes it came out too Sean Penn."

"So who is the guy?" I asked. Part of me always became impatient with this type of client, although they paid well. "What does he do in the film?"

I should have known better. Scripts are state secrets and all the art director gave me was: "Travis Bickle in Kafka's *Metamorphosis*."

I wanted to laugh, but didn't.

No family, no interest in girls.

"*Metamorphosis*?" I asked.

"Yes," the art director explained. "Because he is one thing, then changes into another thing. A very dramatic, colourful change."

I was thinking of the stages, which I tried to remember while sipping my coffee. Egg, larva, pupa, adult. The last stage brief, a moment of beauty. The struggle to emerge followed by that instant of first flight.

"Say . . ." I said, as the idea fluttered into my head, bursting into the fullness of what it could be.

Perhaps the most appealing aspect of the idea was the way that something I had been tricked into finding could be used to lead me on towards my own discovery. That by resisting the collector's impulse, I had yet been rewarded.

I went to the flea market the following Saturday, first thing in the morning. I took an enthusiastic breath of the fragrant air inside the turnstile and jogged the length of the warehouse to the Shickey Shack. He didn't let on that he recognized me. But they were still there, the butterflies scattered once again without order across his tables. The naval officer's cap had been refilled. The black butterfly with the blood-red stains sat at the very edge of the table, and I picked this up first, failing to suppress a small smile of recognition.

"The postman," he said wearily.

"This is the postman?" I asked, remembering the name.

He cracked a look up at me. "There's sixty-two in total," he said.

I asked him how much, casually.

"Some people think they're worthless," the man said, scratching his head. "Buncha dead bugs, know what I mean? But to the right person, these are priceless."

We talked back and forth a bit, and I admit faking much greater knowledge of the collection than I had. I said it was on the small side, with a common assortment of specimens, although in pretty good shape. He saw right through me, apparently, and upped his quote to a hundred and fifty dollars for everything, the specimens, the William Howe book, the collector's log and the killing jar, which he pulled out and proceeded to explain all over again.

I held on to them for a week before phoning the art director. I left them scattered on my desk. I used the book and the log to figure out their names. Part of me also knew that this drove up the drama value of the delivery. I even wrapped them for maximum impact on opening. I kept the books and the killing jar—the art director wouldn't be interested in those—but loaded all the butterflies carefully into a small wooden crate, wrapped the box in heavy brown waxed paper, then tied it up with butcher's twine. It might have been shipped in from the Amazon Basin.

"Good God," the art director said, staring at the elaborate package. And when it was open, there was an instant when the small clear boxes spilled onto the table, and it seemed that the butterflies had escaped, that they had been released and would now fly away, each to its own home.

"Remarkable," the art director said. Shifting his pale blue, faintly distrusting gaze to me. "Quite remarkable."

When he asked how much, I suggested he make me an offer. I hadn't thought this strategy over and I had never used it before. But without thinking, I said, "These are worthless or priceless, depending on how you look at it. What are they worth to you?"

Spending somebody else's money, he was not struck that this was disingenuous.

"How about a thousand," he said finally.

I HADN'T HEARD FROM TIKO in almost three weeks, not the longest stretch by any degree, just a disappearance of striking similarity to many others. The kiss. The final words. "So beautiful." The sound of the door closing behind him.

I phoned his agent and learned only that he was "out east." I wasn't at a good place on the sine wave. "A lot of things are out east," I snapped, and hung up.

It made me think dismally of my father, I confess. There had come a day following his death—day 111, day 147, I don't remember—but a day different from every other day that he had been gone. It was the day I woke up not envisioning his absence as a separation, a distance that might be somehow closed through my efforts. Instead, that day I woke up knowing the space between my father and me to be measureless, just as the time that stretched ahead of me into the unwritten future.

I thought of this, and then of phoning Alexander Galbraithe. Something that hadn't occurred to me in several weeks and an impulse I quickly suppressed.

I went to the flea market that weekend, no reason, no objective. No Object of Desire for me to find or miss. I just rolled with the uneasy crowds. I bought the purple glass fishing float. Fifteen dollars bargained down to ten. Why negotiate? I couldn't say.

I walked by the Shickey Shack but didn't stop. The *American Riflemen* were still there, ditto the quartz polar bears. My man was nowhere to be seen, but I knew he was on his milk crate, head in his hands, socks collapsed around his tired ankles.

Past the Shickey Shack were the darkest corners of the warehouse, such undesirable real estate apparently that not all the tables were in use. Here is where the new worthless junk and the madly compiled personal junk gave way to the utterly unsellable junk. Headless golf clubs, TVs with cracked screens, torn couches, bent bicycles. These were the people selling anything they could lift and carry here, their own things. These were the people burning furniture to stay warm, selling organs, consuming themselves.

At a table against the very back wall I stood and inspected a computer with foreign characters on the keys, no English. A skinny man in a faded grey suit offered to demonstrate. He turned it on, typed in the password—the name of his father? I wondered, a favourite drink or food from home?—then flashed up the various programs, all written over with the same language. He finished the demo with a winning smile. I made a sympathetic face. We both shrugged.

I turned away from the table and left the flea market. Out past the pessimistic vendors, cutting through the sluggish crowds, under the dead hanging pigeons, through the turnstile and into a light afternoon rain. Driving unnecessarily fast across town, it occurred to me that the skinny man had only one potential flea-market buyer for his computer: himself. And he already owned one. There was a painful irony in his linkage to that thing from his home, his past, a painful emblematic power in his attempt to sever the connection.

I found myself stopped in front of a well-known antique dealer on Granville Street. Not a place I used often any more. The woman at the counter recognized me, but could not place me. When I gave her my card, she nodded immediately and said, "Yes, of course, Doves of Townsend. I knew your father."

She had more knives to choose from than I could bear to consider. And in all of these, she had one set of Les Frères.

They were in a square black wooden box, with a very worn blue satin lining. The knives themselves were immaculate, like something gifted with eternal youth, for-ever fresh as the mundane world aged around them. A set of two Les Frères steak knives, the black inlaid pearwood handle at once familiar. I picked one up, turning it over in my hands. Letting my fingers ride over the sculpted golden dove figurine. Three-dimensional, very real. It released smoothly under my thumb, the blade unsheathing, extend-ing, locking rigidly in place. Still very sharp, I noticed.

Sharp enough to cut flesh.

And then I was crying at the glass counter of an expensive antique store on Granville Street. Weeping. Inconsolable, although the woman did not try. She only stood at a distance, respectful of my grief. I suppose she didn't have to share it to sense that it came from memory. From a life already lived.

IT WAS MY IDEA TO GO to dinner. Thinking about it now I realize it's just possible he might never have called me again. Let it go finally, released to the future.

So I phoned him. A jet roared in the background.

There is a French bistro downtown, dark but comfortable, the food hearty in the Parisian style. Walls covered with photographs of famous people, some who had visited the restaurant. Others who could not have, but who one might imagine spending an evening here. Jack Johnson. Carl Sandburg.

I knew this to be one of his guilty pleasures. A quiet table at this bistro, a companion. *Steak frites* and a bottle of Burgundy.

I arrived first and took a seat in the corner I had reserved, at a small table covered with a thick white cloth. I sat with my back to the wall, under a photograph of Sigmund Freud, enjoying a clear view of the restaurant and the door.

When he came in, the maître d' bowed just slightly at the waist, and they exchanged a few words. Then he turned into the room, spotted me, and began his weightless navigation through the tables. The *Queen Mary* approaching the jetty, all double-breasted grace and size.

"Clare. My dear." His lips floated down to my hand. Then to my cheek. He smelled just faintly of soap. Of wool and oak.

I kept my surprise until the main course arrived, the filet a delicate island in a pool of dark demi-glaze. The pile of potato-straw *frites* a cloud at one corner of the plate. Seven pomegranate seeds and a spray of snow-pea pods providing balance.

The waiter produced steak knives, and when he had gone, Alex held up his glass and said, "Santé."

We touched glasses, sipped.

"Now wait," I said. And I pulled out the black box from the seat beside me and slid it across the table to him.

This time, his surprise was genuine and warranted. He untied the red ribbon I had tied around it, and when it was open he looked down at the knives for some time without touching them. "Oh my, oh my," he said. And when he did finally take one of the knives in his hand, he only held it, unopened, touching the clasp.

"Real," I said.

"Oh quite, yes," he said. And he looked at me with a small smile.

We walked afterwards. I held his arm, which meant reaching up just slightly. It was cold but clear now, and we walked from the restaurant all the way down to the water, then along the sea wall as far as English Bay. A boat churned past, heading to berth in False Creek. There was phosphorescence in the water. We talked only a little. Alex held the box of knives tightly under his other arm, as if they made him very proud.

At the beach houses we turned out onto the sand, and found a log to sit on. It was enormous. He helped me up onto it, then sat himself, his black-and-white shoes comfortably reaching the sand.

Neither of us said anything for some time.

"They're very beautiful, Clare. Thank you."

"You've been good to me," I said, not looking at him. "And I appreciate it."

"I am devoted to the Doves of Townsend," he answered. "For a long time, yes?"

"Doves," I said, holding up an imaginary bidding paddle and speaking with what had been my father's imperial cadence. "Doves of Townsend."

Alex smiled at the memory. "A name for which you once gave me a very colourful, if not entirely truthful explanation."

"Did I?" I asked, not remembering immediately.

"Oh yes," he said. "You told me that in Townsend there were doves that lived their entire lives in the rafters of the train station. When they died, you told me, they would fall onto the trains and be carted off throughout the countryside. The opposite of homing pigeons, I think you said."

"Gosh," I said. "Did I tell you that, really?"

"I think perhaps you were in a black mood that day," he said.

"Quite possible," I answered. "Although it could have been worse." And then I told him how I had remembered this story in the flea market, looking up at the pigeons that had been caught and suspended after death.

He cocked his head at me. "Where you found my Les Frères, perhaps?"

I let the corner of my mouth twitch into a small smirk. "I'm not that lucky," I said. "Not twice." But I told him where I had bought them, and how I got there after an unusual trip to the flea market. "Just wandering around without objective," I said. "Very unlike me."

31

His soft eyes were resting on my face, my hair. "That can't always be bad," he said. "Wandering without objective, that is."

It wasn't, and I admitted it.

"You know?" he said, exhaling a tiny breath of resolve. "I left you a gift there once."

"A gift?" I feigned surprise.

"Yes," he said, looking out at the sea. "I left you something there that I wanted you to find. Something I wanted you to find by accident."

I didn't say anything.

"Aren't you going to ask me what it was?" For all his immense weightlessness, I could feel him next to me now. I could feel his gaze on me, on my skin.

I turned on the log, shifting to face him. "What it was?" I said.

"I thought you might wonder."

I put a hand gently on his arm. "I didn't know when I first found them that they were a gift," I said. "But I figured it out once I got to your office."

He looked back at me curiously, processing this.

"The ashtrays," I said, squeezing his arm.

I wondered if I had embarrassed him by knowing about it, if I had spoiled the kindness he had shown. But he didn't say anything right away. He slipped his fingers into his jacket pocket for what I expected to be one of his cigars, and brought his hand out closed around something small.

"Ashtrays." He said the word as if he had just learned what it meant.

"I don't mind, Alex," I said. "Maybe I was a little angry at the time, but I'm not now."

"The aeroplane ashtrays," he said again. "I'm fond of them."

I nodded.

"They look very handsome in my office," he went on. "I receive compliments daily."

"I'm glad," I said.

"But I wouldn't give them as a gift," he said. And he shook his head slowly, thinking of how improbable this would be. "Not to you. Besides, would they really be a gift if you didn't keep them?"

I was still nodding for some reason but I wasn't certain.

Alexander Galbraithe opened his large hand. My eyes were drawn immediately to the middle of his palm.

It was a small clear plastic box. In it, I recognized the fragile stamp of colour. The blood-red spots on black wings, the tendril antennae with their clublike tips.

I took the single butterfly from him, staring down at the case, hearing the sound of their wings as they exploded from the box, released back to their grasslands, their forests, their mignonette, mustard or passion vine, each to its own corner of the world.

"Oh, no," I said.

HE'D HAD NO DOUBT I would find them. That once there I would search the place thoroughly, ask questions. "I was confident they would haunt even you." But he smiled as he said this.

One of the sixty-three, he kept. There had been two postmen in the collection. And with that one, pressed from his large palm down into my own, he considered the gift given. And I accepted it.

And yes, sometime later I did track down my art director and I did ask if I might buy the others back, but he couldn't find them. "What do you mean, can't find them?" I didn't get angry. I kept my cool.

They hadn't been sold, he was certain. They hadn't been thrown out that he recalled. He thought that the prop master might have returned them to the antique store where they had rented the furniture.

Did he remember the name of this store? Well . . . he could find out and get back to me.

"Surely you can find some more?" he said. "How's Tiko?"

"Probably not," I answered. "And I have no idea. Respectively."

Alex laughed silently when I told him. He said, "I don't mind that someone else will have discovered them, found them beautiful."

"They are beautiful," I said, still wishing, wishing. "I could have kept them so easily, they made me want them."

"Clare. Dearest," he said, his warm hand on the side of my face. "Of course they did. Their purpose is their beauty. It's what they're for."

I still have the books and the killing jar. The postman I keep on my desk as I imagined the others would have been kept. From time to time I imagine them out there, want them to return, and then I may spend a week or two looking in shops, asking around. No one has ever seen them, and I know that the more time passes the further away from me they will have flown.

I went into a shop once, idle, directionless, on a Saturday. I asked about my butterflies. Described them: a collection maybe, in small plastic cases? The proprietor considered this very carefully, then produced a stuffed toad and asked me if I wanted that instead.

It doesn't matter. The postman, where I am now, is very real. It sits there on the corner of my desk, and every day it tells me a fascinating story.

# FRANCISCO'S WATCH

In 1955, my father left St. Andrew-on-Hudson, the former Jesuit novitiate in Hyde Park, New York, to pursue a non-monastic life. At this pivotal moment, as he turned away from becoming a Brother just days before he would have pledged eternal vows of poverty, chastity and obedience, his mentor, Brother Francisco, gave him a watch as a blessing and a personal gift. Francisco was originally from Madrid, blind and stooped, and the watch suggested that he supported the difficult decision my father had made. It was a tacit statement of support but one that my father wore on his wrist as if it were a written endorsement.

My father told the story often.

"Nicholas." Brother Francisco came tap-tapping into Dad's room with his whited-out eyes on the perpetual horizon and a gaunt hand extended, something gleaming on his wrist. "Here, Nicky, help me off with this." He held my father's shoulder for support, reaching up to do so. Dad was a big man. Full name: Nicholas Lacroix. French angles and a handsome jawline. A monk that got the eye. A monk now poised do a range of unmonk-like things including a decade in New York painting and, some years later, an ill-fated K-2 siege climb during which he broke both wrists.

"A watch? Brother . . ." Pretty golden ring around a bulging crystal. Lizard strap. There were tiny red date numbers, from one to thirty-one, etched around the very perimeter just outside the hours.

"I know, I know." Brother Francisco was saying. "Put it on. It feels good doesn't it?"

It did. Hefty.

"Nineteen thirty-four Movado Triple Date. Do you know Movado? Founded roughly seventy-five years ago in the Jura Mountains of Switzerland at La Chaux-de-Fonds by Achille Ditesheim. Now, while we wait here and listen for the footsteps of time, you will watch minute by minute as each one approaches. You will see it come around the bend, watch each second sweep into sight and then run by and into the past. That will be something for you, Nicky."

"Well, well." Dad was still stunned. Staring at his wrist. "Look at this."

There was a kiss on both cheeks. Then the blessing. Brother Francisco leaned his cane against the bed and took my father's wrist in his hands, one palm covering the watch.

"Oh, Father," he said. "No man may know the hour, but Nicholas Lacroix will now, at least, know the hour."

Jesuit monk humour, I always thought, although my dad told the story straight.

I took it in to have it cleaned once, years later. I had just turned thirty-eight and I was painting in my studio on a Tuesday afternoon. Checking the time on my wrist, idly, I was swept with my memory of this story and, acting on impulse, I washed up and walked around the corner to visit Heinrich, the neighbourhood jeweller.

Heinrich worked out of a serious, tiny, precise shop on Homer Street not far from my studio, where he did a busy trade appraising and repairing old watches. Opening the door to his shop, you had to watch not to hit Heinrich, who might or might not be hunched over his workbench, staring down the workings of a petulant Patek Philippe. To remind customers of just how small the shop was and to provide himself with a warning in the event they forgot, Heinrich had a little bell rigged to the handle, and a sign: Open Most Carefully.

"This is a nice watch," Heinrich muttered as he looked down at Francisco's Movado. A flop of hair was thrown down from the top of his head, almost to the green velvet desk, as he focused in with his monocle.

"This is a very nice watch," he repeated. He turned it over, reading it first with his fingertips. And then he clamped a silver wrench to the hexagonal back piece, twisted firmly in a single soft motion and exposed the mechanism.

"Where did you get this watch?"

Heinrich let a vaguely accusing silence hang in the little room as he gently probed the workings. "See here," he said without waiting for an answer, without lifting his head, indicating with a tiny steel screwdriver something that had been etched inside with the finest point. So fine that it could not be read without a magnifying glass. "It says here, 'No man may know the hour, but Nicholas Lacroix will now, at least, know the hour.' "

Heinrich looked up at me and let his tubular black monocle fall from his socket to the end of the beaded chain alligator-clipped to the collar of his white cotton shirt. "What do you suppose that means?" he asked me.

"Nicholas Lacroix was my father," I explained.

"I see," he said frowning. "He is dead now."

"He died, yes," I said.

"Did he know the hour, I wonder?" Heinrich looked down again at the watch. Then slowly, gently, he reassembled the pieces. "It needs no cleaning," he said. "It was cleaned in New York City in 1954 and is still very clean."

I raised my eyebrows.

"Inside here," he explained. "Old jewellers used to make a mark just inside the cover. Date and place of cleaning. Marked at the same time as the engraving I should think."

I took it back and strapped it on.

"You want to know what it's worth." Heinrich then stated.

I shrugged. It was true, I did.

"It's worth between seven hundred and a thousand dollars," he said.

"That much?"

"If you sell it to me," Heinrich went on, "I would pay you maybe seven hundred dollars. But if you came to me to buy one, then I would look around for you and you might have to spend as much as a thousand when we found one. This is a rare watch. Take care of it."

I left Heinrich's shop, his bell tinkling its little reminder to be most careful.

Then I walked slowly back to my studio with my precious watch, which had travelled from the Jura Mountains of Switzerland to a shop in Barcelona. Into the collection of Count Teo de Castillo. From there, upon the Count's death, to the wrist of his son, Almo de Castillo, who became in time Brother Francisco. From Brother Francisco to a drawer under his bed in the St. Andrew-on-Hudson Jesuit Novitiate in Hyde Park, New York. From there, by way of a propitious decision and a generous gift, to one Nicholas Lacroix. New-minted as a civilian, as a man with ambitions and a sense of the time before him. Who would wear Francisco's Movado in New York as he experimented with (among other things) pop art. The same Nicky Lacroix who would much later have one small successful show, a series of twelve fire hydrants, all of which, the story goes, were sold to the newly famous Andy Warhol.

The watch came to me eventually, in a padded package from an estate lawyer in upstate New York.

To me. Painter. Royal fuck-up.

"COME IN," I said to her.

We went to cheek-kiss, as had long been our practice, but she turned her head just slightly and we half lip-kissed.

"How did you get home?" she asked me, pushing her red hair off her forehead.

I was distracted that afternoon by large events in my life and walked away from her, across the studio, and stood by my window looking down into Hastings Street, watching the drug dealers.

"I lost my father's watch," I said to her. "I just can't believe it. It was the only thing he left me."

I turned back into the room. She stood squarely in the middle of my painting area, a thin girl with long legs and a light pink complexion whom I have used as a model at various times over the years. The previous night I slept with this thin girl, my model, and her slender ankles crossed one over the other in the small of my back. Today my wife, Gillian, would return from Toronto, where she had been engaged in business that I understood to be worth millions of dollars.

"I am so sorry, David," Sophie said to me. Her hand dropped resignedly to her side and she came across the room and sat in my fan-back chair, flopping down into it, her legs extended. "Where do you think? In the cab? At Café de Paris?"

We had been there. I distinctly remembered checking the time on my wrist between the appetizer and the main course. I glanced at my watch and the robust charm of it seemed meant for precisely this occasion. This rosy presence opposite, the slender strength I wanted to feel under my hands. The ticking timepiece marked our certain progress towards her bed, towards the completion of something that suddenly, very clearly, seemed to have been incomplete between us for a long time.

"I phoned. They didn't find anything."

"How about the Casbah?" she asked.

"I walked over. The bartender let me search the entire place."

We had sat together at the front bar in the Casbah. By now we were gently touching one another as we spoke, a hand on an arm or a knee. I don't think I looked at my watch at the Casbah.

The bartender remembered me and helped me look under tables and behind the bar. When I was done I thanked him, and his sympathetic expression brought home to me the barrier I had passed through. I realized that we were speaking on a new day, a changed day, a day whose morning had been like no other; my heirloom watch gone, my act of betrayal consummated.

"Lost ads?" Sophie was asking now, speaking up to me from the cushy softness of my chair.

"Lost," I recited from memory. "One antique man's wristwatch. Movado day-date-time model with black lizard strap. Very great sentimental value. Reward offered. Call David Lacroix."

Sophie's eyes drifted away from me and out the window. We drifted together into silence for a moment.

"I feel terrible," Sophie said.

"In what way?" I asked her.

"I feel guilty," she said sharply, as if I should know, from feeling the same.

"I feel terrible too," I said, and it was true, but it was muddled somehow, a less crystalline feeling than I might have expected. I felt primarily afraid.

"And still," Sophie said, "I can't believe I'm saying this but I had a great time. It was nice except for the wrong aspect of it." She shook her head and smiled at me.

I stroked her hair back off her forehead, just as she had done a minute before.

"So what will you do?" she asked me. "What will we do?"

I could only sigh. It felt like the fullest expression of my place and feelings.

"Did you take a cab home?" she asked me finally, after seconds of silence. "You should have woken me."

I had walked the early morning streets for a while, in fact. Then, when I saw a cab approaching from the distance I flagged it and rode home in silence, thinking about Sophie. I undressed in our bedroom, my wife's and my own. It was six or seven in the morning and I thought I would sleep for another hour or two. I was looking sleepily at a pile of laundry spilling from a square wicker hamper, thinking Gillian would be home by six that evening and that before then I would have gathered and steadied things, cleaned up the apartment and done some laundry, got the pasta water boiling. I didn't think that I cared deeply for Sophie at this point, only knew that I felt strong, resilient and powerful in the morning, having been with her the night before.

I checked my pockets idly at first, wondering in which one I had stowed Francisco's Movado. Jacket pockets, pant pockets. Finally in the pockets of my raincoat, which were all empty.

Left it at Sophie's, I thought, and then in a tumbling instant I knew that it wasn't there either. We undressed one another. I remembered every detail of it. I had lost the watch before we even kissed a real kiss, before our tongues conspired to touch.

I DIDN'T TELL MY WIFE about either event. The one matter was mine to keep or reveal. In this respect our marriage would sit, for a period, like a stone in a catapult.

45

I could leave it alone or touch the lever, send Gillian and myself through space to some unknown landing point.

As for the watch, I have several and I simply wore another. It would be entirely unlike Gillian to say, "I haven't seen you wear that Movado in some time." Which of course she then did, a perfect enactment of the glancing, refractory way time progresses in human lives. She'd never specifically noticed the watch in my fifteen years of having it, in our fifteen years of marriage, my father having died weeks following the simple ceremony.

Precisely what she said was, "Whatever happened to that old watch of your dad's? I promised Robert at work that I would tell him what kind you have, because he says he wants to buy an antique watch for himself and I went into your dresser and I couldn't find it. Is it a Bulova?"

I said no, it was a Movado, and that I had left it with Heinrich the German Watch Man to have it cleaned. The moment I made this statement, I realized that I was a bigger fool and a stupider liar than I'd ever realized before. There were now angles and intersections in my story that I would have no control over and I had needlessly complicated my life still further. I thought, looking at Gillian's face just then, I should be hit by a cement truck. My life should end soon.

I had a bad day, knowing with rising certainty that I loved Gillian and full of the fear of her leaving. Fear that if she left me I would be a penniless, utterly lonely painter without accomplishment, instead of being merely a restless unhappy painter who hadn't captured the public imagination in a few years.

Still, in all this, my head was filled with thoughts of Sophie. Inside and outside me, Sophie swam in my fluid atmosphere.

About the watch Gillian said, "Oh well, when it's cleaned let me take it to work to show Robert, all right?"

"Of course," I said. Liar. Fool. Already lonely.

I WAS PAINTING NOTHING of value, not clinically depressed but with a mood between blue and black. I decided to stop everything I was working on, right where I was, and begin a new project: a from-the-ground-up reappraisal of the nude.

I called up Sophie to see what her modelling schedule was like. We had not continued what we started the night I lost Francisco's Movado, and since a whole month had passed and I had purged myself of compulsive thoughts about her, I had convinced myself that the risk of relapse was minor. It would be nice to work with Sophie again as good friends, I said to myself, even if we knew one another in a different way than friends typically do.

Eventually we talked about the watch.

"Did anyone call?" she asked.

"No," I said.

"It was a Bulova, right? They're expensive, aren't they?"

I said they were plenty expensive but that no, it was a Movado, considered among collectors to be a second-tier maker (under Rolex, say). Still, I said, it had been my father's and before that it belonged to Brother Francisco and thus it had measureless sentimental value. She knew this story already.

"I miss it like a person who has died," I said to Sophie. "There are times I don't believe it's gone."

"I wish you'd find it," Sophie said sadly.

"I look compulsively at a spot on my dresser where I used to keep it," I went on. "I look there every morning as if it will be there. I look, knowing it's gone, and still I look, imagining that it will return by my looking."

"Like the apostles after the ascension of Christ," Sophie said.

Sophie was a lapsed Catholic. It always struck me that there was more Catholic than lapsed about her. To describe yourself as lapsed, however, did provide some ideological flexibility.

"Christ said he would return, and from that point onward the apostles began to look up at crossroads, looking far down the road in each direction just in case Christ was approaching."

"I see."

"It became habit," Sophie went on. "This looking up into the distance at intersections."

"I see," I said again.

"Well, I'm sorry, it just reminded me of that. You looking at your dresser for the thing that has departed."

Sophie agreed to pose for me again. The idea was that she would come over every Wednesday for a few hours in the afternoon. At first it was just art, we had straightened out the whole physical attraction thing over a coffee one afternoon.

Then after a couple visits it returned. I think back and I imagine it coming in the door with her that particular Wednesday, our third session together. After that we had sex every time before working for a few hours. When we weren't together, I found myself again thinking about her. She was on every canvas around me. The parts of her I sketched in charcoal were littered over my easels and benches and across the floor near the windows. The rose-stem strength of her. The pink-blood health. When I left the studio in the evening, I took her with me like a hot feeling on the skin after walking by the sea on a cold day. A scrubbed healthiness that only very slowly faded as the hours passed, until I eventually felt only like myself again.

SOPHIE WAS OVER, we were lying on the futon that I have set up behind a divider. The phone rang.

"Oh, damn."

"Don't get it," she whispered.

But I had to, in fact. The Ferrell Gallery promised to phone Wednesday and I had promised to be in. Cynthia Ferrell and I had a mutual friend who brought the gallery owner around one day unannounced on their way to get sushi together. They ended up staying for over an hour, looking at almost everything, oils, sketches. Cynthia said

49

she liked what I was doing a great deal. She said the nudes were "confessional," which gave me a start.

I asked her what she meant.

Private, she said. Obviously very personal.

Of course, untangling myself from Sophie's long legs and wrapping a shirt around my waist meant I didn't make it in time to get the ringing phone. So I waited a minute then checked my voice mail, but there was nothing.

"Damn," I said again. I imagined blowing this chance because I was sleeping with my model and I was filled with a passing sense of self-loathing.

I went back behind the divider, where Sophie was lying so beautifully on the white sheets. She lay with her back arched a little. Stretching her pink length in front of me, not shy in the least. I looked down at her as the phone rang a second time, then I dropped the shirt and sprinted naked across the room to get it. I remember thinking as I gleefully snatched up the phone that I had been given that rare second chance.

"Hello," I said, very cheerful.

It was a jumpy, nervy-sounding voice that said, "Hey, is this David Lacroix? David Lacroix? Is this Dave?"

I said that it was.

"Dave Lacroix, you lose a watch?"

"Yes," I said. "Oh my God, have you found it?"

My heart, instantly, pounding.

"Where is it? Where are you? I'll come right over to wherever you are." He might have said Hyde Park, I would have been out the door.

But instead he said, "Hang on. You got to describe it to me, right? I can't just give it to you until I know we got the right one."

Sophie pushed aside the divider and rolled up on one elbow, listening as I lovingly detailed Francisco's Movado. I painted a picture of it in the phone space between me and the caller.

Movado day-date-month . . . check. Golden bevelled winder . . . check. Bulging crystal.

I think I even told him about the Jura Mountains.

"Right," the guy said, and sniffed loudly into the phone after each detail. I imagined he was holding it in his hand, confirming my description, and the idea of this made me almost insane with happiness. Through the phone lines somewhere, there it was: alive!

Finally he said, "What colour strap?"

"Black!" I almost yelled. "Black lizard. Not shiny like alligator, more flat black with a greasy texture like boar skin."

"Well . . ." the man said. "I guess it's yours then."

"Excellent," I said looking across the room at Sophie who was smiling at me. Thank God, the prodigal watch returns.

"OK, so . . ." the man said. "Here's the deal, right. I don't actually have it on me right now. It's at a pawn shop, but they're keeping it in the back for me. What happened is, I saw it and I knew it was stolen, watches like that don't show up in pawnshops any other way. So I went and checked back issues of *The Province* and I found your lost ad."

He explained how he made a small living reuniting people with their missing property and collecting the reward. Last week he turned around a Sony video camera in the same fashion.

The man elaborated, "When the pawnshops *know* something belongs to someone else and I can prove it with a newspaper ad, they're happy to use me to get rid of the stuff. The cops closed some places last week, you probably heard they're cracking down."

"Well?" I said. "Which pawnshop? I'm blocks away."

"No, no, no. You can't go in to the shop yourself, these Lebanese guys'll flip."

I asked why.

"They don't know you. Two of their shops went down last week and you might be an undercover cop. As soon as you buy something that they know is stolen, then they're breaking the law." The man took his mouth away from the phone to unleash a series of phlegmy coughs.

"So what do we do?"

"Well, I can go in and get it, right? They know me," he said.

"All right," I said. "How much will they want?"

"Well," he said. "You gotta realize they probably paid twenty for it. More even."

"Twenty dollars?" I asked, incredulously.

"Well, sure."

"That's not much," I said.

My guy paused only a second. "Why? What's it worth?"

"I should get $750 for a watch like that," I said. "Collectors trade the Movado triple-date at a thousand if they're really fine specimens."

I saw Sophie wincing on the futon.

My man was coughing and sniffing at the same time. "OK," he said, recovering, "We won't tell them that, all right? They don't need to know that part. Let's you and me meet. You bring like . . . say a hundred bucks, that should cover it."

"Just say where."

"There's a church across from the pawnshop," my man said, and gave me directions. "How will I recognize you?"

"Black jeans, white T-shirt," I said. "What's your name?"

He thought for second, then came up with "Theo."

I hung up and turned to Sophie. "What?" I asked, regarding the wince.

She pointed out the strategic weakness in telling him how much it was actually worth, but I was too excited to care. "I would pay him that much, you know?" I said. "I would pay double to get back my watch."

"Well, don't pay more than you have to," Sophie said.

"Hey, this is important to me," I said to Sophie. She had irritated me by implying that I should cut some kind of *deal* to recover this object that had been passed down to me in a way that suggested I was truly meant to have it. Buying back such an object at full price, at double the price—an object that had been mine and then had been assumed lost—was like an honour.

She made a motion as if to zip her lips shut, and I went over, leaned down and kissed those pink, zippered lips.

I stopped at a bank machine on the way over, counted out five crisp twenties onto the ledge, folded them neatly once and put them in the front pocket of my black jeans. Then I found the church where he said he would be and I sat in the darkness for about forty-five minutes during which time a single person came in, a crumpled old man who stood in the nave and berated the gloom in vodka breath I could smell from six pews away.

Eventually I went outside. I looked up and down the street, wondering if Theo was watching me.

There were three pawnshops on the same block. I went into one and asked if they had any watches. The man gestured to a case towards the back of the shop. Even though Theo had said it wasn't in the display case, I looked half-heartedly. There were sixty or seventy cheap watches in there, every manner of gaudy and gutless time-piece. It depressed me to think of my Movado in such a place. I ached for my watch then, hovered over my own reflection in the glass case.

ANOTHER COUPLE OF WEEKS passed. It was now almost three months to the day since I had lost Francisco's Movado and I learned that I had been given the Ferrell show. This greatly improved my mood, which had been deep black since my screw-up with Theo. What had I been thinking to tell this Hastings Street rubby that he was onto a piece of hot property he could buy for twenty bucks and sell for a thousand? By now Theo would have bought and resold the watch and poisoned himself with ginseng brandy on the profits. I tried hard not to think about it.

Cynthia Ferrell used the word again. She said "confessional." "They're luminous, especially the small triptychs. Absolutely vibrating with some kind of confessional power."

The show was planned to include two other painters who hadn't been heard from in a long time. Cynthia's idea was a "What-have-they-been-up-to?" show, three of us who had high-profile starts and drifted out of the limelight for one reason or another. One of the other two artists had been a heroin addict when I knew him ten years before, so I wasn't surprised to learn that some of his intervening years had been spent in detox.

"It takes epochs to recover from the changes you inflict on your own system," he said to me when we all met at the gallery to talk about the show. "But it's a beautiful and frightening spiritual process, that sense of your body and your mind trying to reconstruct themselves after you have consciously, wilfully tried to destroy them."

I took Gillian out to dinner to celebrate the upcoming show. I insisted she choose the restaurant, and she chose Café de Paris. We'd never been there together and someone at her work had told her that it was excellent and romantic. And it is both those things, although I might have expected French bistro staff to be a little more discreet. A waiter (not even *our* waiter) very clearly said to me as we came in, "Nice to see you again so soon."

Here it had been three months since Sophie and I had seen the man.

On the way out again he said, "All right. Bon soir. See you soon."

"You come here often?" Gillian said, laughing outside on the sidewalk, assuming the guy was being unctuous.

I probably missed a beat, anyway it was nothing I said but rather the quality of the silence I left that held something for Gillian, which she then interpreted instantaneously. Not the smell of infidelity or anything nearly so dramatic, just a sense that she had read events and people incorrectly. This is the business person in Gillian, I think. And in this case it meant a sudden awareness that what she had thought was an obsequious waiter was in fact an unusually attentive and smart waiter.

She didn't have to announce all this. I just knew she had changed her mind about the waiter, so I came clean. "I went there with Sophie," I said, but then I fudged the dates. "Just a couple of days ago. That night I came home a bit late, I simply forgot to tell you. She's been such a big part of what's happened here, me getting the show and everything. I thought I'd buy her a bite to eat, although I suppose I could have invited her along tonight to celebrate with us."

I didn't like lying again, but I wasn't comfortable saying we had been there during those days three months before when Gillian was out of town. There was no obvious reason for me to have been treating Sophie at that time and anyway, it was a small lie in the context of all the larger lies involved. Gillian took the final joking reference to her coming out with us and laughed. "No, you shouldn't have invited her," she said, taking my arm. "I think she has a crush on you."

So that was that. Well, that and the fact that Sophie broke us back down to friends the following day, which hurt more than I might have guessed.

I had just made a big point of telling Sophie about the Café de Paris story. "I told Gillian we went there after all the hard work we'd been doing, she's fine with it."

That was the moment Sophie chose. "Part of me really does not want to do this. . . ."

I got a little teary, which embarrassed us both.

"Oh, David," she said, and held my head, patting my ear.

"You should have a proper boyfriend," I said after a few minutes. It occurred to me that I hadn't thought sufficiently of Sophie's needs in all of this. "You deserve someone who is really yours."

"Maybe," she said, not overwhelmed with the suggestion that a man was her root requirement. "But it's not really that anyway."

"What is it?" I asked.

She didn't want to say. I made her tell me.

"I've been reading about marriage," she said. "Breaking one up is like an offence against God."

This was more of her religio-babble, I assumed, which as a rule I didn't interrupt. "How would you know?" I said this time. "You're not married."

"Well, I can read, can't I?" she said. "And I see it in you. And worse, I see the role I'm playing in splitting you off from Gillian. I'm breaking apart the symbol of your creation."

"Sorry?" I said.

"It's one of the key sacramental implications of marriage," she said. "A human relationship in which there is this fusing, this union, this creation of a new joint entity. Ideally it offers us a metaphoric glimpse of our createdness."

"I don't even believe in God," I wailed, besides which I didn't think I understood what she was talking about.

"It doesn't matter what you believe," Sophie said. "We're talking about what I believe."

I kissed her a couple of times, the last times. I felt that I loved her and after she left I also felt as if a huge cloud of pain were hovering on the horizon.

THE MORNING OF THE SHOW I went to my studio to collect myself for the big event. I didn't call Sophie, although sitting in the fan-back chair with my feet on the window sill I felt the urge. In fact, I almost dropped to my knees when the phone rang. I immediately thought of her and her antique Catholic sense of the world and her God hovering over all of this and I almost converted right there.

Had I prayed (I didn't in the end, I didn't want to miss the call) I would have simply prayed, *Please God may this be Sophie.* But without the time for this pitch to my creator, I instead leaped twenty-five feet across the room and grabbed the phone before the second ring.

"Dave Lacroix?"

I recognized his voice and remembered his name immediately. "Theo," I said.

"You remember me," he said, sounding pleased.

I was angry and yet this was countered by overwhelming gratitude that he had called. "I went to the church and waited."

"Look, sorry about that," Theo said. I guessed he was at a pay phone on Hastings Street, within blocks of me. I craned my neck uselessly at the window, there wasn't even a pay phone in sight.

"What happened?" I asked.

"I had to deal with something."

"I bet," I said. The balance was tipping back to anger. "How much did you get for it?"

"What?" he said, sounding genuinely confused.

"My watch. You went and bought it for twenty dollars and sold it somewhere. I'm just wondering how much you were paid."

"Hey, wait," Theo said indignantly. "I'm no thief. I haven't done anything with your watch."

"Oh, sure," I said.

"I swear to you," Theo said. "It's still in the back of the pawnshop where I saw it. I went and looked at it yesterday."

"Well, what happened to you then?"

Theo sniffed loudly and I could hear voices and street noise in the background.

"Don't hang up," I said.

"All right," he said, "but don't yell at me. This is my time I'm spending to contact you."

There was some more silence. "I won't yell," I said.

"I got arrested," Theo said finally. "You happy? They kept me for a few days, but I got released."

"For what?" I asked him.

"Some bogus crap," Theo said. "So you want me to get this watch for you or not?"

"Yes, I do," I said.

"All right, you know where to meet me."

"I'm not going down to that church," I said. "We're not doing this in a church."

I suggested he come up to the studio. I had guessed right that he was blocks away; he was exactly one block away on Cordova Street.

"You live down here?" he asked, sounding dubious, as if he didn't trust people that came from his own neighbourhood.

I waited on the street outside my building, scanning the street, and sure enough I knew him the second he rounded the corner. He strode into Hastings Street climbing the slight incline towards me, arms swinging wide, gangly walk, ape-sized head with a grubby ball cap on. He had filthy too-tight jeans and a zip-front kangaroo jacket under a jean jacket. Basketball shoes, although not Air Jordans, just a beat-up set of Converse that were likely the only shoes he owned.

He came bobbing up the hill towards me, a springy step full of misplaced energy and confidence. About ten yards off he tossed up a hand and yelled, "Yo, Dave." He seemed to be in fine spirits.

We stood on the street outside my building.

"So what's the drill?" I asked, fingering the cash in my pocket.

Theo seemed a little nervous, although bouncy. He suggested we go inside.

"Cash transaction," he said. "We might want to get off the street."

There's no lobby to speak of in my building, so I took him up to the studio.

He sniffed around a little. Uttered the same critical comment in front of each canvas. "Right on."

"All right, already," I said. "Can we deal with my watch?"

He came over and stood in front of me. "Say the word, give me a hundred bucks and I'll take care of business." He was swinging a cupped hand up into the palm of his other hand, smack, smack.

It's not that I hadn't thought about the man's honesty before. The fact was he'd thoroughly convinced me that his sense of truth was more dangerously variable than my own. Still, I hadn't clearly contemplated the moment of transition. The very precise point in time at which the cash left my hand and went into his pocket and he walked out the door with it.

"Look," he said, on top of my concerns. "There's no other way to do this. It's like a drug deal. The cash and the stuff can't be in the same place. I take the cash, I meet the Lebanese guy in his car outside his shop, we drive around the block, I give him the cash, he goes into his store, he gets your watch, brings it out to me, then I bring it up the street to you right here. That's how it works. It doesn't work any other way."

"How do I even know it's there?" I asked him.

Theo shrugged. "I ain't scamming you. This is my neighbourhood. I'm around here all the time. I cash my cheques at that Money Mart over there. I score my dope in the park across the street. I can't be scamming in my own part of town. I'll probably see you next week."

The truth was he looked vaguely familiar. I might have seen him countless times before. "I don't know," I said. I turned and walked a few steps away from him. "I wish you hadn't fucking phoned me."

Theo didn't say anything, or if he did I didn't hear him. The bastard had me thinking that Francisco's Movado was down there, and having seeded this thought, Theo knew I needed to find out for sure. Any outcome was better than sinking back and trying to accept that what had been lost remained lost without ever having checked. Which meant, of course, I had to fork over the cash.

"You think I'm a junkie?" he said, which I didn't, in fact. I thought he was a cokehead at this point. "I'm not a junkie." And here Theo pulled up the sleeves of his jacket to show me his arms. "No tracks."

Theo stood in front of me with the insides of both his arms exposed.

I gave him sixty dollars in the end, promising the balance on his return. I counted out three twenties into his dirty palm. "If you're scamming me, Theo, have a good fucking time with my money, all right?"

I slammed the door after him.

He phoned me ten minutes later. He said, "Well, Dave my man, your gamble paid off. He's just in the shop getting the watch now. I'm waiting in the park for him. I'll be up in a few minutes, you have that forty bucks ready for me."

"All right," I said. It was really too much to have hoped for, I thought at the time, but Theo was going to come through for me.

I never heard from him again.

I CALMED DOWN BY THAT EVENING. The opening was very well attended. I sold two pieces without even meeting the buyers. They came early and left early, snapping up both of the small triptychs.

"You two have met," I said when Sophie approached Gillian and me. This might be the ultimate Terror Meeting for other men who get themselves into my position, the meeting of the two people whose universes contain the anti-matter of the other. Mutual assured destruction and all that.

Not here and now, though. Sophie was so sincerely devoted to the sacramental imperatives involved that she had reassured me on this point. "It will be perfectly fine," she had said. "I actually really like Gillian, I think it is totally great how successful she is."

"You two have met."

"Oh sure. Hi, Sophie, you look wonderful."

"Thanks, so do you, Gillian."

"Well," Gillian said, gesturing around the gallery. "You must be feeling a bit naked at the moment."

"Nobody has even picked that up," Sophie said. "Here are these pictures of me but the treatment is so . . . personal somehow . . . so personal to David, that it's really only him people are seeing. Strange, I suppose, people looking at pictures of me and seeing David."

"What are you doing after?" Gillian asked. "Maybe the three of us could get a drink."

"I have to meet somebody at eleven," Sophie said,

making an apologetic expression. "I almost have to go now."

"What time is it?" Gillian asked me, surprised to think it might be nearing eleven.

Of course, I wasn't wearing a watch nor would I ever again, I had pledged, having been taken by that demonic character not for the watch itself, or for the sixty dollars, but for the hope that had briefly flickered around the thought of its return, a hope exponentially more valuable and fragile than the watch itself.

But since I normally wear a watch I looked at my wrist automatically the way one does. And so my blank, hairy wrist stuck out of my suit sleeve naked, where it was contemplated for several seconds by the three of us.

Once again, events glanced off in an unexpected direction. Gillian was struck with a thought; Sophie was struck with a different thought and they articulated both in unison.

"Did it ever get cleaned?"

"Any call on those lost ads?"

Silence.

"Lost ads?" Gillian said.

Here was an exemplary moment, in which Gillian's multivariate world view took on data and slightly reconfigured. Sophie wasn't as gifted in this regard, and not realizing Gillian didn't know about the lost watch, plunged innocently ahead along the same track.

"Well, sure, from when he lost the Bulova at Café

de Paris. I feel so bad that I was with him but we'd been working so hard."

"You lost your father's watch?" Gillian said. "That's terrible, David, why didn't you tell me?"

"I did," I floundered.

"When was this?"

Under pressure, I could only come up with the one occasion we had spoken of it. "Just after you got back from Toronto, remember?"

"And you were at Café de Paris?" Gillian said, shaking her head, then looking at Sophie. Even by her standards, she was taking on a lot of new data. Her recalibrated model of the situation took a second or two to rerun the numbers.

I gave Sophie a look conveying the data she needed to know it was goodnight.

"You were out with Sophie while I was in Toronto?" Gillian said to me, still standing there in the lobby of the Ferrell Gallery.

Somebody walked by me quickly, tapped my shoulder and said, "Nicely done."

"I thought I told you," I stammered.

"No," she said. And then she excused herself to use the ladies' room.

"I sold three in the end," I said in the car later. "Both the small triptychs and one of the big canvases. You know who bought the large one? A guy named Francisco. Funny."

Funny indeed. So funny I didn't even think of the loop slowly closing here.

"David," my wife started, and with that she moved us through a wall of sorts. A shimmering wall, a plane of time that demarcated the events that preceded it cleanly from the events that would follow.

Epoch-shift, I found myself thinking, listening to the heavy words my wife was now saying. An epoch-shift described by the dropping away of items that characterized the receding epoch. Not like the shift from fauvism to expressionism. Not like the relationship between pop art and its antecedent abstract expressionism. Those had been growths, movements onward. Actions that embraced and accommodated new components within revised versions of an old system.

Not like that. Instead, Gillian opened her mouth and formally ushered us into an epoch of perpetual loss, a transition that could not be observed approaching because it did not bring with it any references to the past. Nothing swept around the bend to be either admired or loathed in advance. An epoch merely fell away and was replaced by nothing.

And I had no means to know the hour of its passing.

I HAVE THOUGHT ON MORE than one occasion about travelling to Hyde Park in New York State, just to view the place where Brother Francisco had worked and where my father was first a Primi, then a Secundi, then relaunched with Francisco's Movado as a civilian. Where his decision to turn away from the eternal vow of poverty, chastity and obedience had been made. It would be worth visiting in the sense that I think of his parting from the Jesuit Order as holy, blessed by Brother Francisco and by the God they both served, the God of whose existence my former lover Sophie remains devoutly convinced.

But I haven't made this trip since I learned recently that the novitiate moved to Syracuse some thirty years ago. The old building in Hyde Park still stands. It now houses the Culinary Institute of America. Perhaps I'm concerned that the traffic of new novices in their white jackets and checkered pants would blot out any sense of the building's original spirit, or that the smells emanating from the once-holy site would mask any epiphany.

I suppose I could go to Syracuse. To the new novitiate. And there I might stand outside the gates and feed off its vital emanations, imagining the forces that drove my father's devotion and then, while he remained a believer, his quiet turning to secular pursuits.

I might think on the blessing he received, on the watch that was its Swiss-made vehicle.

## SMOKE'S FORTUNE

After some talking, Fergie offered us forty dollars to shoot the dog. Smoke haggled with him, standing in that little screened porch tacked onto the front of Fergie's house, but he just said the dog was dying anyhow and swatted at a fly. Smoke said we wanted forty dollars each, and that we knew the dog had bitten a kid, and that the RCMP said kill it. But Fergie didn't budge even though we said we'd bury it and all. He said, "I know I can't kill the bastard anyway. Here's your forty dollars. You boys take it."

So we took it, Smoke and I. Then we got my Ruger 30-06 out of Smoke's truck and went to the shack by the yard where Fergie kept all his wrecks and parts of cars. He kept two dogs in there. They were fenced, but I guess there was one kid smarter than that fence. When Fergie found the kid, and then the dog with blood in her mouth even he knew what had to happen. And Fergie was a guy crazy for his dogs.

Frank Hall was in the shack propping up the desk with his feet, and he laughed when we came in.

"Here come the hunters," he said, and came over to the counter. "Don't get bit now, you hear?"

That was Frank, always winking and ribbing, but Smoke flipped a bit. He grabbed Frank's jacket and pulled him hard up into the counter so some coffee spilled. I was glad I was carrying the rifle so nothing went off or anything. Frank just laughed again like he couldn't care, and got a fresh toothpick out.

The yard was set out like a football field. Blocks on the fifteen-yard line, exhaust units on the forty, stacks of bodies on the forty-five. All with some roads for the trucks running out into the junk and then back into the corner by the Haffreys' land.

The dogs knew Smoke, but since I'd only started with Fergie in July, I carried a deer steak. This was Smoke's idea. I wasn't too sure really. If they didn't recognize me I figured the steak might give them the wrong idea. So I hung back a bit while Smoke went ahead looking for the dog.

"This fucking heat," I heard him say.

"What," I said.

"I can't see through this heat," he said.

"It's hot, all right," I said swinging the steak.

We kept on walking through the blocks. There was about a half acre of them I guessed. Up ahead I could see the stacks of pipes, then the rads, bodies and smaller parts all grown up with weeds and grass. Fergie kept a yard for certain, everything neat and separated and lined with rosehips.

"Smoke," I said.

"What."

"Listen, I shouldn't be carrying the steak and the rifle. I mean, I can't shoot her one-handed. I figured maybe . . ."

But Smoke came back to where I stood and said to me slowly, like it didn't need saying, "We find her, you throw the steak, then you shoot her. It's easy."

I looked at him.

"I'm here to do the finding," he said. "They like me."

This was how Smoke got you to do things. He made it real obvious, and then kept on telling you anyway. So by the end of his telling, you were wishing he'd be quiet and let you do it.

We went on walking, through some trucks and into more blocks. I guess there might have been a thousand old engines there, all black and rust-coloured. Right where we were, the grass grew up through some of the cylinders. They looked pretty in all that junk, which was mostly just oily.

Smoke was poking on ahead, into the big stacks of bodies. It was well-known junkyard knowledge that you watched yourself in the stacks. Frank always told about Marcel, who came out from Quebec and was crushed under a stack. He was tugging at some piece of dirty junk and pulled about three trucks down on himself. Right out from Quebec, had a job for maybe three weeks, and pulling on something he was probably barely curious about and boom. So I was watching Smoke a bit because he would tug on stuff even though he'd probably been in a junkyard as long as Frank, or even Fergie. That was Smoke's way, tugging on things even when he was in the stacks.

"Here, here, here," I heard him say, like he was coaxing something, and then I saw him back out from under a big cab-over with his hand out. I stayed back near the blocks, holding the steak, ready to throw.

Smoke came back further and a dog came out of the grass. I could hear it panting and breathing all hanging with saliva the way they do when it's hot. This was all the sound, next to Smoke saying, "Here, here, here. Yes, yes. Easy boy."

When they were right in front of me Smoke just held his hand out, dangled it in the dog's face and waited. Then I'll be damned if the dog didn't start smiling, only all I saw was that whole face change, and the eyes squint back and tight, and the teeth drop out of the black lips, and the mouth crease back along the sides. I have to admit I dropped the steak and brought the Ruger right up fast thinking about squeezing not jerking the trigger, and letting the bastard move at you before you fire.

Smoke turned his hand over and cupped the dog under the muzzle and said, "Just show them slow, like that, see?"

Jesus, I was like a stone. I think I even turned grey-coloured.

"Hey, that's great Smoke," I said.

"What are you going to do? Shoot me or what?"

"No, hey," I said lowering the rifle and stooping to pick up the steak. "No."

"This here's the one that likes me," Smoke said, all grins.

"Yeah, well, I guess I can see you've met."

"Here, I'll go put this one in the pen so's we don't have to catch him another four times. Give me some steak."

I propped the rifle between my knees and managed to get my knife out. I hacked off a bit and tossed it.

"OK, I'll be back. Have a smoke or something. Don't wander around and get lost."

"Right." I said. And I sat down on the nearest block and smoked. It was too hot to smoke actually, but I was feeling like having one. Sometimes when I want a smoke the worst, I don't even like it when I light up. It'll even make me feel sick sometimes. I figure that's just like me to feel sick about something when you want it the most.

Smoke came back patting dust out of his pants, looking all keyed up again. He was glad to find the one dog. Now he was thinking about finding the bitch, and it wasn't getting any cooler.

"OK, OK, OK, huphuphup. Move it out!" he started shouting like a crazy person. "Here pup, here pup!"

"Jesus, Smoke, you'll get her all riled."

"Relax on the trigger, old son. I'm finding dogs. Come here, dog!"

So we went off further, looking. Right into the back parts of the yard where the real junk was. Some of Fergie's stuff back here didn't move too often, I figured. The back of some old Seville was rusting off to one side, fins slanting up through the weeds.

Smoke was poking, pulling on things like nothing could ever hurt him. Under a pile of fenders twenty, thirty feet high, he pulls up a piece of a radio or something and says, "Well, shit, look at this." I think a fender even fell off about a foot away and he just shuffled over and said, "Hey, easy now."

"Smoke."

"Yeah."

We had stopped again, I was getting dust down my shirt.

"Smoke, we're getting way the hell back here."

Smoke came over and took a drag off my cigarette and then took one out of the package in my shirt pocket, and lit it off an old Zippo he carried around. I've seen Smoke use about three of his own cigarettes over the years and that includes the one he keeps behind his ear. He's never without the Zippo though, he loves that old thing.

"Well, she's out there, son," he said.

Then, as he dragged on the cigarette, Smoke got to thinking and he sat down on the grass, quiet, and I slid down so my neck could crook between the manifold and the block on this old motor. There were clouds floating by really peacefully. Maybe forty clouds across the whole sky.

"Smoke, you figure that cloud's a hundred miles across?"

"Where?"

"There. That one that looks like a couch or something."

Smoke started craning his neck all around, trying to think of an answer.

"Well," he said finally, "you know, I think they're actually a whole lot smaller than people think. The sky's actually smaller than people think too. You take Fergie, say, thinks he's a smart guy. Now he'll tell you that this sky's so big you can't even start to understand it. But it isn't. It's really quite small to some scientists. And getting smaller every year."

Smoke kept on talking. I was remembering about last Saturday at the Tudor. There was a lady there I'd never seen before. Really pretty, in a skirt, looking around her like she was a little scared or something. Like maybe she got a flat going through town on her way to Red Deer and ended up here. Sitting at this bar, sipping a Coors, waiting for someone from the garage.

Well, Smoke caught one sight of her and went right up to her like she was waiting for him in particular. "Are you the lady with the flat?" he said, like Magnum P.I. or something. You know, here's a time when I'm thinking, Maybe this lady had a flat. Smoke, he's thinking, Maybe, maybe not, no difference. And I get to wondering sometimes why it is that Smoke thinks he can ask people right on if they have a flat just because they're pretty.

Then Smoke shifted over in the weeds and looked down at me. I noticed he had stopped talking.

"You entirely comfortable, son?" he said.

"Why yes, Smoke," I said. The exhaust manifold felt smooth and cool on my neck.

"Well, don't you wake up if you can kill that bitch sleeping."

"Oh, I'm not sleeping."

"Well, what do you think?"

I stalled a bit, wondering what I might have missed. I pulled myself up a bit, looking around for the steak. It was all ground with dirt and I wondered if a rabid dog would still like it.

"What about this steak?" I asked Smoke finally.

Smoke looked at it.

"Doesn't look too good, does it?"

"Not to me," I said.

Smoke shrugged and looked around.

"Say, I'm going to beat the brush around here a bit, maybe drive her back toward you so you can get a shot at her." He squinted a bit into the weeds.

"Uh, well, Smoke, I'm not too sure here . . ."

He was on his feet, gliding into the grass.

"Smoke, Jesus!" I jumped up. Smoke stopped and turned slowly, following his nose around like he was finding me by smell.

"Listen, I mean, why don't we fan out together?" The idea of wandering around these stacks with both Smoke and a rabid dog cut loose seemed like craziness.

Smoke looked disgusted for a second, like I was about twelve years old for being spooked by a dog. "You got the fucking gun," he said. "You just use it when the time seems right."

I stood there for about a minute after he left. Not moving. Swearing quietly and keeping my breathing even and shallow. The grass stretched out around me, yellow and burnt, stained with oil so the heat made your head swim with fumes. The sun kept rising higher overhead like it wasn't planning to set that day.

I backed up, holding the Ruger against my thigh, feeling the rough patterned grip on the stock grab little tufts of my jeans. I was feeling backward with my left hand, until I felt the big stack of radiators behind me. I crouched down, watching the dry weeds and thinking.

The rads had a lot of sharp edges so I stopped and pulled on my hunting gloves, which let your trigger finger hang out. Then I slung the rifle flat across my shoulders and began looking for a place to start climbing. The rads were stacked in a huge pyramid, maybe forty feet high. I put my boot up on one and pushed, knocking one off higher up. It came sliding down the stack, and I rolled to one side. It hit my shoulder and then the ground.

I started again. Trying to stay on top of the metal pieces as I climbed. My boots gripped on the rough edges all right, but as I got higher I was knocking them off left and right, kicking twisted chunks of metal down into the lane. I kept thinking, Fergie will kill us if we don't clean this up.

When I got to the top, I was afraid to look down for a while. I pinched my eyes almost shut and wormed my way onto a flat area at the top of the stack. Here I shifted around and got myself cross-legged. Then I slung the Ruger off my back carefully, trying not to shake too much. I sat like that, with the rifle up, stock up against my cheek, elbows on my knees. Then I opened my eyes wider and started looking around the yard.

Smoke was pretty small from up there. He was moving up and down the lanes, cutting across the grassy bits between the bodies and the blocks, trying to sweep through the yard toward me, and flush her out. It was kind of hypnotic, like watching a spider wait out a fly. Only now I wondered whether Smoke was the spider or the fly or what.

He was right up to the exhaust pipes, all jumbled with the weeds. He was bobbing his head again like he was smelling something, taking a quiet step or two every so often. I nestled the rifle into my cheek. The wood was oily and hot from the sun. Through the scope I could see Smoke and about two feet all around him. With my other eye open, though, I could still see the rest of the yard. My dad taught me that. A lot of people think your scope eye stops working if you do that, but it doesn't. You start seeing better. As you stare and you don't blink, you suddenly start getting every little movement all over the yard. And in the middle, this circle of larger detail.

I could see Smoke breathing slowly, his cheek sucking in and out. I could see the brick-red sunburn across his neck and the line of dirt around his collar. Across the top of my sight, I could see a truck on the highway, maybe a mile away. You could barely hear it growling, but I could see it moving and see the black exhaust jump out the pipe every time he took another gear. I could see them both, Smoke and the truck.

Smoke kept on crawling through those pipes. Near the far side of the pile he slowed right down and froze. His one hand was up hanging over a tailpipe, the other behind his back, his nose pointing. I tracked the crosshairs of the scope over his shoulders into the grass, then back into his open hand. His hand went into a fist, my left eye was shaking, trying to see all over the yard and concentrate on Smoke at the same time.

Suddenly he jumped to the left, swinging his hand down and pulling the pipe with it. They crashed and rolled across the dirt and he leaped backwards and rolled on one shoulder, coming up in a squat with his hunting knife hovering in front of him, blade up. The crosshairs hung in open air for a moment, a foot in front of his face.

In that second when Smoke was still, I saw her. In my left eye, in the big picture. She was there, where we'd dropped the steak, maybe twenty yards from Smoke. She was muzzling the meat, pawing it. Trying to figure out why it smelled so good and looked so bad, I guess.

She wasn't looking too good herself. All matted and caked around the mouth, dripping drool on herself when she shook her black head. Her sharp snout had flecks of grey, her chest was muddy and her legs shook badly. Her hair was dull, and she panted as she pawed the meat, then jumped back and shook her head from side to side. Just a half-crazy old Doberman, mad at the world and hungry.

When she heard Smoke dump the exhaust pipes, she stopped and listened. She turned and thrashed on her back in the dust then stood up again. I didn't move the rifle too much, just let it coast over as Smoke started out down the lane again and cut into the weeds towards her. I was dead still except for that, that tiny movement of the barrel; Smoke walked along slowly, whistling softly, wondering where I was, maybe, crosshairs on his shoulder. When he crouched down, I'd freeze entirely. No breathing, both eyes locked open, I think my heart stopped even.

I guess I kept meaning to do something, but I didn't want to. I felt almost sleepy except for my face smeared into the Ruger. Pretty soon they were both moving again. Smoke in the scope. The bitch in the yard. I was seeing them both, eyes running with tears. When she saw Smoke through the weeds she went still and tight, low to the ground, like a piece of steel sitting with the others. I was thinking about shooting her then, but I was afraid the bullet would skip right off her, ricochet around, maybe hurt someone. Her lips went back into a grin; her teeth hung with dirt and saliva.

Smoke was batting at some weeds with an old antenna. I was looking at his scalp with my right eye, thinking I could feel the itch of the dirt and grass in it. I scratched it lightly with the crosshairs. From the back up across the top where it was tangled, down into the slick sideburns and the tuft in the ear.

And I was watching these two tangled bits of hair and dirt and saliva get closer together and thinking about how my finger, soft on the trigger, was going to do something soon, very small, and stop them from hurting each other, which seemed a shame, although also very natural.

And then she moved up fast, coming off the ground like a jet, real low at first and then wide and high. Her front legs in and close to her chest, her head forward, brows over and down to protect her eyes, her mouth lipless, showing every tooth and every rib on her black gums. Streaming saliva. And I just sat there until I saw her pass from my left eye into the right, and when she burst into my scope I shot her.

And then she seemed to vanish, and I lowered the Ruger, and Smoke had spun around like a drunken wrestler and was sitting in the grass, his knife still in his belt, his face blank, his mouth open a bit.

I climbed down and walked into the lane past the broken dog. Smoke was on his feet again, grinning. As we stood there he took a cigarette out of my pocket, lit it off the Zippo, and said, "Nice piece of shooting, son." And I guess I knew he'd say something like that.

## POPE'S OWN

"Well now," the man from Kinsale said, returning his pint glass to the dark wood bar. "I am to understand you have some knowledge of our Brothers."

There was a certain insinuation in the Irish cadence, Gillian thought, not that she would take issue. "I have an associate," she began, as neutral as possible.

"Do you then?"

"Chekhov McGuigan."

She knew this would get his attention but that he wouldn't let on. And sure enough, the man from Kinsale scratched the edge of his jaw, silvery with afternoon beard, and murmured. "Ah, well then. McGuigan. Went to Canada, didn't he?"

"Chekhov said Brothers was the best washed-rind semi-soft in existence although, no offence, I'll believe that when I taste it. He said it was known locally as Pope's Own, that it was a closely guarded secret, that I might start looking in the Union Hall area, and he also mentioned your name."

"Did he say all those things now?"

Gillian sipped her Murphy's stout and decided to play silence. She had just dumped everything she knew on the bar between them, for one thing, but she also guessed there was going to be some peacocking around here before they got down to issues. Sometimes you just had to let the boys dance and jab for a while before they finally surrendered and told you how much, for how many, and when. This wasn't a lot different than a hundred (a thousand?) meetings she'd had with chief financial officers and accountants and brokers and lawyers over the years except this was not so much about money as it was about, well, cheese.

The barman came over. "Gillian Lacroix?"

"Mackin," she said firmly. Her birth name never felt better.

"How they found you here I'll never know," the barman said, and pointed to a cream-coloured dial phone at the end of the bar.

"I'm staying up the road," Gillian said. "I told one or two people before I left. Will you excuse me?"

"Of course," the man from Kinsale said.

"Yello," she said into the transatlantic squelch.

It was Tremblay. She turned her back to the man from Kinsale and looked down the length of the panelled room towards the front door. Piggy's was dead empty. Odd to be in a bar when it was sunny out, even a bar with a relatively sunny name like Piggy's, but the streets of Union Hall were just as empty. Earlier that morning the boats had come in and there had been a slow-motion flurry of people in front of the garage that served as fish processing plant and out-door market. Gillian caught the tail end of it, bought some monkfish for dinner. By the time she'd walked up the hill to the house she was renting, made some calls and returned, it was like the small fishing port had been evacuated.

"How are you making out?" Tremblay asked. He was concerned, she thought, calling at 7:30 in the morning Pacific time. But Gillian's investment adviser had been expressing concern for her behaviour ever since the divorce, and just as she had given up correcting his nervous reversion to her legal, married name, she was getting more or less used to this from him too.

"Tremblay," she said quietly, "I'm just sitting down with Mr. Clooney now."

"I'll let you go, but one thing," Tremblay said. "Something McGuigan was saying. I think we have ourselves another bidder here."

"Over there?"

"No, over there. In Dublin. He's a businessman, that's all I know."

It was bad news, but Gillian rolled with it. Chekhov had described a pristinely beautiful piece of West Cork farmland with a large, well-kept stone house and buildings, cheese-making equipment, knowledgeable staff and a working herd of dairy cattle. It was a rare, complete package, and another bidder wasn't such a surprise.

The call was also well timed. Gillian calculated that the phone had rung just as Clooney was about to puff himself up with how impossibly exclusive Brothers was, how not just any purchaser would do. Now as she got off the phone, Clooney would have to take a big breath and start all over again.

"Sorry," she said, sliding onto her stool.

Clooney had a little Murphy's stout cream on the edge of his trim moustache. Fiftyish. Handsome in a tattersall-shirt-and-sportscoat way that remained boyish. He had a mess of black Irish hair she thought went nicely with the green-shouldered hills covered in shaggy goats and yellow broom. He opened his mouth to continue.

"Chekhov says hello," Gillian interrupted. She imagined this like the left-hook counter you throw just as your sparring partner telegraphs an overhand right.

"Does he? Well." Clooney accepted another pint of Murphy's without word or payment. "Was that him, then?"

Gillian didn't answer, she watched instead as

Clooney's left index finger dipped unconsciously into a vest pocket and withdrew a single bead of a rosary.

*Why do they call it Pope's Own?*

*A religious man our Clooney, Chekhov had said.*

*Fanatic?*

*No, just Irish.*

"May I do something?" Gillian asked. And then without waiting for permission, she took a hanky from the sleeve of her sweater and very lightly wiped the Murphy's off the tip of Clooney's moustache. She didn't have to look over to know the barman caught that one.

Clooney suppressed a blush. It was hard to do, Gillian imagined, but she saw it bloom ever so slightly before being pinched off.

"I'm sorry," she said again. And in a way she was sorry, although she got the reaction she wanted. She was sorry, perhaps, to have deployed that kind of a feint even in service of this.

Clooney sighed. "Tell me about yourself," he said finally. "They'll want to know."

NOTHING TO TELL, really, Gillian thought. Nothing more than the standard investment-banker-turned-quality-cheese-importer story. Nothing to tell beyond the fact that not a single core feature of her life had survived the preceding two-year period beyond her sparring partner.

"You're hitting a bit harder, girl," Maria told her a year before, shortly after the divorce was finalized.

"Sorry. I feel really loose."

Maria temped and was only in her twenties. They met at the boxercise class Gillian enrolled in before David moved out. She became more interested in the sport after the split. This was not entirely a matter of unresolved hostility, although there was a measure of that. Gillian thought it had more to do with reasserting authority over things, over herself.

Maria and Gillian hit it off. They decided to spring for private lessons together. First time in the ring with sparring gloves on, Gillian remembered that Maria put the instructor on his butt. They froze in a cock-eyed triangle, the two of them staring down at Franky. A trickle of purple blood emerged from his nose, and you could almost see the birds and stars and the little bombs with fuses swirling around his head.

Maria said, "Oh, my God, I am like . . ."

Franky scrambled to his feet, complimenting her through his mouth guard. "Thas'good. Thas'essackly it."

Over drinks later Maria said, "I caught him coming in, what can I say? The guy was moving like a sofa." Gillian thought of a stunned Franky sitting flush on his ass—it's always the punch you don't see coming—and she laughed so hard it actually hurt. Of course, she was out of practice laughing.

"You were management?" Maria said a little later. "Like your own office and everything?"

Gillian nodded and stopped smiling. That was then.

"What's with cheese? I have to ask."

Gillian looked at her younger friend. She felt sisterly, and she wondered a whole range of things in a single instant that seemed to wind up at the question, What suburban jerk was Maria dating at the moment?

"You know," Gillian said. "It just became really important to be in charge of my whole day. From morning to night. I answer to me."

"Well, sure," Maria said, hands up like, *You don't need to explain that.* "But you're gonna stay interested, selling people mozzarella?"

"Selling anything I can actually touch and smell," said Gillian. She might have added, anything the existence of which I can myself verify, but this was the harder part to explain to Maria. David being gone was more than a hole in her life, he made a blank spot she could not be sure had ever been full. The piece he removed came out of her present and—by transfiguring himself utterly, by rendering himself unknowable—David had expunged himself from the past as well. The operative word for the future became *tangibility.*

There was a period of chasmic anxiety attacks, but these eventually subsided and were replaced by the conviction that she must do something with her hands, something real and unimpeachably good. She quit her job. She cashed in the West Vancouver house and bought a tiny condo downtown and a piece of land up the valley with good out-buildings. She sourced the cattle, spec'd milking and cheese-making equipment, then ran into the administrative blockade known otherwise as the Milk Board. It seemed the cheese manufacturing industry in Canada—presumably while nobody was looking—had been tamped down hard under a grid of quotas and regulations and you pretty much had to commit civil disobedience to make and sell a batch of unpasteurized cow's-milk Camembert.

She was forced to give up the whole idea, the closest to depression she had come through the entire preceding six months. Then her therapist found out through circuitous connections about Ye Olde Cheese Shoppe. Thirty years in the business and Mr. Brian "Chekhov" McGuigan was finally hanging up the slicer. A little dusty perhaps, a little prone to stodgy Stiltons in ceramic vases, but McGuigan's was situated nevertheless on a busy corner in fashionable Point Grey. Gillian thought, Martha Stewart would buy cheese here if the place were redecorated to look like Dean & DeLuca's, and if everything were expensive enough.

Her therapist was thrilled. "It's really great to be able to help. I mean, really help."

Gillian closed the deal with McGuigan personally. It tapped her out, cashwise. She had literally nothing left. But she was no longer in therapy, and standing in front of the Gillian Mackin Fine Cheese sign—copperplate lettering on a farm-green background—Gillian thought she might never have been so aware of the potential for fulfilment.

*Hardly recognize the place, Chekhov McGuigan said, on hand at the opening.*

*It's all the customers, she said, bantering in the way they had adopted.*

And it was true, business was good even without David's strained patronage. He was apparently selling more paintings a month now than he had sold in the six years they were married—paintings of the model he had been sleeping with, no less—and he was compensating by buying more cheese a month than he'd consumed in the same period. The facile selfishness of his quest for absolution notwithstanding, Gillian was grateful that he bought the expensive stuff: *lait cru* Pont Levesque, an appellation-controlled Bleu de Gex that had to be coaxed out of a supplier in the Haute Jura, even the handmade Gorgonzola-Brie cross from the farm in upstate New York owned by Wolfgang Puck that came in at $67 a kilo without much margin.

*I wouldn't bother with that one if I were you.*

*Why not?*

*Well, it's a bit of a fake cheese isn't it? Gorgonzola-Brie. You'll be selling Cambonzola next.*

*I am selling Cambonzola, Chekhov. Quite a lot of it actually.*

*Ever hear of farm cheese? Real small-batch stuff. Comes alive in your mouth. These friends of yours would pay whatever you ask for it.*

The last time she saw David, he said, "Anything I can do for you here, I want you to ask."

"Well . . . thanks," Gillian said.

91

"I mean it. Things are good for me." He tried not to look too pleased. "New York and everything. I know you don't need money, I just . . ."

"I need," Gillian said, "for you not to come here any more."

It left her short of breath to have finally said it, but there was no doubt she caught him coming in. David's face went dreamy and confused, like Franky when Maria tagged him. "I only . . ." he said, clutching his paper bag full of expensive cheese as if that might hold him up. "I just . . ."

She stared at him and waited. There was simply no goddamn way she was obliged to explain herself. Bleed.

*Don't be angry, Chekhov said later. For yourself, don't be angry.*

So that was the end of David. But it didn't matter anyway, she thought, because by then she had been given a nice write-up in a local food magazine and business was ticking along. It took a year to lay down the base, but Gillian Mackin Fine Cheese prospered and even began to pay Gillian Mackin a salary, which she used to hire Maria.

And then it happened. A Thursday, she remembered, about a year and a half in. She was checking a delivery from the warehouse in France. Maria was up front. It was a good delivery, an overdue delivery. Gillian was standing with her clipboard, marking off all the colourful packages and boxes that she had pulled together from master cheesemakers in the Jura, the Haute Savoie, in Normandy and Paris. Wheels upon wheels that she and Maria would now cut down to portions and sell inside four weeks. She could even pick who for what. Who for the Crottins de Chavignol. Who for the downy soft-rinded Coulommiers. Who for the serious discs of Reblochon.

She imagined the pride of each of these cheesemakers and the certain pleasure of each of her many customers. A pleasure that she facilitated, the cheese midwife. The thought filled her with a sudden, sweeping anxiety she had not felt in some time, to think of all these exquisite creations that she purchased and sold, that passed through her hands more or less unaffected, and which were then greedily consumed and gone from her forever.

Anything the existence of which I can myself verify, she thought. Her first impulse had been right, to make, to bring to life, herself. That was verification. That was tangibility. And here she had been once again deflected—just as she had been during all her time with David—shunted to the banal and selfless periphery of the creative process.

Maria said, "Take a break already. You ever go to a Club Med?"

*Well, my dear . . . Chekhov said to her when she tried to explain.*

SHE COOKED THE MONKFISH in a bit of white wine. She made the most perfect potato pancake the world had ever seen. Then she carried her plate outside to eat dinner with the cows that speckled the green hills in all directions.

Being halfway around the world was good in itself, but this was rapturously peaceful.

Clooney showed up early the next morning as agreed. He glanced quickly at the table on the lawn, now covered in dew, then back to her as she locked the door and approached him. On the driveway, hearing the gravel crunch underfoot, Gillian had a sudden awareness of her movement across the ground, of the microscopic trace mark she left on the great green back of Ireland. It was not uncomfortable, this sense of closing a distance between herself and Clooney, as his tweedy frame cast a long shadow in the light of a new day.

She climbed into his red Fiesta. Then, self-conscious about her own silence and the gyroscopic sensation that remained in her, she looked around the tight interior of the car and said, "Cosy."

"It'll get you there and back again," Clooney said, snugging the seatbelt around his waist.

"And to various undisclosed destinations," she said.

"Indeed."

"Your turn," Gillian said, as Clooney swung the Fiesta onto the narrow road. He accelerated quickly, shifting into second and then third, as they roared toward the crest of a hill, tall stone walls flying by very close on either side.

Clooney was a bit of a pioneer in these parts, it seemed, a connoisseur celebrating the culinary output of the country long before it was fashionable and for more years than he claimed to remember. Handmade pâté from farms in Kerry, walnut oil from Wicklow, cheese from every county in the Republic, all out of a tiny shop in Ireland's gourmet capital south of Cork City.

"For years only to foreigners," Clooney said. "Or restaurants where foreigners liked to eat. That was Kinsale."

"And now?"

"Well, now even the Irish are fancying finer things," Clooney said, managing to sound disapproving of the national success story that he embodied. An odd gourmet, she thought. Country lanky, with the simple faith revealed by that unconscious finger to the vest pocket.

"So, I was approved?" Gillian tried. They were skimming through the hills, deeper into the green and gold of West Cork. Towards Brothers.

"Well," Clooney said, a little dry. "You've made the short list."

"List?" Gillian said, feigning alarm. "How short?"

Clooney did not answer. In Skibbereen he shifted all the way down to first. The streets were clogged and sprouted from one another at odd angles. There were farm trucks parked on the sidewalk in front of the town hall. "Heart of famine country, this," Clooney said. "But I suppose you've seen the television shows and know all about it."

"Why don't you buy Brothers?" she asked, when they were pulling out into the country again a few moments later.

"I'm not eligible," Clooney said. "I suppose I'm also too old for a new game entirely."

"Well, look at me," Gillian said.

Clooney smiled. "I have already. I think you're very young indeed."

"What do you mean, eligible?" she asked again.

Clooney didn't answer this one. He didn't seem ready to take a risk on her. Outside the countryside was spilling past, fragrant, verdant. She still felt light.

"Can we talk about the cheese?" she asked him. "Pope's Own from Brothers Farm?"

Clooney didn't say no.

"Washed-rind semi-soft?"

"It is that."

"Like anything I've tried?" Gillian asked.

"Perhaps a bit like a Morbier," Clooney said. "But different as well."

"And how is it I had never heard of Pope's Own before Chekhov told me about it?" she pushed.

Clooney stopped the car on the shoulder just then, so close to a stone wall she couldn't have opened the car door. He produced a black kerchief from the glove compartment in front of her knees. "You won't have heard of it because it's never been for sale before," he said.

He raised the black handkerchief towards her eyes.

She tried to treat it lightly. "This is all very dramatic, isn't it?"

"I'm sorry," Clooney said, from quite close, his hands now behind her head. "But if you do not buy the farm, the seller does not wish its location revealed." He smelled just faintly of soap and bacon, not unpleasant in total. But even as he tied the kerchief in place so gently, Gillian had to fight a surging impulse to tear the thing from her eyes.

The car began to roll again. The breeze came through the window and her breathing slowed. They were on pavement for a short time, then on a rougher surface, perhaps gravel, whereupon she found herself shifting this way and that in her seat, once jostling to the right and rubbing shoulders with Clooney himself.

He wasn't telling her what he knew, Gillian thought. And that told her something else entirely.

*Pope's Own? It sounds like a race horse.*

*Chekhov put his hands flat together as he thought of it. There's nothing in the world quite like this cheese, he said finally. Golden paste like the sun on Derby morning. A trace of purple runs through the centre, like the blood of the Republic itself.*

*Why Pope's Own?*

*Chekhov came out of his reverie. Because Brothers Farm is owned by the Church at the moment, that's why. His balding holiness and a crimson gang of cardinals eat every wheel of it.*

*Gillian understood finally. How did that ever come about? She asked.*

*Chekhov frowned as he thought about how to answer. I understand, he said finally, that Brothers was given to the Church over thirty years ago by an elderly cheesemaker who had seen a vision to the effect that this was what God wished of him.*

*Crazy.*

*I shan't disagree with you on that score.*

*And why would the Vatican be selling Brothers now?*

*Chekhov seemed to lose interest suddenly. I can only imagine they have their divinely inspired reasons.*

*So cheese aficionados from all over the world are descending on West Cork for the first ever taste of . . .*

*Chekhov cut her off. It won't be like that at all. They have a man, Clooney. He will arrange a very quiet sale.*

*And why me? Why not yourself?*

*Just get to Clooney, Chekhov said. Tell him only who you are and that I have sent you.*

*That's it?*

*You might also try Matthew 13:45 on him. In a pinch, I suppose. A religious man, our Clooney. And then he recited it for her.*

*It seems a little cheap. Gillian frowned. I can't say things I don't believe.*

*Oh, certainly you can, Chekhov said. It feels so good when you stop.*

She jostled against Clooney as they rounded a bend. He joked with her dryly. "Just another kilometre or so. Would you like anything to read?"

She stayed in the jostle position, leaning a little on him. "I might have drifted off," she lied.

They stopped a few minutes later. The tires had just changed tone from the conversational scratch and ping of gravel to the hollow rumble of a stone drive. She heard a gate close behind them.

When the black kerchief came off, she was blinded. She climbed out of the Fiesta, holding the door, and blinked into the splintering haloes of blue that fizzed on her retina—she had an image of Franky on the mat, the two of them looking down at him—and then her new surroundings slowly rose to her vision.

She was in a small courtyard in front of a tall house, stone with blue wood shutters and a slate roof with many chimneys. There were rose bushes flurrying over the lattices that had been built along the side walls. There were some farm trucks parked against a hedge opposite. A garden bordering a cobblestone drive, a narrow walkway that disappeared towards the farmyard. And rising behind the house in a broad, calm sweep, there was an expanse of green pasture that stretched up to the far ridge line.

When she pulled her eyes away from all of this she saw that there was another man there, standing with Clooney on the far side of the car.

"Meet Ferghal, our foreman," Clooney said. "Ferghal, this is Miss Mackin."

She rounded the car to shake hands with Ferghal, who grinned widely. "Cheers. Yeah. God bless." He had a thatch of sandy hair and was wearing a white T-shirt with red suspenders, black wool pants and green rubber boots with the tops folded down.

"Just working the morning milk now," Ferghal said, motioning them to follow him. He led them past the courtyard to the nearest building in the yard. And here, before their bags even came out of the car, they stood at the low doorway, and Gillian could see the large table vats where the milk was being coagulated over steam heat. Half a dozen women in gowns and hairnets bent silently to their various tasks, the hush reverential.

CLOONEY EXPLAINED HOW IT would work. Sunday, an envelope would arrive from Dublin with the other bid. That gave her all of today and tomorrow to inspect the property and the books. Ferghal and Clooney would be available for any information needed on the equipment, the buildings, the herd or the cheese itself.

She put in a call to Tremblay first and got him out of bed. A Dublin real estate agent was what they needed, she told him. He might try using the Internet. Get some recent sale prices for a property of similar size with a large house in good condition, working farm attached. "Any kind of farm," Gillian said.

"Location?" Tremblay said, yawning.

"I don't know exactly, to tell you the truth. Somewhere in West Cork."

"By when?"

"Tomorrow, your noon?" she said. "Please and thank you."

"I'm assuming these monks of yours run a *profitable* cheese operation," he said then, awake enough to start worrying about her pressing tone of voice, about the impulsive quality of her request.

"They're not monks," Gillian said, finding again that Tremblay's attentiveness made her irritable. "Brothers is just the name of the farm. Brothers Farm. Pope's Own is the cheese."

Tremblay didn't care about any of this. He was waiting for his answer.

"I'm going through the books this morning," Gillian said, wanting off the phone.

Of course, books were just paper on one level. Clooney spread out a plan of the property on the Brothers House dining-room table and brought two hard-bound black ledgers out of the next room. He left her with the words "Well then, I imagine you'll want a few hours with all of this."

Which she emphatically did not. This might have been her old job, the mental framing of reality through the manipulation of financial results. She sat at the table, frozen above this brocade of written entries and blueprint lines and legal descriptions of the property, wanting only to look up from the pages and out the window to the fields beyond the rose bushes.

Really, she thought, what was there to say about a company that sold everything it made to the Vatican at a price negotiated thirty years before? Of course Brothers was losing money.

"All right, all right," Gillian said, finding Clooney outside washing the Fiesta. "I've had enough."

Clooney put down his rag. "So soon?" he looked genuinely disappointed.

"Not enough of all of this . . ." Gillian said, waving

her arms around her, aware that he might have taken her to be displeased with the farm itself, the cheese, the whole operation. "I only meant . . . all that." She motioned back to the house.

Clooney scratched his chin. "I see," he said.

And so he found a pair of rubber boots for her in the Fiesta, and they walked for the rest of the day. From the big house up through the pasture to the ridge line at the north end of the property. From there into the back meadow where the herd was grazing its way methodically towards an evening milking. From there they followed a small stream to the low stone wall that marked the west side of the property. And this guided them south again to the creamery buildings, the paddock, the courtyard and the big house.

They had dinner in the big house. Ferghal had gone and they were in the hands of the Brothers' septuagenarian housekeeper, Annie, who (if she was to be believed) cooked, cleaned, gardened, mowed the lawn, fixed the roof and once chased off a prowler with a pair of hedge clippers. Annie had decided she liked Gillian.

She served them lamb chops and roasted potatoes, then sat watching them eat as if Gillian were someone whose arrival she had hoped for, anticipated for a long time.

After dinner Annie said only, "Well?" And Clooney nodded.

She disappeared behind the kitchen door, where Gillian heard the scraping of crockery, a brief clatter of silverware and then silence. They both stared at the door. When she re-emerged, Annie carried a white plate, which she slid soundlessly onto the table.

"Mustn't muzzle the ox," Annie said.

Gillian stared down at the small triangular cheese, maybe seven inches a side. The rind was as orange as the sun had been that morning when she locked the house and turned to find Clooney out of the car, standing, watching her.

"Go ahead, love," Annie said.

Gillian took the small knife and rotated the plate slowly. When the cheese was aligned with a corner facing her, she made two symmetrical cuts on either side of it, and gently pulled free a diamond of cheese. She turned it on one side to see more clearly.

It had the palest of yellow flesh, and horizontally through the centre of the paste ran a capillary of royal purple. It was a startling contrast, making her wonder how the trace of purple had been introduced, but also drawing her eye to how the colours highlighted each other: the yellow somehow a greater promise for the blood-like residue, for the suggestion of prior despair.

"It's beautiful," she said.

"The sun on Easter morning and the blood of the Irish saints," Clooney said with a small smile.

"Is that what you think?" she asked him, cutting the piece into three smaller pieces. "Or is it the sun on Derby morning and the blood of the Republic?"

Annie smiled and nodded. "Chekhov," she said.

"And may I ask how he would have come to taste it?" Gillian asked, looking up at Clooney.

He raised his eyebrows in friendly exasperation, then stared down fixedly at the cut Pope's Own in front of them and said, "Will you be eating some of this blessed cheese, then?"

She put it on her tongue, squeezing it, chewing it almost gingerly. It was full and savoury, no sharpness or acridity, but tangy with the life that blossomed within it.

*It comes alive, Chekhov said. It will remind you in an instant of all that you have been.*

*I don't know if I like the sound of that, Gillian had answered.*

*You needn't like the sound of it at all, Chekhov said.*

She let the flavours swim through her for a moment. There was clover here, she thought, letting her eyes drift shut. There was the scent of broom and a faint saline back breeze. Was that earthy undertone the purple vein, she wondered. The flavours carried her aloft, to a point above the farm where all was visible and yet within her grasp. At once vertiginous and exhilarating. One might crash to earth from here or never touch down again.

When she opened her eyes again, she was not particularly surprised to find Clooney and Annie watching her carefully.

"Oh my," she said eventually. Embarrassed to find only those frail and grandmotherly words. "Oh my."

SHE FOLLOWED FERGHAL around the next day, squelching behind him in a too-big pair of Clooney's wellies.

They took morning milk from half the herd and poured it, steaming, still warm from the cows, into the table vats with the rennet. When it firmed into curds these were lightly cut with long thin knives, drained, then pressed gently into the triangular moulds filling each of them up halfway.

"All right then," Ferghal said. "You'll want to watch this part."

The gowned woman who was working with them produced a steel pail of purple paste. Gillian's eyebrows raised quizzically but the woman said nothing.

Ferghal answered, "Soot and port wine. To protect the surface."

"Soot?" Gillian asked. "As in ashes?"

He nodded, concentrating as the woman gently brushed the surface of the curds in the half-filled moulds.

They repeated the process with a late afternoon milking from the other half of the herd. After these curds were cut and drained, they were used to fill the moulds to the top, trapping the layer of purple ash in the centre.

"After about a week we salt them and transfer them to the curing house," Ferghal explained. "We'll wash the rinds with brine and brandy for a few weeks until they're nice and orange."

At the end of the second day she walked back through the Brothers pastures again, alone this time, and stood on the ridge line, looking down at the farm. The cows had been released into the fields after the second milking, the seven employees from nearby towns were pulling out the front drive, driving slowly over the cattle guard. She could pick out Ferghal making his final rounds before shaking hands with Clooney at the front door and climbing into his small flatbed truck.

Above her, the darkness was coming. Dropping down to enfold this farm and her. And she felt herself snugged down by the descending night, pinched between the air and the land and fused between them.

She called Tremblay after dinner from the old black-and-chrome phone in the main floor study. He was in an upbeat mood, the Dublin numbers having come back very high. "Bit of interest in West Cork at the moment," he said. "I'm afraid prices reflect it."

He told her. It was about twice what Gillian expected. She winced and looked out through the glass into the darkness. Her own reflection was superimposed over the silhouette of the ridge line, where the stars were just visible.

"You tried," Tremblay said. "That's the important thing."

"You think so?" Gillian said.

"To a degree, yes."

"To what degree, though?" Gillian asked. The comment angered her.

"Gillian . . ."

"I want to know to what degree trying is the important thing. Is trying about half the value of doing something? Is it about a quarter the value?"

Tremblay listened patiently at the other end of the phone.

"Because I'm more of the opinion, at the moment, Tremblay, that it's about zero per cent of the value."

"Fine," Tremblay said. "Tell me where the money comes from and I'll get it to you."

"I could sell the property up the valley," she said.

"Bad idea," Tremblay said. "But it wouldn't be enough anyway."

"Bad idea?" Gillian said, gripping the phone tighter. "What do you mean, bad idea?"

"Investing everything in Irish real estate? Is this the strategy we discussed? Anyway, it's not enough."

"Sell the West End condo."

"You have to live somewhere."

"I realize that," she said. "I could live here."

"Gillian . . ." he tried. "I think you're getting ahead of yourself."

"You have no idea where I am relative to myself," she said, irritated with this resistance. Always accommodating, always deferring to her, he chose this moment to carve a position on something.

"I won't help you run away," Tremblay was saying. He might well have said more after this, but those words obliterated whatever might have followed.

"Run away?" she said, incredulous.

"I know what's going on," Tremblay said. "What this really means. He was a bastard, all right? The world agrees that he was a bastard. That he deserves to fail, to be surpassed by you. For you to succeed . . ."

"You are completely wrong," Gillian said.

"I'm not," Tremblay said firmly. "You're falling for the oldest impulse in the book: flight. It's no more complicated than that really, you're going to run until nothing looks the same any more and then you'll think you've proved to yourself somehow that you have changed, gone past him. But you won't have."

"Nonsense," Gillian said. They were both still on the line, and seconds passed during which explanations might have been attempted, but all she could think of were the obstacles erecting themselves between her and what she had finally found. And as the thought surged, her hand slammed the phone down into the old chrome cradle.

*Just don't be angry, Chekhov said. For yourself, don't be angry.*

*How can I not be angry? Everything should be wiped clean just because he's buying fifty-eight dollars' worth of expensive cheese he probably doesn't even eat? Makes me sick to look at him.*

*That's what grovelling looks like. I'm not suggesting you forgive David, only don't spoil it all for yourself by being angry.*

He answered on the first ring. She didn't even say hello.

"What are you painting these days?" she asked him.

"Cheese?" David said. Then he laughed unnecessarily hard, his voice cracking with the manic pleasure of hearing from her. She supposed he might be thinking of a sunny future just then, a post-marital über-contentment during which he and his darling ex-wife would share friendly absolving banter over coffee, perhaps the odd fuck. So ran the purple vein of her insight as she clutched the phone in the study of Brothers House just then.

"I need to borrow money," she said.

She told him every detail, more than he wanted to know no doubt, but she left him not one spare second to interrupt. She laid everything bare for this man who had himself a proclivity for laying things bare. Not caring. She told him about the farm up the valley, about the condo in town, the price of McGuigan's cheese shop, the value of the inventory. She told him about Chekhov's tip, about Brothers, about the morning milk and the evening milk and the port-stained ash between. About the cobblestones on the main drive, the tended gardens, Annie and the women in their hairnets. About the sky pressing down on her like a lover on the ridge that evening, how it had pinched her to the earth and made her blood prickle in her veins. About—at the end of it all—what she had discovered and what, through her, it could become.

She wrote up the offer immediately after hanging up. And when she was finished she didn't think about anybody. Not about David or Tremblay or Clooney. Not even about Chekhov. She walked the envelope down the hall to the last door on the right and slid it under, into the darkness beyond.

GILLIAN HEARD THE FRONT GATE opening early the next morning, as a courier from Dublin dropped off the other envelope. But she didn't want to see Clooney until he had decided. She didn't want to see Clooney comparing her to some anonymous other.

She walked through the dairy instead. Watching the women cutting the morning curds with their long-tined knives. She watched the whole process as it unfolded again, thinking with pleasure of this gentle and perpetual repetition.

"What's your name?" she asked the woman who had applied the purple soot the day before. Now she was raking the curds, silently.

"Sal," she said.

They met in the front room as agreed. The sun streamed in off the meadow behind him.

"You were low," Clooney said.

She nodded, but couldn't bring herself to comprehend these words. "Low how?" she said.

Clooney sighed. "Lower than Dublin," he explained.

Over Clooney's shoulder she could see that the cattle had been released into the main pasture behind the house.

"I don't believe this," she said. "How close?"

"Does it matter?" Clooney said. "I have a duty."

"How close, God damn it?" she asked.

Clooney stared at her, a little sorrowfully.

"I'm sorry," she said.

"So am I," he answered.

She sat back in her chair, exhaled a long breath. "Who is 'Dublin'? Who is this winner of Brothers Farm? Maybe I could talk to him."

"Gillian," he said. The first time he'd used her first name. "Do you think I'd lie to you?"

She snapped at him. The man she needed in the whole process, the key to this whole thing and she snapped. "I don't take this personally," she said, sharp, voice raised.

"Oh no?" he said. "You're a bit like your friend Brian McGuigan in that department, I think."

She had to think who that was for a moment. Chekhov. And then her mind was spinning forward already. "Who is the other bidder?" she asked.

Clooney squinted and thought.

"You can afford to tell me now, surely," she said.

He scratched the side of his jaw. "Colman McGuigan," he said.

She considered this, recalibrating her view of the situation. "Chekhov's brother," she said eventually.

"The elder of two," Clooney said. "McGuigan the father willed Brothers Farm to the Church some thirty years ago. It was to go back to one of the boys at a fair market price if ever one of them did wish to buy it. One of the boys, that is, or a designate."

"And you set them bidding against each other?"

"The McGuigan boys were born to bid against each other," Clooney said. "The surprising thing is that Chekhov didn't come himself. He must think very highly of you to have sent you along instead."

"This is ridiculous," Gillian said.

"You might say so." And while Clooney sat there, comfortable in his chair, his index finger dipped unconsciously into his vest pocket. So instinctive was this impulse to reach for strength beyond. She didn't care that it was muscle memory at this point, she cared only that it was a telegraph. How dare this man, anyone for that matter, come wading in on her with a left hand at the waist, chin dangling.

Clooney rose slowly to his full height. Lanky at fifty.

"You haven't passed the news along yet," she said, setting up.

"I wanted to tell you first."

"The brothers," Gillian went on, keeping her eyes steadily on a spot in the middle of Clooney's chest. "I mean the McGuigan brothers. They're not believers, are they?"

"Oh, we're all believers in our own way, I suppose," Clooney said.

"That's not so at all," she said. "Not true of Chekhov. Not true of Colman McGuigan either. Chekhov is a bitter ex-communist-Republican and Colman is a successful businessman with his treasure stored up on earth. Isn't that true?"

Clooney appraised the comment. "Perhaps," he said.

"You think either of them understands Matthew 13:45?" Gillian said. And only now she let her eyes drift downwards, intending to playact sorrow and finding it right there, quite real in her throat and behind her chest.

Although she could no longer see him, she could hear that Clooney had stopped moving.

"Or again . . ." Gillian said, and her cheeks flushed just a little as it occurred to her she might forget the verse, and she had to blot everything out briefly. The sound of the breeze, of cattle. The smell of straw and clover, of manure. The light of the country streaming in around them. She imagined herself channelling the scripture itself and the words then came easily: "Or again, the kingdom of Heaven is like a merchant searching for fine pearls. When he has found a single pearl of great value, he goes and sells all his possessions and buys it."

You can hear someone listening.

As she thought back, Gillian knew she had never ever heard David or Tremblay or even Chekhov listen to her as Clooney listened to her that day.

He listened so hard. Listened with everything in him, to everything in her.

# PRAYERS TO BUXTEHUDE

I proposed marriage to Maddy on a Sunday night. We had been to the christening of her nephew that afternoon, an occasion that precipitated all the events that followed, up to and including the proposal.

You might argue that I should have done this a long time ago. Maddy and I have been together five years, since shortly after meeting at Columbia Law School. We were friends first, two West Coast kids in New York City, both sent by enthusiastic parents who were themselves associated with bench and bar. We came back west together, even worked at the same firm on our return, although Maddy eventually took a job with an investment bank. Our lives have tracked along in tandem for these years and we seem more or less compatible.

I find Sundays stressful, with work looming in the morning. For the past year my professional life has been a single difficult file. A multimillion-dollar fire fraud that has half a dozen insurance companies suing the lights out of each other. Downstairs in Documents, there is an entire room devoted to this file, which other firm lawyers have taken to calling Ishmael. I don't know where this started but if I meet someone in the coffee room on a Saturday, they will say to me only, "Ishmael?" To which I will gamely nod.

Saturdays I work, but Sundays I take off—in deference to Maddy, who was indoctrinated as a child on the matter of the Sabbath. I wait out Sundays, everything in precarious balance. I read *The New York Times* and try not to think about my roomful of data.

Something notable happened at the christening. When the priest drizzled the water on the little boy's forehead, both Maddy and the baby cried simultaneously. It was as if they'd been cued. The baby got wet and they both bawled. This provoked a series of unexpected thoughts about my childhood. I thought about being unable to swim. I thought about my piano teacher.

"I can't swim," I said to Maddy in the car heading back to the city. "Ever since I was a kid I've been scared witless of water."

"I didn't know that."

"I became a pyromaniac to counter it. I remember thinking that there were two types of people: water people and fire people."

Maddy looked quizzical.

"I was just wondering how many kids develop aquaphobia after getting water splashed on their heads when they're little babies."

"You were baptized?" she asked, surprised. But then she decided it wasn't worth pursuing and said something about the importance of the ritual being worth the risk.

"Why?" I asked. "The baby has made no choices. And when you throw water on babies, I have observed that babies always cry. Water on the baby. Baby cries. And now I can't swim."

"Just think of it this way," Maddy said. "While other kids were taking swimming lessons, you were taking piano lessons and increasing your cultural depth."

"Or think of it this way," I returned. "While other kids were swimming, I was melting toy soldiers with a magnifying glass and gaining psychosocial complexity."

But she was right. And I might have admitted that I had been thinking about my piano teacher during the christening, although not as a cultural alternative to swimming. Instead, I thought of these lessons and the promise that I had, and I was reminded of how I fantasized about playing for a living. In my teens I used to imagine myself at black-tie cocktail parties, saying, "I am a musician.

Jazz." Although, inevitably, I figured out that jazz musicians don't get invited to black-tie cocktail parties unless they're performing.

Maddy was reiterating her point about ritual verbatim, a rhetorical technique she favours.

"You know?" I said, blinkering to get off the highway. "You might convince me that your view has merit if you supported it with evidence and argument in some fashion."

"Stop being a lawyer for five minutes," Maddy said.

"I'm beginning to think I might like to stop forever," I said back. And for some reason, this made Maddy cry again.

WE WERE IN A STUDY GROUP together at Columbia, just friends. I was still playing piano at this point, trying to date sequined black-haired jazz singers at night and study law during the day. It was a stretch, but I did actually get something like a break in the jazz world.

My best buddy at the time was a cat named King Knight—given name—a piano player I became friendly with by showing up every Tuesday night at the Jazz Cellar. After I got to know King, we would get loaded together after a show once in a while. We would sit at a table near the piano, drink bourbon and argue about things like whether the squeak of the men's-room door was an E or an E-flat. We settled most arguments at the keyboard, playing out our points. Was Billy Taylor better at stride or bop? I played his version of "Let's Get Away from It All" and even King had to back down.

"All right, that swings," King allowed.

One morning during second-year law school, King phoned me early. He sounded terrible.

"Flu?" I remember asking.

"Shit man," King said. "I don't need a doctor, I need a replacement."

"Tuesday at the Cellar?" I said, hugely flattered.

"No man," he croaked. "The Green. Benny Shulman hit me up for a favour backing him tomorrow night and I can't fucking stand."

Shulman was an unreconstructed lounge act, enjoying the rebounding popularity of the style. He wore snakeskin cowboy boots with a tux and had done a few big shows in Vegas years before. The truth was, I could take or leave Shulman.

The Green, however, was a landmark.

"Holy shit," I remember saying to King. "Holy holy holy shit."

So I went. Shulman looked me once over and ordered me up onto the bandstand to play "When I Fall in Love" in A-flat. He said, "I'm not taking a flier on King's say-so." I played it, he nodded once and handed me a set list. That was it. I was in. And, of course, Maddy and everybody else we knew came down for the gig.

Shulman says to me afterwards, "Yeah you play real nice kid." I was a mile high. The gang goes out for drinks, we hop around to a few bars. People are peeling out one by one, off to bed, have to get up in the morning, classes, books, standard law-school bullshit. Pretty soon it's just Maddy and me and I'm looking at her and I'm thinking how pretty she is and how nice it is that she's stayed with me and how brilliant it is that she maybe understands what nobody else understood, which is what the Green meant to me. One night there, and I was going to tell my kids about this, in the unlikely event I ever had any kids but if I had kids, you know, Shit, Maddy would make a great mom.

I kissed her in the cab. One thing led to another. I'm not proud of myself, admitting this, but when we were sitting on her bed and I opened the front of her shirt, I distinctly remember thinking, My God, I can't believe I didn't think of this before.

AFTER SHE STOPPED CRYING in the car, she didn't think I should come over. I had to talk her into going to the Cue Ball for a nightcap and a snack.

"Sundays they have jazz," I said. "Come on, it's early."

We went down and sat at a little table in the long dark room. We ate chicken fingers and nachos. We talked about nothing, really. Ishmael. Her work. Things we had to do before the end of the month.

Over her shoulder, I was watching the stage. They were a tight trio, piano, bass and drums. A seventy-year-old piano player creating a familiar dense and swinging sound, slapping out the strung block chords, the bass laying colour under it all, drums nice and quiet. I recognized "Red Beans," a number Coleman Hawkins had done with the Red Garland Trio in the late 1950s. And here was this old guy in the 1990s. It was comeback time and I found myself cheering for him.

"You know," I said to Maddy, as it all came to me, "I know that guy."

She was starting to enjoy herself again. "From New York?"

"No," I said. "From before that."

"Is he good?"

"Horace Blank is a monster," I said. "Listen."

Which we did for a while, and I pointed out where Blank flared out of the groove along his own licks woven through the bop changes. When he finished the number I clapped loudly, and he looked out across the room and nodded at me.

"How did you meet?" Maddy asked. And so I ordered two more drinks and told her the never-previously-told story of Horace Blank, Mrs. Laurence and related matters.

I WAS TWELVE, TAKING PIANO LESSONS from a teenaged girl who lived down the street. She was sweet, but even at that age I knew I was limited by her. I wanted to audition to train under Mrs. Laurence, who taught music at the University of British Columbia, and whose few recordings I had borrowed from the library. Mrs. Laurence was, among other things, beautiful. White skin, short black hair, thick eyebrows and lips. The cover photo from her Chopin interpretations made it appear she had no irises, so large were her glistening black pupils.

My parents, observing my disinclination for sports, were pushing me into joining the soccer team.

"Balance," said my father. "The balanced individual is an organism made up of three components: body, soul and spirit." And here my father—a judge—traced an equilateral triangle in the air over the breakfast table.

I sat there in the dock, poking my oatmeal.

"Although we are prone to favour just one of the three sides of our personality," the Judge continued, "there is discipline in the combination. Body. Soul. Spirit."

"What's my spirit part?" I asked glumly.

The Judge allowed the question and answered, "Your spirit is the lift under your wings."

"Wings?"

"Wings, which you will build feather by feather during the course of a first-rate post-secondary education," my mother said.

"Post-secondary?" I said.

"Preferably Ivy," came the response.

I cut a deal. Soccer every Thursday after school in exchange for an audition with Mrs. Laurence. If I made it, fine. If not, back to the teenaged girl up the street.

Mrs. Laurence lived in a neighbourhood of modern houses that looked like giant sugar cubes balanced on one another. The day of the audition, Mr. Laurence answered the door and we were shown into a clean square room with mirrors and black flagstones. Three large paintings hung opposite us, each a banner of solid colour: black, white and rust, the colour of drying blood.

"Well then," Mr. Laurence said to my mother, squinting down at her. "You're the Judge, aren't you?"

"That is my husband," my mother said. "I am a lawyer."

He took us up a staircase of polished wooden slabs balanced on a thin metal beam. We passed diagonally across a window looking out over the Laurences' rock garden, in the middle of which sat a small green pagoda. At the top of the stairs we turned left into the music studio, a large bare room with a black Steinway concert grand. The walls and ceiling of the studio were covered in beige sound-absorbent tiles. The piano stood in front of a wall of glass looking out into the trees. The glass wall itself was partly covered with a translucent paper blind through which the sunlight glowed in reassuring orange tones.

Mrs. Laurence examined me. I wasn't sure what she saw, but I was pleased that she looked just as she did on her album covers. Only in person, the heavy eyebrows and the black eyes held me with critical interest. I could also see that she had a smooth body moulded by tight khakis and a thin black sweater.

My mother coughed slightly and I looked away.

"Right," Mrs. Laurence said, a voice both soft and hard. She sat me on the leather piano bench, then leaned over me and put a Kuhlau study on the music rack. She smelled of clay and paper and spices. "I expect this will be easy for you," she said from just next to my ear. "But I want you to take a minute and read it over."

Mother was escorted into the kitchen to read magazines. I waited, dangling my legs and reading the Kulau, chewing my nails and finger skins nervously until I was bleeding from the edge of my right thumb.

Mrs. Laurence returned, smiled at me and said clearly, "Let's say our prayers to Buxtehude then, shall we?"

I played well. In her brief absence I had memorized the simple structure and melody and so I was able to concentrate on each tone instead, my eyes closed dramatically, carving my phrases to emerge and crest and taper with what I hoped was depth and maturity.

I opened my eyes before I struck the final chord, at which point I saw how very much my thumb had been bleeding. Up and down the piano, above and below where my hands now rested, were beads of my blood, a spackling of drops and smears that traced my treatment of Kulau over the Steinway, a tracing just now beginning to dry.

Mrs. Laurence made a wonderful face, not disgust but a kind of stage horror. And then she said, "You play wonderfully. Only you must promise not to bleed on my piano any more."

But she took me. Once a week, Tuesdays after school. I was ecstatic.

In the car, my mother said, "What on earth were you playing?"

"Kulau," I said.

"After that. It sounded like a dog walking on the key-board."

And with this comment, I realized that my mother had been listening carefully from behind the kitchen door while Mrs. Laurence had produced a handkerchief from her sleeve, moistened it with a dab of spit, and gently wiped clean the keys, each one sounding under her touch. I laid down a track of blood for her, but Mrs. Laurence had wiped up the drops in a pattern of her own design and so it had sounded nothing like Kulau to my mother, nothing like the music I had previously played.

"What a dreadful woman," my mother said aloud, but to herself. "An arteest."

I only liked her more as I got to know her.

She smoked. That was exotic, but she also had a pot-ter's wheel in a separate studio on the main floor. A motor powered the aluminum platter, slick clay slithering under her hands as she showed me how. She leaned over me, her small breasts brushing the back of my neck, and I watched the clay begin to cover her hands, climbing up past her wrists in gloves of greyish muck.

Plus, she felt my potential was significant enough to warrant a second weekly session.

"Thursdays after school?" she said, settling back on the cushions of her Swedish teak chaise longue and tuck-ing her sockless feet up under her bottom.

I made a formal appeal to drop soccer. It was denied.

And so I was forced by circumstance to skip Thursday after-school soccer practices.

It was not exactly like breaking out of Alcatraz. On a good day our forwards (delinquent fourteen-year-olds) could smoke four doobies between them before practice. Coach Reijnitzsc had thick glasses and at some point in every practice a soccer ball would inevitably elude his outstretched hands and smash into the bridge of his nose. The forwards would collapse on the turf, giggling insanely. And if everything co-operated, the number 23 bus would heave over the horizon at this point and I would vault the fence, pulling my piano books out of my shorts, and be climbing up through the back garden to the Laurences' house inside ten minutes.

She typically answered the door on the phone, the long black cord slinking back over the flagstones, under the three modern canvases, around the corner and into the back of the main floor and the bedrooms. She would put her hand on the top of my head, gently pull me inside and motion for me to take off my cleats. Then she would extract herself from her conversation the same way, each time. "I have to go, darling."

Silence.

"Someone's here."

Silence.

"Time for us both to say a few prayers to Buxtehude."

And then she would say this to me again, returning from the kitchen with her ginseng tea. "All right then, prayers to Buxtehude." Which I understood eventually to mean, Let's you and I get cracking, let's immerse in this music together. She said this with a wide smile, seeming genuinely glad to see me, glad to hear me play. And if ever I forgot my books before going out to practice, we would work on whatever she was playing at the moment. In this way I learned Chopin, came to enjoy Shostakovich and respect Satie. When it had been established I was breaking out of soccer prison to make my Thursday class with no parental endorsement or financing, Mrs. Laurence waived the lesson fee with a dismissive toss of her exquisite head.

"You are worth it," she said, a comment that was beyond thrilling. It was stirring somehow.

"Who is it on the phone?" I asked finally. The school year was nearly over. We were working on Bach's preludes and fugues, which Mrs. Laurence said that I had memorized in about a tenth of the time a student in high school would take, if they accomplished the feat at all.

She was lying on the chaise longue, blowing smoke at the beige ceiling. "Do you like the preludes?" she asked, clearly hoping that I did.

"Of course I do," I said.

Mrs. Laurence sighed.

"Who do you talk to on the phone?" I asked again.

She looked across the room at me finally, her black hair pooling around her white face.

"He's a professor," she said. "My friend. We talk on

the phone, he and I. What time is it? Don't you have to get back?"

I looked at my Goofy watch. "I still have half an hour," I said.

She smiled and lay back again. "You're playing well," she said, eyes back on the ceiling.

"Is your friend called Buxtehude?" I asked politely, pronouncing it in the correct German way that she used, with the tamped-down *u*.

Mrs. Laurence laughed like a girl. "Oh, lovely," she said, sitting up. Her eyes now fixed me from under a tangle of black. "I must tell him that. No, Dietrich Buxtehude was an organist. My friend only studies and writes about his work."

She put an LP of German organ music on the record player. I remember the dense weaving lines of the fugue. Then she came over and sat on the piano bench next to me. I could feel her breathing, the rise and fall of her rubbing against my shoulder. She said finally, "Perhaps you can hear on whom Buxtehude had an influence."

"Bach of course," I said, and then I asked her very seriously, "Will you teach me Buxtehude?"

"Of course I will," she answered.

"Promise," I demanded.

"Promise." But her voice was growing distant when she said, "In 1705 Bach travelled, on foot, 280 miles in the snow from Arnstadt to Lübeck just to hear Buxtehude play. Imagine, 280 miles in the snow."

"Why?" I asked stupidly.

Mrs. Laurence put her arm around my shoulders as the fugue braided itself steadily to a close. "Because it was winter," she said.

Unlike here, I thought gloomily, where it would soon be summer. And despite Mrs. Laurence's promise, the lessons came and went and we did not learn Buxtehude, and in due course it was June, and then nearly the end of June. At first, my parents tried offering the two-month break from piano lessons as a reward for first-class honours in my grade nine Royal Conservatory exam. But when I objected, suggesting I might not go to the cottage this year but stay back in the city and work on Buxtehude, for which Mrs. Laurence thought I was nearly ready, well then it became an executive order: I would go to the cottage.

Last week of school and lessons. Tuesday I went to my piano lesson as scheduled, thinking only that Thursday would be the last one. Then soccer practice was shifted to Wednesday afternoon for no reason, and standing on the field it dawned on me that even this one last chance to see Mrs. Laurence was being taken from me. And so it was more or less now or never.

On the bus, the driver said to me, "Got the wrong day don't you? Today is Wednesday."

"I realize that," I said.

"Where are you going anyway? I see your buddies over there playing soccer. How are they going to win without you?"

"They'll manage," I said.

"Going to see your girlfriend maybe," the bus driver said, winking at me.

Let him wink, I thought. He was a simple man. A simple bus driver whose life was built around the stops and starts of others. I sat back in my seat and tried to lift my thoughts to music only, the strands of Buxtehude, the lyrical elegance of Chopin. The fiendishly difficult "Pictures" at Mussorgsky's "Exhibition."

"You should never visit your girlfriend on the wrong day, you know that, don't you?" the bus driver prattled on. "It might be someone else's day, know what I mean?"

He had a cruel laugh.

At the Laurences' I knocked and waited, noting how warm the air was becoming. In the garden there were butterflies circling the pagoda. I smiled and waited for the shuffle of Mrs. Laurence's penny loafers across the inside flagstones, the sound of her voice laughing musically with her friend.

There was no answer, but it was unlocked. I took off my cleats and explored, enjoying the silence. Silence except for a faint mechanical squeak produced from the belly of the house. Her sweet clay-smell hung in the air.

I climbed the stairs to the studio. There were pages open on the piano, handwritten pages I didn't recognize. "Buxtehude," I read finally. I had never seen the music transcribed before and I gently touched the keys, hardly sounding the notes at all, sketching them with my fingers.

Downstairs, I registered again the faint squeak. A metronomic noise at about *largo*.

I followed the path I normally saw marked by Mrs. Laurence's phone cord. Past the turgid modern paintings and around the corner into the hall, which was dark but given an ambient glow by its blond hardwood. I slid across these polished boards. With one finger I pushed a door open, peering first through a narrow crack and then, seeing nobody, opening it enough to slip through.

It was their bedroom, clearly. The bed was unmade, its pure white sheets and bolster piled in a breathless heap on the floor. I glanced around, picking up a sheet of manuscript paper that lay at my feet. I recognized Buxtehude at once, but the page was crumpled. There were more here, more than a dozen in all. They were from upstairs, I thought, wondering how they'd ended up down here.

I collected them one by one, and instead of a dawning sense that I was trespassing, instead of any fear that I might be caught, I began to feel that I had arrived just in time. That these pages should not be crumpled and that surely they belonged upstairs with the others.

I slipped into the hall again, the pages in one hand.

The door to the pottery studio was opposite. With one eye to the inch-wide opening I was able to identify the source of the steady squeak. The wheel was spinning, the motor off but the momentum of the aluminum disc carrying it around and around. Mrs. Laurence was there with someone, although I never really saw his face as her bare back obscured the view. He sat on the bench on the far wall; she sat astride his lap facing him. I remember that his naked legs were skinny and came down together from underneath her beautiful round naked bottom. (My heart nearly stopped.) Her back was smeared in clay. Her beautiful black hair the same. They rocked in this position, and then his grey-caked hand slithered up her back and gripped her hair from behind, pulling hard. Her head came backwards all the way, her chin pointing at the ceiling, her eyes tightly closed. Her beautiful face now presented to me upside down. His eyes must have been closed, although I don't remember.

I ran upstairs. At first thinking only that I would set the sheets of Buxtehude back on the piano rack in their right order, and that from this gesture Mrs. Laurence might know that I had been there and might feel guilty about not teaching me as she had promised. But then, standing at the piano and remembering my audition in front of these same keys, I had another idea. I went into the kitchen, searching in drawer after drawer for a knife. I found pens and tuning forks and a magnifying glass but through some kind of panic-induced mental block I could not locate a single sharp blade or anything else that I might use to open a nick in my finger and distribute spots of blood across the keyboard in the perfect calling card of anguish.

Back through the same drawers a second time I paused on the magnifying glass. The instrument was to me, to many kids, not intended for anything except starting fires.

Buxtehude burst into flames with only the gentlest touch of the bright blue-white disc of concentrated light. It was such a sudden burst of flame, in fact, that I dropped the whole sheaf of papers near the windows where I had been standing to focus the sun rays. I stood back, momentarily delighted, but the blackening of the hardwood soon concerned me. I moved towards the window to pick up the papers, the flames now the size of a small campfire, but I burned myself and stood back, perhaps just now thinking I had begun something I could not stop. Then the thin paper blinds caught fire.

*Largo* events accelerated to *presto*. The paper blinds burst into a sheet of flame, spreading quickly to the cloth acoustic tiles, which began to burn one by one, the flames moving rapidly over my head and down the walls on either side of me.

I remember running for a long time. I remember getting to a bus stop just as passengers were leaving the rear doors, and squeaking into the back of the bus without paying. In front of my school, I remember vaulting the fence and squirting back out onto the soccer pitch and standing, panting, just as three stoned forwards surged past and booted a ball into the net.

Coach Reijnitzsc blew the whistle. Practice was over. I went home that night and never said a word about anything. I didn't find out for two weeks that the Laurences had lost half the house, the kitchen, the front bedrooms, the studio (the Steinway needless to say). Mrs. Laurence had escaped without injury, my mother told me. She had apparently been in the house alone.

"Napping," my mother said. "She probably dropped her cigarette."

MADDY DIDN'T SAY ANYTHING for quite a while after I finished. She had a look on her face that was simple to interpret. *You burnt down a house.*

I nodded slowly. Up on stage, Blank was still swinging.

"You were quite smitten with this woman," she said, laughing a little tightly. And then she had questions, of course. Did I confess? Did I feel guilty? What did any of this have to do with meeting Horace Blank anyway?

I had forgotten this was where I started, and so I told her. Mrs. Laurence didn't teach the following year, and I had decided already that I couldn't go back to her. ("You broke up with her. How sad," Maddy said.) We went looking for new piano teachers and some very misguided family friend suggested Horace Blank, who made a dramatic first impression. He asked me to play some Red Garland that had been transcribed in chicken scratch on sheets of mimeographed manuscript paper, but he also offered my mother a drink at eleven in the morning. I distinctly remember him suggesting a Greyhound.

But it was the music my mother had a problem with. "Isn't this *jazz,* Mr. Blank?"

To which Blank responded, "No, ma'am. This is sex in a twelve-bar blender."

And as she turned and marched me towards the door, Blank goosed her.

"So that was it for Blank," I finished. "But I had played my first jazz, Maddy, struck my first seventh voicing, the third, sixth, seventh and ninth. The sound was amazing, absolutely new but absolutely all that I wanted to do from then on. It was a defining moment, or at least I thought so at the time."

Maddy sat back in her chair. Her drink was long gone and she suddenly looked like she wanted to be home. She encouraged me to stay, however. "You should talk to your musician friend," she said, gesturing towards Blank, who was winding down a swinging rendition of "There's No Business Like Show Business."

"I'll call you tomorrow," I said, and then I went over and sat at the bar and ordered a bourbon, feeling dangerously swingy. I could blow off work tomorrow, I thought. I remembered how King sounded on the phone with the flu those years before. I could fake being sick. What an incredibly simple idea! It was crazy people didn't do it more often. Maybe people did. Maybe I was the only one who wasn't doing it, which would make it worse somehow.

I clapped at the break, loud and long. Some heads turned.

He took a few minutes to make his way back to the bar. He was stopping at tables and shaking hands. Smiling and being extremely cool.

"Hey, Peter," Horace called out in a familiar voice to the barkeep, who ignored him for a carefully timed second or two.

"What can I get you, Horace?" he said when he eventually came over.

"Greyhound," I said, from down the bar. Then I lifted my bourbon and said simply, "Mr. Blank."

He came around, sat down.

"This here is Sarina," he said, introducing a young woman at the bar who had floated to her feet as he finished the set. She had a headful of dyed red hair and a sequined blue cocktail dress. My guess was that she wasn't nearly as tired as she looked.

"Pleasure," she said, like she thought we were being filmed.

"I don't think I know Ivy League here," Blank said to Sarina, who took a seat on his far side. "But he knew my drink, and that's something."

"We met once," I said.

"It's an old drink too," Blank went on. "I don't drink it much any more, favouring a blue curaçao on the rocks these days. So did you guess or what? I don't think I made it into any jazz mixology books."

"Jazz mixology?" Sarina said doubtfully, sipping a martini with seven or eight large pickled onions.

"I saw this book," Blank explained. "It had the Bird Blue-Light Special and Coltrane Tea and god-damn Dexter Gordon Sun's Up Shooter, with crème de menthe and Kentucky bourbon and some Ultra Brite toothpaste."

The bartender was looking me over now.

"What did Red Garland ever get named after him?" I asked.

"God help me, Princeton here knows my heroes too," Blank said, looking at me closely. "Garland is a master, and even he never got a drink in the jazz mixology book."

"Typical," I said. "But here's to revivals, nevertheless."

"Here," Blank said, hoisting his Greyhound, "is to revivals nevertheless."

Sip.

"Peter, bring us another," Blank called.

"What are you drinking now?" Peter asked, as if Blank was messing up his whole evening by changing drinks. "Greyhound or blue curaçao?"

"Both," Horace said, inspired. "And one of whatever he's having."

Peter lifted his eyebrows suggesting that this was unwise.

"Both, goddammit. Yellow for yesterday, blue for today. Ask Cornell here what he's drinking."

"Black Russian," I said, getting in the mood. "For the future."

Peter brought the drinks.

"All right," Blank said, taking a sip from each of his drinks. "You say we met."

He enjoyed it in the retelling. He pretended to

remember the Red Garland, denied that he had offered my mother a drink. Then, finally, he laughed and winced when I got to the goose.

"You're not here to smack me or anything nuts like that?" he asked.

"I haven't thought about it in years."

"Hooo," Blank said. "I truly cannot make change for that story. Hope you weren't listening, sweetheart."

"Oh, I'm listening," Sarina said.

"So, you ever find your teacher?" Horace asked me.

"Sure, although it took me a few more years to work around to jazz."

"And you're still playing?" Horace said.

"I played in university, clubs and what have you."

"What have you," Blank said, dubiously. "You ever record?"

"No. I played behind Benny Shulman at the Green once."

"Goddamn Columbia University here played at the Green. Sweet God damn." Horace shook his head.

"What do you think," the bartender said. "Another set maybe?"

"All right," Horace said, climbing down off his stool. "All right."

Then he went up and played a swinging set, not a single slow number.

Before the encore he introduced me and called me up to the stage. I sat stunned in my chair for several seconds, listening to the applause before it registered that heads were turned and expectant faces were looking my direction. It was an honour as great as performing at the Green to be asked to play by a real musician after all these years. And so I did "When I Fall in Love" in A-flat, taking a stab at the version on *Steamin' with the Miles Davis Quintet*. Playing the sorrowful Davis lines from the first verse and shifting to the glistening chords Garland uses to embellish and intensify the second. And of course the bass player grumbled as I stepped on lines he was used to playing, and the drummer just nodded and pulled us all into line. And in the final analysis it wasn't a "Cookin' at the Continental" moment in jazz, but I handled it.

"Nothing too outrageously wrong with that," Horace said to me after the encore, sitting again at the bar. "Blue curaçao and a Greyhound, Peter."

"A little debt to Miles and Red there," I said.

"I noticed," Blank said. Then he looked me over. "Course, you look about as Steamin' as Phil Donahue."

"Oh well, thank you very much," I said.

"What's this all about," Blank asked, fingering the lapel of my blue suit.

I shrugged. "I'm a lawyer by day."

"A lawyer by day," he repeated. "Well, that figures. What are you by night?"

"Nothing now," I said sadly.

"No point trying to be two things," Blank said.

"Maybe."

"Not maybe," Blank said. "God damn, look at you."

"The thing is . . ." I started.

"This is the thing," Blank cut me off. "Life'll drive you to the crossroads. You'll decide."

"My aim is to never decide," I said.

Blank laughed hoarsely. "Oh, you'll decide, Dartmouth," he said.

I thought, The fucker is right. So I said, "Two roads diverged in a wood and I took the more yellow one."

"That's not even how the poem goes," Blank said. "Sarina, my sweet Masdevallia blossom, tell Yale here how goes that poem about the roads and the taking of the one and the not taking of the other and shit along those lines."

"Frost?" Sarina said, stifling a yawn. She told us roughly how it went.

"See?" Blank said, head jerking over at Sarina.

"I see," I said.

"Now what she said, mind, is a small crock of sala-mander shit."

"What Frost said, not me," Sarina said to Blank.

"Whomever," Horace said, articulating the *whom*.

"What's shit about it?" I said to Horace.

"Cakehole said 'a road diverged,' you know? Singular. A road diverged on my spotty ass. Makes it sound like some great thing just happens, one great moment in the forest you look up and the way wafts the steam from your piss, so there by the grace of God wafts you."

"That's not how it happens?"

"That's talking like a chowder pole," Blank said, sipping. "I've been turning left all my life. There ain't no one fork in the yellow goddamn woods, the fork just keeps on forking. Everybody's turning right and you gotta take one left after another. Turn left, then left again, then left again, then left and left again. Pretty soon you're all alone, then you know you were doing the right thing all along."

"Then you know you're going in circles, darling," Sarina said.

"Don't talk like a fool," Blank said. "You're a left turn yourself."

Sarina sniffed and disappeared in the direction of the ladies' room.

"I hate to get mean, just get angry sometimes," Blank said sheepishly. "I like a girl with red hair like that though."

"I like a girl with black hair myself."

Blank looked at me carefully. Then he said, "Yeah, I had that figured."

"How?"

"Pale guy like you. Stands out like welts from a pussy whip," Blank said. "You got your black-haired woman now?"

"I used to," I said.

"So who's the blonde you were drinking with tonight then? You messing her up?"

I was thinking about how to answer this question. "She isn't coming back, is she?" I said, nodding towards the ladies' room.

"Don't suppose so," Horace said to me. Then he ordered us both drinks again. We had gone through them slowly for a while. Then we went through them quickly, three apiece. Now we were going to be sipping slowly again.

"Blue curaçao and a Black Russian and a Greyhound," the bartender said unnecessarily loud.

"All right, man," Blank said to me. "You go on and tell me about your black-haired girl. What was her name?"

"Tell me first, Horace," I said. "Are you a praying man?"

"Course I pray," Blank said sharply. "What kind of bee's fart question is that? Guy who doesn't pray might as well try to play 'Scrapple from the Apple' with a ball peen hammer."

"Just wondering," I said, patting his arm. "You ever hear of Buxtehude?"

"You laying a black-haired girl named Buxtyhooters? Sounds like a dancer."

"Organist," I said. "True master."

"Hammond organ?" Horace said.

"A master," I said again.

"There's only one Hammond master I am prepared to acknowledge, John Brown, and that's Jimmy Smith. Maybe Brother Jack McDuff."

"Fine," I said. "Buxtehude never got famous, that's all."

"Well, all right," Horace said, settling in to listen. "I might have been able to relate at one time. So this guy was good though?"

"This guy, Horace," I said, "if you had the guts to dive right in there, this guy could change your life."

"Heavy," Horace said.

"Prayers to Buxtehude," I began. And then I told my whole story a second time. Blank listened carefully, sipping only once or twice. He liked the ending.

"Hahahahahahahahaha," he said, leaning far back. "Hahahahahahahahaha."

Then he looked at me with that same look. *You burnt down a house?*

"Yes," I said. "Really, I did."

"You were one fucked-up kid," he said finally. "Course I was too, but I only robbed a hardware store. Free nails. Whoooeee."

"What does it mean though?" I said.

"I'll tell you one thing for free," Blank said. "Black-haired women are either the only women you should be with, or they just aren't for you at all."

"Well, thanks," I said.

"No charge," Blank said. "I never got a chance to teach you piano and you play just fine. You probably don't need my advice."

Of course he gave it anyway, people never say *You probably don't need my advice* without immediately giving you what they think is the score.

After Horace left, I phoned Maddy.

"You can't be serious," she said. "What time is it?"

"I feel strongly that I should come over," I said to her.

"You need to get to bed, did you know it's one in the morning?"

"I need to come over," I said.

When I got there she had made tea, which I accepted. I took a sip and then put my cup down, took her hands in mine. I caught my reflection in a set of copper pots she has hanging in her kitchen. One of them was like a mirror aimed right at me. There I was, bending the knee at long last.

"Maddy, I should have done this a long time ago. Will you marry me? I want you to marry me. Do you want to marry me?"

So, technically, I asked twice and asserted my desire a third time, but anyway, one answer was all I was going to get.

"No," she said.

"No?" I said.

"No," she repeated. "But thank you for finally thinking of it."

"Thank me?"

"Yes. Thank you, it was sweet."

"Oh, God," I said. Now I was on both hands and knees. But instead of taking a shot at convincing her, like a genius I said, "I should have known. Blank told me I belonged with black-haired women."

"What?" Maddy said, getting out of her chair rather sharply, her voice raised. "Blank? You asked a jazz piano player whether you should marry me based on the colour of my hair?"

"We were just talking in general terms."

"Oh, that's much better," Maddy said. "Women. Better off with black-haired women? Not even one woman but women . . . don't you fucking propose to me, you . . ."

"Hey, wait . . ." I tried.

"Get out of my house," Maddy yelled.

"Maddy," I pleaded, entirely unsure for what.

And this time, she didn't merely reiterate her position without additional evidence or argument, but added, "Why did you start with this in the first place? Any of it? Me or law or jazz or anything? Why waste everybody's time?"

A rhetorical question, I realized, so I left.

MONDAY. I made it in for 9:30. No voice mail from Maddy, no e-mail. I sat stupidly for a second, trying to remember what I did for a living.

One of the junior partners connected with my insurance file stormed into my office and slammed the door. "Where the fuck were you?" he said.

I was still quite drunk. Maddy's apartment had not been my last stop. "What?" I said.

"Ishmael breakfast meeting this morning. The big guy wants some information and we couldn't even find the fucking files."

This guy was like a wrong note in a slow ballad. I said, "We gotta fucking room full of files downstairs, shoulda taken one of those."

To his credit, the guy looked at me a little more closely. "You OK?" he said.

"Bad night," I responded.

"I see . . ." he said slowly. "Why didn't you call in sick, you idiot? If you had just called me . . ."

I stared at him. "She dumped me," I said finally.

"Shit," he said. "Well listen, buddy, you're going to have to focus here . . ."

"Fuck focus," I said.

"Come on," he said. "Sharpen up."

"Fuck sharp," I said. "I'm 'Walkin'.'"

And I got to my feet quickly and went towards the door.

"You're walking?" he said, misunderstanding me. "Jesus, buddy, you better think about this."

"You know Horace Blank?" I said.

"He's at Blaine Crosby Diller, isn't he?"

"No no no. He's not a goddamn lawyer," I said. Then I slipped, I don't remember how, but I hit my head on the corner of my own desk.

"OK, OK. Look. You're going home. Sit down and I'll call you a cab."

"How about Buxtehude?" I said, holding my handkerchief against my forehead.

My colleague's eyebrows went up. "German organist. So what?"

Remarkably, he got me into the elevator, through the lobby and into a cab without incident. Only there, sitting quietly in the back seat, did I pull away the handkerchief and look at my own blood, watching it turn from its original brassy red to the coppery rust-colour I remembered from Mrs. Laurence's keys.

"Where we going, man?" the cab driver said as we headed into the dense matrix of streets that make up Vancouver's West End.

"Turn left at the lights," I said, staring down at my handkerchief. Then to myself, quietly I said, "Yeah. German organist. So what?"

He went left and then straight for a while.

"Still straight here?" The cabby was trying to get a look at me in the rear-view mirror, but I was hunched down and mumbling, making it hard for him.

"Left again," I called.

"Here?"

"Yeah, that's it. OK, now left again."

"Here?"

"Yeah, straight for a bit. Left at the next lights."

"OK." He was sounding a little doubtful.

We went left again. I was still staring at my handkerchief.

"OK, left again," I called up to him.

We were stopped. "Hey, buddy," he said. "We're in an alley here. There is no left. How about you pay me now and get out of my cab?"

Even drunk I produced a substantial tip, which softened him up a little. As I fumbled with the door, looking down the alley past dumpsters and power poles and all the way to the office buildings on the skyline beyond, he turned around in his seat and asked me, "Is this where you wanted to be?"

I don't remember if I answered him, but the truth was, I had no idea.

# THE RESURRECTION PLANT

Dad struck oil in 1976 when I was fifteen. "Struck" maybe isn't the right word. More like, was struck by. He read an enthusiastic article about it and became, himself, enthusiastic. That was his way. And so we moved from Halifax to an acreage outside Edmonton, Alberta.

I sat on the front steps of our new house and looked at the dead grass stretching away to the fence by the dirt road, the shrubs lining the drive ready to burst into flames. I was stunned by the heat, by the lack of moisture and colour. I felt like an exile. Marooned on a buff-coloured planet full of hostile, sun-toughened Prairie kids.

Mom dealt with it her own way. She was inside unpacking. Not pots or clothes. First, her South American hat collection. Panamas and bowlers. Next, the record player. Dad phoned from his new office in downtown Edmonton.

"Helping your mom, Colin?"

I didn't tell him mom was lying flat on her back in the empty living room listening to the Tijuana Brass. Wearing a Mayan bowler. What I did tell him was that I was going to go look for the river.

"Attaboy," Dad said optimistically. "The Atlantic, see . . . it just goes in and out. The river is always coming from someplace, and then going on to some other place."

There were black-and-white birds that shrieked challenges and followed me from branch to branch partway down the ravine. I climbed through papery grass and some thin silver trees, up over a weed-covered berm, and discovered the mighty North Saskatchewan.

It was brown. I threw dirt clods into it.

MY LOCKER PARTNER WAS TED SHUCHUK. He had a virgin upper lip, never shaved, which aspired to a moustache and achieved only a faint black smudge that disappeared entirely if you looked at it from a certain angle. His closest friend was a failed eleventh-grader everyone called Snowblower. He stored his broken binders, a dumb-bell and stray sandwiches on a rickety homemade set of plywood shelves. Almost every morning I had to brush piles of mouse shit off my books.

Ted spruced up the locker with an Olivia Newton John poster and a Nazi flag.

The gym teacher, Mr. Cartwright, was the first to see the flag, and he cuffed Ted in the side of the head and told him to take it down. Ms. Davison, the drama coach, said hanging up that particular flag was hateful, insulting and immature, but Ted's legal right.

I waited a week before mentioning it to my mom. She wrote a carefully worded letter to *The Edmonton Journal* and the next day there was a long, if somewhat oblique, editorial about the Holocaust. The swastika came down.

"That was my grandfather's flag," Ted said, breathing menthol tobacco breath on me.

"You must be very proud," I said to him.

"Get out of the way, turkey, I'm going to work out." And he began pumping his dumb-bell right in front of the locker. I had to lean over him to put my liverwurst sandwiches up on that tiny top shelf.

My mom said to me, "He can't hurt you. Don't forget that." It was late September. We were walking through a warm wind on a hard blue night.

After Hitler was gone, my mom emerged from her hiding place in the Black Forest and took a boat to Argentina. (This is how she told it.) She was drinking hot chocolate on the lower deck, an indescribable luxury, and someone said, "Eichmann is on this very boat!"

An old woman, her voice shaking with rage at the diabolical irony of it. And my mom had heard this and been sick: all at once, over the rail, a deep hot-chocolate-coloured, evacuating sickness. Then she fainted, toppling like a spent gyro and hitting her head on a deck bollard. She woke up wrapped in a horse blanket, her head pounding, and delivered her signature line, in broken English with her eyes still pinched shut: "Damn to Eichmann." My grandmother and the old lady cried. My mom never did. She said simply, "Then we went to Rio de Janeiro, and I prayed for a husband. Canadian or maybe from California."

I have a photograph from the New Year's Eve party at the Canadian consulate in Rosario where they met. My dad is flushed and brush-cut. My mother looks wide-eyed, frozen in the headlights of her own prayers. He took her to Nova Scotia the next year.

PHIL LEVINE WORE A BLACK kangaroo jacket and carried an asthma inhaler. We used to eat lunch out at the hockey rink, on the visitors' bench. Phil always had a Vonnegut on him, an old dog-eared Dell paperback edition *Player Piano, Mother Night, Cat's Cradle*. Phil's brother once spent an entire year indoors, reading and underlining bits in his Vonnegut collection, then moved to the Yucatan Peninsula. It was enough to make anyone read the underlined bits. So we sat out there at the rink and talked about fascism and nuclear winter and setting things on fire, until a tanker truck pulled up and flooded the rink. Then suddenly there were hockey players everywhere.

"Goofs with dentures," said Phil, who had a fine eye for details.

We went inside.

"Phil's a Zionist," I announced at dinner.

SCOTT MILLER WAS NOT A ZIONIST, but he knew aircraft statistics and had read half of *Slaughterhouse-Five*. Phil, Scott and I ended up in the same science group. Our fourth was Ted. He came over and surveyed his teammates: "Fatso, Nerdball and Psycho Asthmahead."

"You can be Goering," said Phil.

"But I was Fatso last year," Scott said, and Ted hit him without even looking in his direction.

"Anyone know what this is?" Mr. Duke, our science teacher, stood at the front of the class behind the lab bench, holding a brown crust above his head between his fingers. Holding it like it might break. It looked dead, whatever it was. The rad hummed.

"It's a dried dog turd," Ted said, laughing.

"It's a resurrection plant," Duke said. The brown crust didn't deny this. It was curled in on itself tight as a pine cone.

"And if I said it was alive would you believe me?" he asked, and somebody near the window answered aloud, "No-o-o."

"Well," he said, "how could you prove me wrong?"

One of the girls got it right. "Absolutely," Duke said. "Living things need oxygen."

So, we tried to suffocate it. Duke and Snowblower put it under the vacuum beaker set up on the corner of the lab bench.

"If it still looks the same in a week, what'll we know then?" Duke asked. "Anyone?"

"That it's definitely a dog turd," said Ted.

"What'll we know?" he asked again after Ted had disappeared to the principal's office.

"That it's dead," I said aloud. My first unsolicited class answer and, in fact, the right answer.

After school, Ted and Snowblower hung out and smoked in the east stairwell. We didn't talk to them. They hung out with girls, knit-vested princesses with platforms, pooka shells and three-dimensional breasts.

Phil got moods. He'd walk all the way home and not say a thing.

Scott walked between us, always talking, sticking a hand out on either side of him so we all had to stop and listen to him.

"Someone ask me what the fuel capacity of an L-1011 is."

Or, "Got your jockstraps for wrestling next week? No, really, what size did you get?"

After we dropped Scott off at his house, I'd try to draw Phil out.

"Shuchuk's into knives, hey?" I said once.

"And flags," Phil said tightly.

"You know he hung it up again," I asked.

"I know he hung it up again," he nodded.

"I could be a Zionist, you know," I tried.

"With a name like McCluskey?" he said and peeled off for home. I waved at his back.

At night we played Ping-Pong and Yahtzee round robins, and my mom and I listened to talk radio. Every Albertan held a personal opinion on whether the northern lights made a noise. I saw them a couple times and didn't hear anything. They just waved back and forth and then faded away.

At breakfast, Dad read the "Exposed-flesh-freezes-in-how-many-seconds" statistics out of the newspaper: "Ten seconds. Coldest November day since nine-teen-oh-too. Says here scientists have proven it's actually colder than a witch's tit. Sorry."

DUKE LET EVERYONE COME UP with a way to kill the resurrection plant. Carbon monoxide, X-rays, two weeks of darkness, chlorine and ammonia gas. By December, I was rooting for the plant.

"Just burn the fucking thing," Ted said, right in one of those unexpected canyons of silence that a classroom will pass through.

Everyone turned to look at him. Duke closed his eyes and clenched his jaw. We decided to put it in a deep freeze until after the holidays.

The bell rang. "All right. The jockstrap hour," Scott said.

The sponge mat was rolled out in the gym. Phil tripped Scott and fell elbow first onto his back. "Body slam," he shouted. They bounced up, tapped into the finely strung mania webbing throughout the room.

"Get off the mat!" Cartwright emerged from the equipment room. Whistle, stopwatch, green sweatsuit cut like real pants with a wide yellow stripe down the outside of each leg. Red eyebrows the same width as his moustache. Black eyes flicking left and right.

He called me Mr. Vocabulary.

"Ring the mat!" We scattered like ants under a magnifying glass.

"Sutcliffe and Nesbitt," Cartwright read off his clipboard from the centre of the gym, glaring around him for silence.

"Sutcliffe, referee's position." Sutcliffe hit the mat on all fours. Nesbitt kneeled beside him, hands on Sutcliffe's back, fingers spread. There was silence, I looked up at the ceiling. Green rings around the gym lights were a bad omen. Silence hovered. And then the sound of the whistle was swamped by pandemonium.

"Nesbitt!" Scott yelled beside me. Sutcliffe had done a sit-out, sliding out from under Nesbitt's hands and scrambling to his feet. They grappled and fell. All knees and ribs.

"Nesbitt!" Phil and I joined in.

Nesbitt was chest down. Sutcliffe was on his back reefing on a half nelson. Snowblower was chanting, "Sutty, Sutty, Sutty."

Nesbitt's underwear climbed out the top of his shorts.

"Gonch pull," shouted Ted.

And that appeared to break his spirit. Nesbitt resigned with his eyes and rolled. One. Two. Three.

"Who backed the loser?" Cartwright paced the edge of the mat looking at each of us.

Our betrayal of Nesbitt was unanimous.

"I heard some of you yelling," Cartwright said, smiling, enjoying the moment. "Some of you, I know, backed the loser."

After gym, Phil and Scott and I sat in the hallway with our backs against the lockers and ate lunch.

"Meat loaf," Scott said, looking depressed. "What do ya got?"

"Gefilte fish and a Ding Dong," Phil said.

"Very Yiddish, Levine, congratulations. What do ya got, Colin?"

"I'm not trading."

"What though?"

"A granola bar," I said.

"All right. Meat loaf for the granola bar." Scott opened a corner of his sandwich. "It's got ketchup and mayo. What kind of granola bar is it?"

"My mom makes them," I said.

"Oh, forget it," Scott said. "What else you got?"

"A herring sandwich," I admitted.

"Herring sandwich?" Scott said. "What's with the Yid food, guys, how'm I supposed to trade here?"

"Well, I'm kind of Jewish, you know," I said.

We ate and watched the janitor string up red letters that spelled Merry Christmas along the main hallway.

"You spelled it wrong," Scott called over to him.

"What?" he said.

"Your sign is spelled wrong."

He climbed down off his stepladder, wiped his forehead with a rag he took from the pocket of his railway overalls and looked at the sign.

"So how'd you spell it?" he said after several minutes.

"H-A-N-U-K-K-A-H," Scott said. So Phil and I punched him until he coughed up a piece of sandwich. Then we went over to Poon's to buy Sno-Jos.

"What's this about you being kind of Jewish," Phil said later. We were standing outside the store squinting in the clear bright sun.

"My Oma and Opa were, so my mom kind of is," I said. "I mean they're not really, because they're Lutheran, but they could be if they wanted to switch back."

Phil took some Wink Sno-Jo into his straw, covered the end with his thumb and dribbled the green slush onto the sidewalk. "Moms pass the Jewish bloodline," he said. And Phil scraped the frozen green pattern he'd made on the sidewalk with the side of his boot.

WE WENT SKATING IN MAYFAIR PARK after Christmas. Dad bought us all new Bauer Supremes. I asked my mom while we were skating, "When does it warm up here?" I had two pairs of gloves on.

"Don't you like this?"

She skated with her bare hands behind her back.

"It's crisp, it's fresh," she said.

The air felt sharp on my cheek for the first while, then I didn't feel anything on my cheek.

"I'm going numb," I said.

"You shouldn't complain so much," she said. And we skated on a bit in silence. It was true that she never complained, not about physical pain.

"Ted hung that flag back in our locker," I said.

She kept skating. The ice was covered with a whisper of snow.

"Phil's a Zionist," I said. Still she just skated. Bare hands behind her back. Ear muffs, no toque.

"I want to be Jewish," I said finally.

Then she stopped, so I stopped. She looked at me.

"What do you want to be?" she asked.

"Jewish," I said.

"No, what do you want most of all. Right this minute."

"I'd like to be warm," I said, without thinking.

She smiled a sort of halfway smile I couldn't interpret.

Then she said, "Well, that's not so complicated then. In the spring you will get what you want."

PHIL AND I PLANNED A CAMPING TRIP out to Elk Island Park to see buffaloes in the spring. I was talking about this on the way to school and he cut me off.

"I want you to put this in your locker," he said, just outside the schoolyard gate. It was a taped-up Birks box. I held it in my glove. It seemed weightless.

"What is it?" I asked.

"It's the resurrection plant," he said.

"No, really," I said.

Phil stopped walking. "Do you have to know? I'm asking you a favour. A favour I couldn't ask just anyone. Hide this box in the back of your locker. Forget about it. As my brother, do me this favour." And he took my hand and shook it slowly and firmly, something he'd never done before.

"Well, I don't have to exactly know about it," I said. "Except maybe if it's explosive or flammable. I'd like to know whether to put it on the upper or lower shelf." Phil didn't smile. At school I dropped the box behind Ted's shelves and blew into my cold hands.

"All right," Phil said, grinning, happy. I felt guilty-good. Plus we were late.

"Glad you could join us, gentlemen," Duke said.

We sidled in like desperadoes. The room stayed silent after we sat down. No one was looking around.

"One of us is a thief," Duke said. And I noticed that Ted's chair was empty.

By the time I got out the door after class, and sprinted

to the locker, Ted was hunched over, digging into the papers that filled the bottom shelf.

"Where'd you put it?" Ted said to me.

My legs actually felt weak. I was hyperventilating. "Behind the shelves," I said.

Ted leaned into the locker. "Oh, here it is." And he pulled out his dumb bell, turned around and started pumping it up and down solemnly.

"You been using this?" he asked me.

"No, I haven't at all. I promise."

"Just be cool," Phil said from behind me. He sounded cool.

There was a muscle on the right side of Ted's neck pressing out and relaxing rhythmically as he pumped. I stretched around him to put my science binder away.

"Hey, turkey," he said. "I need your notes from today."

"Sure. Where were you?" I asked.

Ted looked disgusted. "Principal. It was nothing."

"What was nothing, Shuchuk?" Phil leaned into our conversation, a big fake smile pasted on.

"Mind your own fucking business, Levine."

"No, seriously, I want to know. I mean, we never talk, you know. How was Christmas, get any cool stuff at all? Guns? Grenades? Gas maybe? Hey, nice flag."

"Hey, happy Hanukkah, Levine, all right?" Ted turned to his locker.

"And back to you, Shuchuk. Happy, happy, happy Hanukkah."

Ted was walking away.

"What a pin-dick," Phil said. He was wheezing. He took a drag on his inhaler.

"What's your problem?" I said to him.

"No problem," he said.

"What did you do? What did I do?" I asked.

He smiled, took another drag.

"Take it easy, McCluskey," he said. And we walked after Ted down the hall towards the gym.

Cartwright was pacing the circle at the centre of the mat, spinning his whistle. "And now," he said to the assembled class. "A special match."

Every light in the ceiling cast a green ring.

Cartwright was grinning broadly. "Will you welcome please, the Snowblower."

Whoops. Ted was on his feet. "Me. Me. Me. Let Snowblower and me go."

Not likely. Never friends. Cartwright's eyes were flicking around the ring. My arms goose-pimpled.

"In the blue trunks . . . Mr. Voca-aaa-bulary."

Snowblower's face went flat with surprise, then hardened into something like sadistic amusement. I stood slowly, trying and failing to hold Cartwright's stare.

"Oh man, that's unfair," Scott said.

"Thanks," I said. "Any advice?"

"The balls," Scott said, "definitely the balls."

"His that is," Phil added. "Kick them, or pull on them."

"Oh, and if you hit him like this, you can drive his nose bone into his brain," Scott said, demonstrating on himself.

"Snowblower, referee," Cartwright barked, smiling at me from behind his whistle as I entered the centre ring.

I spread my hands on Snowblower's sweating back. The whistle sounded far above us and I did exactly as taught. I lunged for his far arm, reaching under his chest, got it, and drove with my shoulder against his ribs. Snowblower rocked a bit and settled. Then he stood up and shook me off. I was hanging from his neck. He grabbed my head. I jerked downward and escaped.

We circled. I could hear Ted screaming, "Snowblower. Snowblower." And Scott foghorning away on my behalf.

Then Snowblower grappled, lifted me and dropped me on the mat. Damn. My face was going to burst. He was working on my right shoulder. I twisted over onto my chest, crossed my legs, tucked in my hands and elbows. My last defence, the Armadillo.

Snowblower was scrambling around my back. I felt one hand on my neck, one on my ankles. I felt his head butt into my side, just above the waist. Phil was looking at me. He shrugged and shook his head. Snowblower was bending me like a bow and arrow, pulling on my head and feet, pushing with his head. I flipped onto my back, a husk, airless. Pinned.

Everyone was shouting. Cartwright helped me up and put a towel in my face. "It's just a nosebleed," he said.

I pulled the towel away from my face. The white terry cloth was sticky red in the middle, still connected to me by a slick string of pink mucus.

I GOT WHAT I WANTED MOST. It did warm up.

Above the dirt-brown snow drifts, the skinny poplars next to the fire station were muscling out buds. There was a mouse population explosion at school. I began losing ground to the shit at the bottom of our locker. There were mice in the halls, streaking for cover in the corners behind doors. Disappearing into the wall under the water fountain.

On a Monday I slushed up the street, the air light and breathable, past sand-crusted front lawns.

Duke came out of the storeroom and stepped up behind the lab bench. He took his time, cleared his throat. Ted not being there didn't even register with me until I saw the blue Birks box.

Conversations slowly stopped, heads turned, seats were readjusted. Phil and Scott were the last to stop talking. I had forgotten the thing existed, and recognized it now like a toy lost in grade four and rediscovered. Like the Bluenose II model in the box in the basement that I had found before Christmas and repacked. That I had recognized every detail of, and immediately wanted forgotten.

He stood with the blue Birks box in his right palm. Then he reached over and pulled the lid off and rolled a blackened briquette-sized lump onto the desk. There was no question what it was. Burnt to a nub of its former size. We might have doubted. We had all doubted, I suppose, but the resurrection plant was now most definitely dead.

"At least we found it," Duke said. "The mouse exterminators were looking for nests in the lockers and . . . and the person responsible . . ." His face was a quilt of red and white splotches. "The person responsible has been expelled."

Phil showed nothing. He stared straight ahead, and so I did as well. Scott's jaw was slack. Around us, people seemed to breathe relief and delight, in unison.

The next part happened fast. I went to the locker after the three o'clock bell without talking to Phil. I was thinking of going home. Of confessing to someone or going to the Yucatan or both. And then I opened the locker and saw the flag gone. And something did flush through me. Like I had won something. Pride. Anger.

Scott came up behind me. "You going over to the fire station? Phil's already there."

And when we got into the poplars, it seemed like everyone was waiting for us. Ted was shadow-boxing Snowblower, dumb-bell biceps evident under his Edmonton Eskimos T-shirt. Phil stood a few yards away in the long grass, shaking his wire-thin arms by his sides.

"This is nuts," I said to him. "This is very stupid."

"And your better idea is?" he said to me.

"We'll get killed," I said.

Ted approached through the thick grass to where we stood. "I didn't burn that fucking thing. He told Duke

I did. He's a weasel. You're both weasels. You're both dead weasels."

"I never said anything to anyone," Phil said.

"Fuck you, Levine."

"Fuck yourself, Shuchuk."

"Right now, man, right now."

"Don't you think—" I started a sentence I didn't have an ending for anyway.

"Hey, you're next, all right?" Ted said right into my face. He was at one of the angles from which I could see the moustache. It was filling out.

Snowblower was smacking Ted in the arm, bop, bop, get him, man, you're gonna kill him. A crowd fanned hungrily around us.

I looked at Phil, who gave a shrug.

"Let me have the first go," he said.

So I got out of the way and they did that mandatory circling manoeuvre. I can't say they were really sizing each other up. Ted was doing it for effect, swinging his fist near his waist, his stance open and confident. He was appraising a certain kill, thinking about maximizing crowd value maybe, but at his own speed.

Phil was just waiting. He could have been waiting for the bus. Except his elbows were tucked in at his sides, his white-knuckled fists trembled at eye level and he was leading left. A useless formality before going out with good form.

The crowd's calls for blood became persuasive, even

from those who didn't want blood, those who probably wanted to go home but couldn't or wouldn't, because leaving at that moment was inconceivable. Girls hopped up and down on the spot. The few junior high school kids there, boys, were pushing each other back and forth, infected by what lay ahead.

"Ted. Ted. Ted." No one was yelling for Phil.

"Kill him, Phil," I screamed. And Phil stepped off his back foot, closed quickly and threw what everyone in the lot must have known was a one-in-a-million haymaker. A sweeping arc. A hate-filled cartoon of a punch, with enough power to remove an opponent's head as long as he'd been immobilized first.

Ted didn't even look at it. But he brought a fist up from his waist hard and fast into Phil's throat. A short, blunt movement. Phil's right arm feathered off Ted's shoulder and followed him to the grass. His face was white, his eyes pinched shut, his hands around his own neck, breathing like a stick in bike spokes. Then Ted kicked him in the stomach, a considered, methodical kick. Phil moved his hands, rolled tighter. Ted kicked again. The side of the head. It sounded like *clack*.

Phil rolled away, bloody face in the grass.

"Enough. Fuck," I said and ran toward them. The air was alive with movement. The crowd was draining out of the lot around me.

Scott was crying and yelling, "If you killed him, my dad'll sue." He was on his bike already.

I rolled Phil over. He was bleeding, but breathing.

Snowblower came over. "Oh, leave him, he's fine."

"You better not've fucking killed him," Scott yelled again, his face red and wet, and then he pedalled away. Standing up for speed, not looking back.

"You later, Vocabulary," Ted said, standing over Levine and me.

"Me now, cheese dick," I heard myself say as I stood up. Clearly I had lost my mind. Maybe I wouldn't feel anything. I felt strong. Maybe I was coursing full of some kind of Judaic adrenaline, making me impervious to pain, to fear.

"Come on, Brownshirt," I found myself saying. "You want to hit me. Hit me. Fucking hit me. What? Knock me down, pussy. Burnt a fucking plant so now you're a tough guy?"

Ted took a step back toward me but Snowblower stopped him.

"Don't," Snowblower said. Ted shook his arm away. "Listen to this little shit."

"Come on, gas me, you Ukrainian fuck. Try to kill me, Eichmann."

"Oh, I'm going to enjoy this," said Ted.

"You want Duke to come out?" Snowblower had Ted by the arm again. "Let's get out of here, man."

"Bastards took my flag. Let me kill him," Ted said.

"Come on, Eichmann, I'm not fucking afraid of you," I said.

"Leave the girls here," Snowblower said, almost softly.

They walked out of the lot, Snowblower pulling Ted through the grass. I wanted them dead.

"Anytime," I yelled after them. I was delirious.

But they didn't come back.

"Nice work," Phil said. He was sitting up behind me holding his throat and laughing. It looked painful. He had to go into his Adidas bag and get out his inhaler before he could speak again.

"Eichmann?" he said, wheezing, bleeding, laughing. "Fucking Eichmann."

Then Phil reached into his bag again, took out the resurrection plant and handed it to me. I had never felt it before. It was crumbled, a little worse for the wear. Tender to the touch, like dried cedar. But all there. A tough little plant. Completely unburned. As alive as ever.

"Just do something with it. Anything," he said to me.

"I thought this was burnt. What's that in the school?" I said, confused.

Phil winced and strained some blood through his teeth into the grass. "A pine cone. A burnt pine cone," he said finally, coughed, spat some more. Laughed another painful laugh.

"Jesus," I said. I felt light, and I sat down suddenly, then lay back in the grass. The sky full of horsetails.

I kept the resurrection plant for three days before I talked to my mom. Even then I didn't tell her anything, only that I had something that wasn't mine. She said, "Is it from a store?" And then when I shook my head she said, "Does it have a proper owner?"

I said that's its real owner thought it was dead. And that made her think for a minute. "Then put it where it belonged before its real owner even knew it was alive."

Of course it only needed water. I carried the resurrection plant down into the river valley. I found a spot near the sludgy bank. Buried it halfway in the moist brown soil, full of bugs and worms. The bowl-blue sky held out space above me. And in less than a week there was a fist-sized bush that sprang roots and pushed itself deep into the prairie.

The magpies still follow and fall away, their insults tapering. Their cackles trail behind them as they turn back toward the highway, toward roadkill and other concerns. The papery grass still catches in my cuffs and laces. The muddy bank gums my leather soles.

I kneel. It has grown as high as my chest.

I hold the branches, which I think smell of musty pine and pepper. The branches aren't dry. Aren't lifeless. They're full of the earth's moisture. Full of the water that the earth holds from the air. Moisture churned by beetles and fertilized by generations seeking to be reborn.

# THE BOAR'S HEAD EASTER

My mother and father lived in Chicago the year before I was born, and during that time my mother had a lover. I discovered this fact reading her journals. Not something I would normally have thought to do, but I'd been given a set of keys to her filing cabinets by her nurse Francine, who came on duty full-time when my mother's arthritis worsened sharply. Even after I had the keys, I didn't think to use them immediately. It didn't occur to me that I could walk down the now little-used corridor to the north end of Mom's very grand condominium on Beach Avenue, open the den door, slip across the dark wood floor and match keys with the many locks on that bank of dove-grey filing cabinets. I wasn't avoiding the discovery of a secret. I knew my mother wasn't well and that, in her own indirect fashion, she would have instructed Francine that the keys were to be mine. But to go through her papers—to read the many words I knew she'd written on the life lived—I thought this would amount to a summing up. An act of resignation to the end and betrayal on my part.

But I found myself alone in the apartment late one afternoon and the scene unexpectedly set itself, demanding particular action. Francine had taken my mother out for her daily hour of fresh air along the sea wall. I wasn't working that night, staying instead to prepare our dinner. She was still lively in conversation at this point, although she didn't walk well, and as Francine wheeled her out into the fifth-floor lobby, my mother turned and called to me, "Oh, Jake. There are beers in the fridge for when you inevitably grow thirsty. And of course, chef, please avail yourself of any other item you need. Everything to be found in its appropriate drawer."

She wasn't giving me permission to snoop, I realize. It could just as easily have been an invitation to find the Glenfiddich she still nipped against Francine's wishes, the bottle lying nestled under the tea towels.

My mother—whose taste in food groups other than Scotch ran to the bland middle of the twentieth century—had requested chicken pot pie and potato salad for dinner.

I had filled the pie shells, sealed the tops, cut the vents and slid them into her ancient semi-functional electric oven. I had found the earlier offered beer and cracked one. I was taking a long sip and thinking of her—she and Francine would just now be wheeling down into busy English Bay, sea breeze on their faces, filling and exciting their senses with the saline message of rolling open, of distance to cross—and my musing was swamped sharply by an awareness of my own surroundings. The large and still apartment. The smell of wood and upholstery, of dust and paper. The projected silence of an ill-lit den at the end of a dark parquet hall.

The journals were there. Three dozen slim green leather volumes filling the lower drawer of the cabinet nearest her desk. They were wedged in tightly. I guessed they hadn't been looked at in some time, no surprise. These were meticulous but ordinary records, or so I thought after thumbing three random volumes and finding weather reports, descriptions of parties, the itineraries of trips my parents had taken together. Nothing unusual. Nothing out of her character. Nothing, that is, until it occurred to me to reach back in the drawer, to feel for the spot where I thought Chicago might rest. And pulling out this record, the year of my conception—having just set aside a volume that covered trips to the Vatican, to London, and the details of an entire bridge tournament—I found myself leafing through pages dedicated almost exclusively to food. Chicken pot pie smells just now starting to make their way down the dark corridor and here were elaborate recipes on every page. Wine-tasting notes, vintages noted. Restaurant addresses.

I began to read these pages with real curiosity and then with a mounting sense that there was a finding to be made at the root of it all. I didn't see it for many minutes, turning pages there, crouched next to the filing cabinets, but eventually I did begin to see something like a solution to a riddle emerging from the pages. A single name, where few others had been mentioned. It was scattered at first, but it rose in density as I read until, many pages in, I found myself stopping and staring at it. Seeing it whole and alone for the first time. Seeing it lift almost physically from the surface of the paper, rise in relief like those coloured numbers you're supposed to find in the field of dots during a colour-blindness examination.

*Klaus.*

He was identified as a chef, and referred to only by his first name. Spare physical descriptions. Grey eyes, lean build, military bearing. The core material I had to help me imagine the man—who had become a stand-alone thing, part of no scene but very much part of my mother— were his recipes. Game, mostly. Old-world dishes like antelope saddle, venison stew, hasenpffer. Recipes my mother had carefully compiled over the year they were in Chicago. One lakeshore spring to the next, when they returned to Vancouver and my birth. Dishes she had never made, never spoken of, since.

JUNE 30, 1962

*Boar shank seems quite barbaric, doesn't it? I have an image immediately of* Homo erectus *squatting near a fire. Still, this is what they produce at the Boar's Head, a lovely place in the Loop. The owner and chef is Klaus, an equally lovely man. After we'd eaten, Edward and the Archbishop were absorbed and the chef appeared at my elbow. Quite unexpected in his unstained whites. I mightn't have thought he noticed me sitting there in silence, but apparently he did and suggested a tour of the kitchen for my amusement. And there he told me a secret or two about boar shanks. He even poured me a glass of wine, which we sipped next to the stove. Châteauneuf du Pape, which is all about where the Pope went during exile, or some such story. There we were sipping wine together while the apprentices and the servers swarmed around us.*

*Tomorrow for lunch is quail, he told me. Edward encouraged me to go when we got back to the hotel this evening. He's swamped in diocesan scheming. I have no appointments.*

THAT'S MY FATHER I'M seeing now. Dead fifteen years. For the fifteen years before that a man routinely mistaken for my grandfather. Crouched beside my mother's filing cabinets and hearing her words ring off the page, I see him more clearly than I have in a long time. He's taking out his lapis cuff links and putting them in a black leather travel case. He's standing with his back to her, in front of the dresser where he has laid out his things in front of the mirror. Pocket watch, clothes brush, collar tabs.

"Go," he says, ignorant of a critical moment passing. A moment during which he should have paid attention. Should have turned to see her in her deep blue satin dressing gown, a beautiful woman half his age. There he is, looking down at his shirt studs and thinking of something else. "Certainly you must go."

*And so here we are. Wild Boar by Klaus:*

*Allspice, Juniper, Bay, Sage, Tomato Concasse*

*A bottle of sturdy red. (Klaus says a vin de pays from Bordeaux is good. The reduction of the wine is not so great that a vintage must be used.)*

*Brown the meat sprinkled with a teaspoon of sugar. (Not for sweetness but for colour.)*

*Braise two and a half hours and Klaus assures me that the meat will fall from the bone.*

I cook for a living. These lines I can read between.

SYD AND I DECIDED TO make a pilgrimage to Chicago for the Easter weekend. I told him I wanted to visit an old restaurant, research for the game cookbook I had decided to write.

I just told my mother Chicago, nothing else, and she said, "Are you swimming upstream like a salmon?" Her eyes steady in mine.

I answered that I was keeping Syd company. Holding the light meter. He had a list of shots he wanted to bag.

Amtrak bar car, El train, buskers in the Loop. He'd selected his Leica M-6 from among his many cameras, gone and had it specially cleaned. I bought spiral-bound notebooks for jotting ideas and flavour observations. And two days before the weekend, a black rainy Wednesday, we walked out along the sea wall towards the train station carrying our duffel bags. We were in a get-going mood, striding, talking. The glass towers of Yaletown rose to our left. The black water of False Creek lay on our right, stippled with raindrops. Syd was already thinking about the place we were going to explore, describing the architecture: cornices and gold inlay, Gothic steeples, plays of light along Michigan Avenue. His boots clicked on the concrete and he ran a hand across his shaved scalp.

I kept looking up towards the station. "Did Erin decide to come in the end?" I asked him.

"She's waiting at Noodle Express. Are you going to watch me shoot? It'd be fun. I could shoot you. I could shoot you in front of that place you're looking for. I could shoot you in the kitchen. Maybe this guy'll let me shoot the kitchen. What the hell's it called?"

"The Boar's Head. It's a game house."

"I remember. Friends of your parents from way back. You sure he's not dead?"

I was sure. I had called. I got a crisp, ageless voice on the first ring. Absolutely and immediately my man with grey eyes and military bearing. But a voice just as clearly impossible to put together with anything I really knew,

177

although it took up residence in my inner ear for several days after our short conversation.

I told Klaus that I cooked, that I was interested in game. In what he did. I stammered out my name, first only. I said I was from out of town although I didn't tell him I was coming in from halfway across the continent. From Vancouver.

"What about this coming Easter weekend?" Klaus suggested. "Sunday, of course, we are full. But Good Friday a lot of people around here eat fish. I could squeeze you in. Show you this thing that is what I do."

I could hear the kitchen behind him. I knew he was busy. But there was residual curiosity there too, a feeling I didn't think many rookies would be likely to inspire in Chef Klaus.

"Where did you hear about us?" he asked.

I hadn't thought to make up an answer to this one. My heartbeat rose and plateaued somewhere above 100. "I read about you in a magazine," I said. A little fast.

He laughed. He genuinely enjoyed a lie built around the idea that his fifty-year-old restaurant might still be getting *reviews*. "Well . . . we're honoured."

I hung up the phone, then snatched it up again. It lay in my palm for the full thirty seconds it took me to realize that I had no one else to call.

"So this is for a cookbook?" Syd was saying, now a pace or two ahead of me. "You stealing the old man's ideas?"

He heaved open one of the station doors and we wheeled into the hollow foyer, then around the corner into Noodle Express where, just as he had told me she would be, Erin was waiting. Hunched at her table under the fish tank, looking tense. Wrapped in a black fisherman's knit sweater, half-eaten bowl of soba gone cold in front of her. She was smoking, holding a sheaf of term papers written by the ESL students she tutored. The top one was scored with red marker.

"Hi, Syd," she said. "Hello, Jake."

I'D KNOWN THEM two and a half years. Syd took pictures of the restaurant for our first big magazine profile and review. There I was, Sous-Chef Jake standing next to our executive chef, in colour. When the issue hit the stands I called him up and we went and drank a bottle of Veuve Clicquot at Au Bar. We talked about photography. We talked about food. But even talking about food Syd was talking about the image of food, the appearance of things on the plate, the arrangement of snow peas and slices of cactus fruit fanned around a thimble of halibut mousse he'd been served the night before at the all-new very expensive restaurant in the all-new very expensive boutique hotel on Alberni Street.

Erin showed up near midnight. Syd introduced us, and I remember her steady, appraising stare. She sat down and said to me, "I had a bowl of soup at your restaurant once. Tuscan bean. Delicious . . ."

179

"She liked you," Syd said a few weeks later. "Cheers." He had a fast, direct way with friendship and we lived vicariously off one another's career progress. There had been other good reviews. Syd's work was showing up everywhere. He came down when I was on shift and ate at the bar near the open kitchen, watching my movements with the eye-flickering interest of an image collector. There was a particular way I threw a blade down a steel, apparently. My eyes Steadicamming the action around me while the Global nine-inch diced air in front of my face. There was a way I bumped shut an oven door with my hip and a way I spun a finished plate right to the centre of the aluminum pass.

When *Details* picked up his pictures of Winona Ryder, Erin and Syd and I went out on the town. I was glistening with confidence as sharp as a freshly cut onion.

The restaurant crashed and burned six months later. Erin called me at home. "Where am I supposed to get my bean soup?" Her first words in our first phone conversation. We talked for an hour. I had this idea, way back then, to write a game cookbook.

"Nobody eats wild stuff any more," I told her.

Erin thought people probably didn't eat wild stuff any more because they didn't want to catch it themselves. She also thought this was probably a pretty strong indication of how little the world needed a game cookbook.

"What does the world need?" I asked her. It was clear to me that she knew.

The world needed me to start cooking again. The world needed me not to mope in my sweatpants, watching high cable channels, which, Erin told me, she knew perfectly well I had been doing. But when I got off the phone, all I could think was that she was telling me she thought about me from time to time.

We talked on the phone occasionally after that. And if I bumped into her walking down Davie or along the sea wall we always stood for ten minutes catching up, then went for coffee and stretched the time out to half an hour. Sometimes more.

"Holy smokes, gotta go." One or the other of us would say these words and there would be the kiss on the cheek. There would be the hand on the shoulder, the half smile, the knitted brow. And then she'd be off.

Looking at her in the bus station with her red-scored term papers, talking up at Syd, who had his hand on the back of her neck, I noticed the same crimp in her brow. A little black crease across the flour-white skin.

WE HAD TO BUS SOUTH to Everett, where we could catch the Amtrak to Chicago. Erin and Syd sat together in the seats behind me, silent. At the border I watched the drug dog from customs sniff through the luggage they'd pulled out of the belly of the bus. A thin, elegant dog, a pretty animal for the job, with a manner nothing like the bounding overexcited Labradors you sometimes see perform the same task. No harping encouragement from the handler. No evident pleasure taken. But as he picked his way through the luggage, through each potential discovery, he made as if to conceal his role in things. Over a maroon Samsonite, he took the gentlest whiff, lifted his head, eyes to the horizon, thought of other things. Moved on.

JULY 3, 1962

*Such heat. Such pressing on the skin, such shrinking into useless shadows. Perhaps I stayed long after dinner at the BH tonight for the cool. For the entirely refreshing darkness. Perhaps. Does it matter? I have come back quite late to the flat and find Edward is still at his meeting.*

*They go to Tzarina's now. Of course. The deacons want to speak Russian while they eat and do their business. They want a headquarters.*

*Don't like the Russian food. Or Russians, who seem to prefer no women at their little powwows.*

*Ate hare.*

WE WENT TO ODIE'S OARHOUSE across from the train station in Everett to have beers. The street fell down a hill into the bay, which was full of logs and piers and cloaked in seagull turd. I liked the oldness of the place. The worn-out realness. Ranier at seventy-five cents a glass. We had a couple each. Smoking and talking and relaxing. Erin's marking lay next to her on the table, untouched. She shook her head at something Syd said, drummed a tiny rack of fingers. On holiday, trying to lose the threads of work.

"So give us one," Syd said to me, and as I began, he got out the camera, and unsnapped the cracked leather housing, opened the front and peeled away the mirrored lens covers.

"Bear loin with vinegar and raspberries." I said. "Marinate and roast."

Erin laughed lightly, then got up and moved past us towards the washrooms in the back, past the Olympia Beer signs, the unemployed loggers and the video poker machine. I continued while Syd opened fire with the Leica.

We almost missed the train, but it was empty and we easily found seats together. After dropping our bags we went straight to the bar car. We drank seven-and-sevens, faking like rube Canadians abroad. Syd was on about something he called Chicago's monumentalism. Edifices of optimism and power, big straight towers.

Erin leaned back on the red vinyl bench and listened. She looked relaxed but still tired. When they went back to the coach to sleep, I stayed at the lounge-car window until two in the morning. I tried to jot notes. I was trying to think about my bear loin, working through the marinade again: shallot, garlic, raspberries, buckwheat honey . . .

The glass was black. Out there the bears would be coming out of the mountains. They'd be lumbering alongside the track, dancing across boulders, and melting into the trees. I pressed my face to the glass, saw nothing. I opened a mickey of bourbon and sipped, imagining wilderness.

I WOKE EARLY, AS THE TRAIN jogged across switch tracks and shuddered to a stop in Havre, Montana. Morning had just reached us, a flat harsh light stretching from the horizon ahead of the train. Syd was asleep on Erin's shoulder but she opened her eyes when I got up, smiled without moving. Her face was smooth as an ice sculpture, no lipstick left now, hair swept forward during sleep.

Outside the car it was a frigid Montana Thursday morning, all directions. Havre was small, brown, old. From the platform I could make out a liquor store, a football stadium. A dozen dirty trucks parked along the main street. There was a line at the phone booth, but I still had time to check in with Francine. Fine, fine. Everything was fine. A little cold; it was nothing.

I ate breakfast alone in the crowded dining car. A flavourless shingle of scrambled eggs, grits and sausages reanimated with Tabasco sauce and a pint of tomato juice. It was a heavy, one-flavour morning, but when I emerged from the swaying washroom I felt fresh and unified.

There was a standing area at the bottom of the car. The prairie was rolling past. Ahead, the sun had risen, burning like a beacon over the Midwest. We swept by an unpainted grain elevator. Rows of pipe stacked beside it, weeds growing through the silver tubes, combing the air, bending and swaying in the hard, unrelenting light.

OCTOBER 19, 1962

*If shot when rutting, elk must be aged almost twice as long to get the smooth-grained, tight flavour the animal is prized for.*

SYD CAME AND FOUND ME in the lounge car. It was nearly noon.

"Do you have any Visine?" he asked, squinting. He had a uniform black stubble from chin to crown.

He returned, scalp shiny as a mango. I put my notebook away and we looked out the window together for a while. There were burnt swaths of prairie next to the tracks. Stripes of black that hurtled under the windows for miles. Beyond the black, dried hay escaped into the fields.

Every fifteen minutes or so we'd shudder past construction crews, yellow hard hats turning with the train. Silent observers outside the glass, flashing in and out of our sight. Like a handful of stones down a well, there and gone.

Syd wanted to take pictures of passengers. Erin was writing in the lounge car.

"Writing what?" I asked, as we passed through the hissing doors into the next car.

Haiku, he joked, motioning for quiet. We were in the narrow hall that ran down the side of the first-class compartments. Syd straightened the camera strap on his shoulders and tucked his T-shirt into his jeans.

"Sydney Parrell, *National Geo,*" he said to the woman who opened the door. "We're shooting for a piece on train travel. May we use your image? Ten minutes. This is my assistant, Jake."

She had an open, honest face. Broad and unwary. Edith Grower left the door propped open with a PanAm bag but she let us in. Syd sat Edith in the jump seat next to the glass and planted himself in the roll-down couch. I stood beside to her, holding the light meter next to an earlobe elongated by decades of its own weight. I made small talk while Syd shot. She was sixty-three, widowed, going just forty miles more. She had been visiting her daughter Ronette in Seattle. Her daughter who had just had a baby. Her daughter without a husband. Her grandson without a father. Edith looked into the landscape, her reflection superimposed on the burnt earth. I heard the whisper of the Leica as Edith's face flowed into the landscape as if it had no borders.

Steps down the corridor, Syd summarized: "Cool face."

NOVEMBER 1, 1962

*Went into the kitchen again today. Not a guest really, any longer. It was a rather gradual change and then, at once, startling, fast moving. It is a magnificent place, with aged chandeliers, of all things. I sat on a cutting board and watched, stayed well out of the way. I told Klaus he moves like Nureyev, which provoked much laughter among his young men. Afterwards, he boned quails and wrapped a thick slice of bacon around each. Roasted very quickly.*

*Some rather beautiful and difficult things can be made in a surprisingly short period of time.*

SUNSET RESISTED THE STAIN OF NIGHT, then crumbled from the sky. I met Erin on the stairs coming up from the washrooms. She looked rested, peaceful, holding a toothbrush, a tube of Colgate sticking out of her jean jacket. We stood on the same step and talked. I asked her about her writing.

The crease was gone from her forehead. She had a different perfume on. When the train shook I smelled it, something in the zone of nutmeg.

Poetry, she admitted, something she'd written a lot of, years before. Let it go. Now it was something she was trying to regain. She looked away out the window into the rose-dust air that lingered over the fields. She asked about my plans for Chicago. About the Boar's Head.

"It's not exactly for the recipes," I told her. "I'm looking to find out how something is done, something old and lost. But I don't even know what this old thing is precisely. I suppose I'm hoping to make a discovery of some kind."

The lights blinked off in the car. Erin was a shadow in front of my face, but I could see her nodding slowly. Wondering.

"When will you go?" she asked.

"When are you free?" I asked back.

The words flew away from me, past my lips and into the simmering air. Erin was looking at me carefully. There was a prickle behind my stomach and the wall shifted against my back. I adjusted the weight on my feet.

"I don't know our schedule yet," she said. "Ask me tomorrow."

"Sure. Of course," I said.

We were silent for a few seconds, and then a shadow appeared at the head of the stairs. Someone wanting to get by. Erin leaned forward. She kissed my cheek, left a tiny nutmeg stamp, barely wet. Slipped by me and disappeared downstairs.

I pulled up the leg-rests on both the seats in my section and spread out my coat, preparing for sleep. I looked through the glass but the light was gone. We were scudding across a black sea, drumming with the energy of the rails. I couldn't see anything.

FEBRUARY 3, 1963

*Impossible rain and cold. Rivers in the streets. The city is telling us to leave, but of course we won't. And now I fear the balconies will flood and freeze, shear off the building in a single slab. All along the Lakeshore is a river of traffic, although there will be no freezing of that flow, coursing into the city. Ebbing for a time but always returning.*

GOOD FRIDAY.

I slammed awake, my eyes jiggling in their sockets as the train crossed a junction and slammed into a fog bank. I guessed we were only a couple hours short of the city. After breakfast I watched the station signs lunge out of the mist and disappear. A station house, yellow trim, gingerbread gates. Station wagons, wood siding matching the houses beyond. When I went and got some water from the cooler downstairs, I stood in the little alcove near the bolted exit and watched the dance of colours along the track.

When the mist cleared, Chicago announced itself with garbage, sent out in looming seas. Old clothes, cars, cardboard boxes and the gutted carcasses of household appliances. And tires. I stood, rocking back and forth on my heels as they flooded past. Dozens. Hundreds. Acres of black rubber stretching away from the tracks, the handwriting of a demon, sister to the one that burnt Montana.

And then we were in it. Sweeping down from the north through concrete tunnels and under sagging roadways, surfacing in desolate yards full of bricks and gravel and shopping carts. The rails shrieked outside the glass like wild birds. Across us fell the shadows of buildings, impossibly high.

We burst past the charred shell of a warehouse and crossed the North Branch. A sticky, viscous meander. Useless even to commerce. Union Station didn't announce itself. We slowed to a crawl. Rounded a half-submerged corner past a thirty-storey building with lattices of wrought-iron fire escapes spidering down its sides. Then the city disappeared as we went underground and trembled to a stop.

In the station Syd went to look for Erin's checked luggage and a phone. I drank a double espresso at the station coffee bar. Across an acre of high-gloss marble, Erin sat on a bench in the middle of the main hall, staring up into the dome, eighty feet overhead. As I watched, she pulled her legs up onto the bench and lay down, her arms behind her head, a smile colouring her lips as she basked in the hugeness of her space.

MARCH 20, 1963

*Easter at Tzarina's, I am told. Wives.*

*Edward has sorted his affairs here. The Diocese has written him a very large cheque, which he spent several hours in the Bank of Chicago wiring in different pieces all over the world. Afterwards he said to me, as if this would be of immense relief, "And now back to sleepy Vancouver for a stretch."*

*There is so much nothing to say it has begun to feel like an enormous thing.*

SYD'S COUSIN WAS IN ARUBA, but Syd had the keys to the apartment off the Lakeshore. Goethe Street.

The cab swept into the semicircular drive, and under the straight red awning stretching to the curb. The building was smaller than those around it. Stockier. It had windowboxes and gargoyles. Great Titan faces with lolling tongues.

Syd was out of the cab, up the walk and under the awning. He had his black morning head stubble back, and he hadn't laced his boots. He had substituted a long yellow raincoat for his leather jacket, and the camera rode up under his armpit like a shoulder holster. Erin and I watched from the cab as the white-haired doorman tottered down the walk to get our bags.

We settled into our rooms. They both had private bathrooms and balconies looking south into the city. I sat in a wicker deck chair and watched down Goethe Street as the traffic swept along the lakeshore, past grey beaches and into the city. Coursing.

We had late-afternoon drinks in the living room. Syd sprawled across the black leather sofa, swirling ice in a tumbler of Scotch and spilling ash.

I told them I was going over to the Boar's Head that night.

"If the invite's still open, we'd love to come," Erin said to me.

We walked through the darkening streets, wet from an afternoon rain. Traffic hissed past on Michigan. Syd was reeling a bit already and throwing his arm around Erin at intervals. She had her hands deep in the side pockets of her raincoat and sometimes turned slightly to look back at me or get directions.

"Left here, down to the end of the block," I'd say, consulting the little piece of paper in my pocket. Folded and refolded, worn supple. I found the door where I knew it would be. I imagined I had seen it before. A green awning stretched out to the street, the letters of "The

Boar's Head" cracked and faded. The door was heavy black wood, with a brass handle. Two rubber trees in earthen pots flanked the entrance like commissionaires.

The restaurant was set for a full house, but we were the first. We waited in a little antechamber by an oval desk. Through the doorway I could see into the old-fashioned dining room with its heavy drapes and upholstered chairs arranged around white-clothed tables. There were stag and bear trophies on the walls and a fire burning in a dark brick hearth. I rang the silver bell on the desk and waited. Nothing moved for a minute, although light came from behind the kitchen door and hanging on the air, as if on a heavy forest mist, was the dirt and blood smell of boar.

I suppose I had been planning for the moment in my own way. Thinking vaguely about how we would make a cool and unobtrusive entrance into this place of cooking history. And although I resolved to myself that I would not press, I was prepared to take in my careful impressions of Klaus—this man who lived in a green volume in a dusty den in an increasingly empty and silent apartment on Beach Avenue—to make a judgement-free assessment of him in his place. To use this later, in a calmer moment, to gently distil into some kind of essential, intoxicating truth about my own history.

But at the point Klaus appeared, emerging from the kitchen with a fluid stride, I found my eyes locked on him childishly instead. Straining to see what I had earlier read. Straining to see through him, through the page, and back to my mother from a different angle. And here he came towards me: seventyish, wire-bodied, brush-cut and mustachioed, straight-nosed, straight-toothed. Handsome by a centuries-old standard. All this adhering to the catalogue of things I'd been expecting. But when he was near, his hand extended to take my own, from that range I observed that his eyes were not the soft grey I'd expected from my mother's writing, from what I thought would move her, draw her, but were darker eyes altogether. The darker seams in a slab of marble, not cold precisely, but speaking of silty residue, of everything he knew.

Erin cleared her throat. Syd laughed nervously.

"Chef," I said, sticking out a hand to take his, my scalp tingling with sweat.

"Klaus," he said, smiling now at the very corners of his mouth, his eyes lingering on me in turn. Careful interest. "You are my young friend who read about us in what must surely have been a very old magazine."

"Jake," I said, feeling the moisture move to my hairline. I made to introduce him to Syd and Erin, seeing as I began that some seconds had passed, the vinyl record of this moment skipping a groove, and Erin's hand was already in both of his. Klaus's waist cracked just slightly in a bow.

Syd introduced himself, overly loud.

"Sydney," Klaus said, shaking firmly. And then, registering the almost-Chicagoan tonality of Syd's voice: nasal friendliness, flat confidence. "From Evanston?"

It occurred to me then that he might be having fun

with us. The baronial handshakes reflecting his amusement that some kids thought they'd discovered his decades-old restaurant. Or did he think we were here *ironically*—this new idea passed through accompanied by a little panicky surge, sweat prickling under my eyes now—here to see some kind of *retro* performance?

"Vancouver," Erin said. And with this word, Klaus's expression changed. His chin came up high, the first half of a large nod of understanding. He turned slowly back to me. But he'd lost pure fluidity of movement and the chin remained high. His own calculation in progress.

Behind us, another group arrived. Four more large bodies pressing into the small waiting area. Giving off the brusque heat of hungry Chicago. They were talking among themselves loudly, but conversation broke as the door closed behind them and one of them nodded with deference in Klaus's direction.

"Evening, chef," he said. His overcoat lapels bristling sable.

"Gentlemen," Klaus said to the new guests without looking at them. We were frozen there in a cocked hat. He exhaled. His chin came down. Dark eyes flickering across my face.

"A beautiful city," Klaus said to me. "Vancouver."

Erin was politely pushing this line of conversation, thinking maybe I was overcome. Had he visited? Did he know that I was a cook in Vancouver?

"So I understand," Klaus said.

The maître d'hôtel appeared. Briskly formal. He took our coats and ushered us into the dining room. I pulled out Erin's chair for her at the table near the fireplace and we sat. A bit nervous, a bit excited. A bit awed by the formal, glittering regiments of cutlery, candlesticks and glasses. An unfamiliar table even to me, although it managed to inspire a gentle feeling of security.

Klaus chatted with the men at the door, saw to their seating. Then made his way across the dining room towards us again. He nodded the maître d'hôtel aside and took our drink orders. He brought Syd a Mortlach. Opened a bottle of sherry and poured for Erin and me. We settled with our drinks and his ease returned.

"Tonight, we will show you what we do here at the Boar's Head," he said. "What I have been doing for over forty years. We are a little old-fashioned. I know we never became a tapas bar when we should have . . . or maybe sushi? But I think you are interested in things that are old, yes?"

I flushed. Erin smiled at Klaus and then at me. Syd was reading his menu.

"Besides," Klaus finished. "It looks formal, but all you must do is eat."

We went for the *prix fixe* dinner, all courses included. And then it began. A waiter appeared from behind the portholed kitchen doors with a white tureen of consommé, which he ladled out into blue enamel bowls and served with a glass of Amontillado.

We talked about poetry. We talked about a gallery showing Syd had set up for Vancouver on his return. I explained the consommé techniques that result in it being perfectly clear.

Rabbit and wild rice pie followed, a careful slice plated table-side, garnished with sorrel. Sauterne the surprising choice here but perfectly, opulently balanced, full sweet to full savoury. Endless taste playing through the mouth. Butter lettuce salad next. Tossed with hazelnuts and oranges, the individual servings piled artfully with silver tongs. A glass of crisp white Bordeaux, not too cold. Citrus echoed nicely in the fragrance.

Back to poetry. Erin smiled, reluctant. I couldn't help myself.

"Go on," Syd said. "Give the man one. Do the one about the power outage."

I remember two parts, that float now independent of the whole.

Erin said, *We find old rhythms in the blackness.*

And the very end, three simple sentences. Looked at one way, not poetry at all.

She said, *I am in the living room. I hear the clock tick. I am losing my balance.*

The roast boar was wheeled out on its cutting board surrounded by ramekins of carrot mousse, deep brown wild mushrooms, bowls of buttery spaetzle and peaches stuffed with gooseberries. The serving was efficient and precise—boar, spaetzle, sauce, mushrooms, mousse, peach garnish, spray of chives. A hot plate guided soundlessly onto the tablecloth in front of each of us.

"*Bon appetit,*" the waiter said, and withdrew to his station near the kitchen doors. I glanced up to follow his quiet progress across the room and saw that most of the tables were now full.

Erin took a small, tentative mouthful, but her eyebrows went up sharply as she chewed. She was looking rather intently at the empty fork tines hovering above her plate.

I had a piece of boar in my mouth. I was chewing slowly. It was releasing itself into me, the only way I could think of it. There was the allspice. There was the juniper and the bay. The sage, the diced tomatoes. The sturdy vin de pays and the teaspoon of sugar. You could almost taste the time it took to cook. The two and half hours, the thirty-some-odd years. The shadow of my mother cast across Klaus's forearm as he stirred the sauce. The whisper of his words. Her eyes on his face. And then, a flash of myself as a boy. We're in a Vancouver restaurant. My parents' conversation is a well-tailored garment of silence. My mother takes a bite and looks around. My father politely asks after her meal. And I am swept away from them in that moment by my own mouthful of food. The most perfect bite of my life thus far—a bit of lamb shank, I think, this was in the Carvery—and I have been struck dumb with a sudden understanding of what lies ahead. Of what my life will hold.

I swallowed the boar, my insides warming. I looked across the now bustling room towards the kitchen, wondering if my inspiration began behind those doors. When I returned to my meal, I saw that Erin was quite close. She was leaning over, looking at me, enjoying something in my expression that she could see and I could not.

"What?" I whispered to her.

"Was that you making a discovery?" she whispered back.

SYD SLURPED UP MORE GOOD Scotch after dinner, clear single malt catching firelight and smoke and the glistening bone-handled blade that rested on the edge of his plate.

Erin and I finished with apples and slices of cheddar cheese. Dishes of blueberries and cream. A rich glass of port, slyly beautiful, heaving and weeping gently against the sides of the glass. Klaus came out and offered to show us the kitchen afterwards. Syd was leaning back in his chair, eyes half closed. "I can't move," he said.

We went back, Erin and I. The last orders were going out. The wave had broken. We stood in a cavern of stoves and ovens, prep counters and waiters' stations stretching down the walls. Down the centre of the room ran a long cutting block, hung with knives and ladles and clusters of copper and black aluminum pots. The floor was tiled in white and blue slabs. Above us, three unnaturally large chandeliers hung by triple chains from the high plaster ceiling.

"They came with the place. Crazy, no?" Klaus said catching my eye.

I shook my head and smiled.

Klaus took three glasses out of an overhead rack and poured us each another port from a bottle near the stovetop.

"Only cook with what you drink," he said as he handed us the glasses. I could feel the evening surge forward in a delicious unbroken crest. Erin had now wandered away along the prep tables, sipping and admiring the kitchen. Klaus and I were speaking of other kitchens I had seen. Of Vancouver. I admitted to having no job at the moment, told him I'd come here to research a cookbook, which provoked him to look at me almost gently, a laugh playing across his lips but not emerging.

Yes, Vancouver was a beautiful place. Yes, it was the kind of place a person might return to if they were raised there, just as Klaus said. But I told him also that I was unsettled there. That it was impossible to know if I would stay.

"You have family still there?" he asked.

I would not have assumed even then that the connection was forged, our link through her complete, had not a moment come in our quiet and certain conversation—the unnaturally relaxed, almost intimate exchange between a fifty-year veteran and a rookie, utterly green by comparison—when I noticed that both Klaus and I were speaking, sipping, our eyes sharply fixed on Erin.

She was at the stovetop, looking over the black surface. She was smiling fully at some thought—perhaps
imagining all that had started there on its way into the dining room—and a flush had risen in her cheeks. She swept
the hair back behind an ear, leaned against the chopping
block with one straight arm, her dress falling away from
her shoulder and breasts in an unwaisted sheath.

New effervescence had risen behind the marble grey.
New to me.

WE WAITED INSIDE THE front entrance for a cab, and Syd
leaned heavily against the front desk, smoking silently. Erin
was tending him. When the car arrived, I climbed in and
waved to Klaus, who stood under the awning and saluted
me with the touch of a single finger to his forehead.

Syd slept immediately and I had to help Erin coax him
into the elevator and from there into the apartment and
down the long hall into their bedroom.

"I'm fine," she said, when I asked. Her voice lowered.
She sat on the edge of the huge bed. I watched her in the
half darkness, the room swimming in silver and black.

I made to go, remembering where Syd had left his
cousin's Scotch, resolved to drink it.

She stood up to say goodnight. I stepped back towards
her, and as she leaned forward to kiss my cheek, her hands
swung forward and I caught the tips of her fingers. Held
them for an instant shaking them gently.

"You really tired?" I asked.

"No," she said.

"You want to stay up a bit?"

She looked over her shoulder at the bed, and at Syd. His shoes were kicked off near the night table. The blanket pulled up to his chest and between his legs in an instinctive foetal curl. The light of the room lay across all of us like an opium cloud. I gathered her fingers into my hand and pulled her into the hall.

We found a half bottle of wine in the kitchen and drank it from the neck, passing it back and forth on the balcony. The air was close. The sky dark with water. I looked over at Erin and at the light from the living room as it passed through the lattice in the windowboxes and broke into white diamonds across her shoulders.

I brushed the white skin and felt tiny beads of sweat moisten the back of my fingers. She turned her head and the collarbone rose out at the base of her neck making a cup that I imagined filling with rain. I wished it would rain. I wished the balcony would break away and throw us into the rain that gathered in the sky. I felt her hand in the small of my back. In her mouth I tasted loganberry, cream and port. I smelled spice, and the scent of hair and carpets. I imagined myself in a caravan, crossing a great desert towards the sea.

APRIL 12, 1963. *Good Friday*

*Tzarina's is a dark, dark place. Full of melancholy Russians. We were given the celebrity booth near the front of the restaurant,*

*with high backs and utmost privacy once you are seated. Nobody
ordered or talked much until the Archbishop arrived, which he did
with several priests in tow. They swayed in with their enormous
robes and gold crucifixes in the middle of their chests. The temperature in the restaurant dropped several degrees. I half expected
chanting to begin.*

*Dinner was large parts caviar and cod. There is a grainy
mustard sauce they favour here that does not sit well. Tonight I
am up and at the window looking south. I have already lied twice
in the past week. Tomorrow I will lie again and tell Edward I am
sick and cannot go to Evanston with them all. They have booked
a hotel on the lake where we will stay over Easter, when the
vodka will be poured and a great number of nostalgic tales will be
told. This is their idea of a reward before we leave. He will offer
to stay back. I'll insist.*

I WOKE UP LOOKING THROUGH the cold dryness of the
sheets I had pulled over my head during sleep. There was
sand in my mouth and eyes. The sun filtered into the
air around my face and my breath grew hot but I lay
unmoving, thinking, waiting for silence in the apartment.
I listened as they showered, and as they made toast, as Syd
brought in a paper, as they dressed to leave. Syd called
from the kitchen for Erin, there was shuffling in the hall
and the tap of a fingernail on my door. I lay absolutely
still, barely breathing. My head sang, and I closed my eyes
and stared into the shield of my eyelids. Then I heard the
front door close and the rooms fill with silence.

I wrapped myself in a bathrobe and avoided my own glance in the mirror. I found leftover coffee and then, standing in the living room, I responded to an impulse and phoned my mother's number. Francine didn't answer and I hung up on the answering machine in frustration. I made my own slow breakfast. Cracking each egg carefully into the simmering water. Cutting the hot toast into triangles. I tried to read the paper but put it down, and stood on the balcony looking blankly at the city rising above me to the south.

Erin left a note saying they'd be near the Tribune Tower.

*Come find us . . . Ciao.*

I planned my route south to avoid Michigan Avenue. I could cross the river on Wabash and miss them altogether, but when I reached Grand Avenue I turned left and cut across towards where I knew they'd be. I stood behind a bus shelter across the street and watched Erin recording something in a log, taking light readings and talking with Syd. I had meant to give them room to finish the shoot, but when Syd broke down the tripod and they looked ready to go, I didn't move.

I sat at the bus stop, as they discussed where to go next. Erin would brush a strand of hair away from her face or blow it back with a gust of breath from the side of her mouth. Then she would put her hand on the waistline of her skirt, just at the top of the zipper, or touch her collar bone while they talked. They moved to cross the river. I walked along the store fronts opposite.

Syd set up for some shots of traffic on the bridge, Erin stood behind him, judging the landscape, Indian-print cotton rippling around her legs, her waist angled and wrapped in a sash of red cloth. Then she crouched next to Syd and pointed at the road work toward the north end of the bridge where road crews were patching sections of decaying concrete. Occasionally a stolid-faced passerby would stumble or shuffle across the rough parts of the sidewalk and flake off chips of the bridge decks into the unnaturally turquoise river.

Standing up from behind the camera, she swept her hair back from her face and tied it back with an elastic. She looked around briefly. I turned to look into the window of a record store and felt her eyes drift across my shoulder blades without hesitation.

They moved south, I moved with them. Standing in crowds at street corners, or in doorways. At Adams Street I crossed the road and watched them from the steps of the Art Institute. When they crossed the road and approached the steps, I slipped through the heavy glass doors and into the lobby. When they approached the doors, I paid and entered the exhibits. They lingered at the front counter, then paid. I retreated into the modern wing past Pollock and Balthus. I escaped them down a corridor of abstract. Found a stairwell. Found a new floor, much quieter. Went through three glass doors and into an exhibit of Nils-Ole Lund architectural collages, shapes in shapes. And there were the voices again. Distant echoes. Closer. Then coming round the curved wall on which the images hung.

I fled again to the stairwell, flushed with heat. One floor down I stumbled into a hall full of armour and muskets, crossbows and daggers. At the end of the hall, past a phalanx of pikes, winked an exit sign. The breeze outside seemed to ice the sweat on my chest.

"Oh hi, Francine, it's Jake." And then I went blank. The machine beeped before I could think of anything else to say.

I slammed the phone down, frustrated again, and I stood in the booth for a moment, shaking and cold. I imagined where she might be, but I couldn't pull in a picture. I closed my eyes and plugged my ears and nose, trying to remember at least a smell. Nothing. I felt dead.

I walked west and south until I wasn't sure the streets were still safe, turned around and hiked back. Night was falling and the shadows of the buildings on my left stretched enough to cross the street and meet their brothers opposite. The air was damp and heavy with the smell of cars and buses. My breathing slowed. The rails screeched on the overhead tracks and I didn't start. The sound made a shield that I slipped behind, across State, under the carrion smell of ribs and deep-dish pizza. A taxi ran a light and I danced to safety behind a pylon. I was invisible. I found the Boar's Head without even fingering the paper in my pocket.

He came out of the kitchen wiping his hands on a white towel.

"No reservation. I'm sorry, Klaus."

"Don't be sorry." Klaus smoothed the fringe of his moustache with his bottom lip. "Come into the back for a while."

I stood frozen in the entrance hall. My face felt dirty, my hair unwashed. Klaus spread his hands.

"You want to cook. It's at least a small part of what you want to do while you're here."

We walked through the restaurant. The magnificent tables of white, silver and crystal were being assembled. And I followed him into the kitchen under the chandeliers. It was a familiar symphony. The clip of knives and the creak of oven doors, the crash of pots and the low roar of flame.

I washed up, shook some hands, Klaus gave me the walk through, and I slid into the evening like I was making an omelette. Working the plates to which I'd been assigned. Jumping to the sauté station when the orders came through. A piece of hare saddle, a sauce with green peppercorns. Watching Klaus the whole time too, as best I could. Trying to find the things I should know about him by his movements. His way of knocking shut an oven door with the inside of his left knee. The slight twist when his plates went up onto the pass. And when he paused to steel his blade—I stopped mid-action, a piece of saddle half off the flame—his eyes floated free and over the kitchen while his wrist accelerated the blade into a blur in front of his face.

Close to midnight, Klaus called me over and we stood near the waiter's station while he filled our glasses from the chef's bottle he kept there. The last orders had gone out. The steam and chatter of the dishwashers murmured from the back of the kitchen. We talked across the range of topics that would be covered at this point in the evening. How it had worked. What had pleased him. What had not gone according to plan.

He worked the conversation onto the topic of my future without trying to conceal his purpose. He had a very particular and surprising idea.

"You told me you were not working," he said, when I hesitated.

"True," I answered. Flattered. Stunned.

"So what's to prevent you? Forget the green card, I haven't hired an American in twenty-five years."

I was nodding, but not quite to the point of saying yes.

"How is she?" he asked, finally. "Your mother."

I told the truth. Her body had failed her in some ways. She didn't walk well any more. I could see her getting smaller.

Klaus didn't look at me while this information was being delivered. He watched his kitchen. He watched the stations being wiped down and the clean saucepans finding their way onto the hooks where they had begun the evening. I realized that he had satisfied a very old urge in asking, scratched a very long-standing itch while carrying on the business of what had filled the decades since it started.

"Neither of you wrote?" I asked.

"We did. For a short while. Then all at once it seemed to make no sense."

"How long did it take?" I asked him. "How long does it take?"

He took a sip of his port and looked over at me. "It varies, I imagine," he told me. "The further into the forest you go, the longer it generally takes to find your way out."

I waited.

"Sometimes you don't come out."

The sous-chef approached tentatively, stood a short distance down the tiles. Klaus saw him and waved him in, friendly. They ran through the evening, the night manager's duties. There was a clogged drain in the dish pit; the sous had arranged for plumbers. He confirmed orders to fill and prep lists for tomorrow.

"Good, good," Klaus said.

The sous nodded to us both and hustled back to it. Klaus and I waited to find our original conversational orbit. He opened his mouth, stopped.

"I read her journals," I told him. "Not one to talk, my mother."

"No," he agreed.

"Recipes mostly."

He smiled. That seemed right to him. He took a breath. "So?"

I thought hard.

"Don't answer right away," he said, refilling our glasses.

"I don't want to make a mistake," I told him.

He sucked his upper lip thoughtfully. "Neither do I," he said. "But it's not something that will destroy you or me either way."

I walked all the way to Goethe Street in the light rain. Slipped into the dark apartment, down the muffling hall, past the light under Erin and Syd's door, and into the cool, dark cave of my room. I didn't touch the light, but went straight to the bed. Like a sleepwalker returning to the dream bed, a ghost returning to the grave. Lying down, lying still on the white sheets, resolved to wait for morning.

APRIL 15, 1963

*So this is what it's like then, to lose something. Or perhaps I should say: so this is what it will be like.*

I SLEPT LATE, DEEPLY. But when I woke up on Easter morning, there was another note.

*You could find us off Dearborn on Monroe . . .*

Which I did, near a fountain and a sculpture in orange steel, in a pulsing downtown square. Easter Sunday crowds, a colourful, lighter prairie air, and cracks of blue showing between the tops of buildings like fragments of painted eggshell. Erin was sitting on a low brick wall, perched, watching. Syd was shooting a busker. An accordion player with a greasy beard and a bass drum on his back.

Syd was on his knees, then on his stomach, sprawled on the brick. Two or three people would watch and then move on to other performances in the square. I stood back near a planter and watched. Erin smoked, then shifted on the wall, stood quickly, hand on her back and turned. She found me immediately, and I walked towards her into the sunlight. A smile. A stab of lipstick, the black jacket, the boots rooted to the pavement, the smooth white forehead and softening eyes.

"Hi, stranger," she said, and we sat together on the wall. My arm went around her shoulder for a second, squeezed and let go, releasing nutmeg into the air like I had stirred a pot of mulled wine.

"Where have you been?" Her eyebrows leaned into a tender frown. "You've been like a ghost."

I looked across the square at Syd. He had the busker sitting cross-legged on several spread-out pages of *USA Today*. Looking upward into the camera Syd was holding over his head. I tried to shift her focus. "How are we doing here?"

"Oh . . . well," Erin turned her head to match my gaze. "Saturday morning on Michigan. Saturday afternoon in Oak Park." She flipped the pages of her journal with a moistened index finger as she spoke. "Today is Buskers in the Loop."

Syd was walking in a circle around the accordion player. Snapping shots, the images washing over him like smoke.

"I haven't seen you since Friday," she said. "I've been thinking a lot about that."

"I roasted a mountain-goat leg last night," I told her. "Thick cream sauce with Stilton cheese."

"You cooked at the Boar's Head?"

I nodded and she looked at me for a long time as she drew her own conclusions.

"You're staying here," she said, finally.

"I'm not sure what else to do. I don't have any other ideas."

Again the pause. Everything I told her caused Erin to consider where we might go next, in words, in life. It occurred to me that I wasn't thinking about the conversation like that at all. My intentions were clear to me and becoming clear to her.

"How could you not have any other ideas?" she asked.

We were staring at each other. We were sitting so close to each other, shoulder to shoulder. I could smell her. I had a taste memory of port in her mouth. Sweet sweat.

"That hurts," she said, the thickening of her voice confirming the fact. She turned away and held a hand to the side of her face, shielding herself from the public square. Tears rolled free of her eyes. Big drops to the point of her chin.

"It's not that I didn't think about other ideas," I said.

Syd looked over from across the square. His brow creased, but when he saw it was me he grinned, waved. Erin's hand still shielded her face.

I waved back to Syd.

I started again: "I've been thinking about you for months. For over a year."

"I know. I know."

"I never thought anything would happen."

"I know. I know."

"But there's a connection here. Something old going on."

Erin raised her face. Squinted at the sky. Syd's accordion player was wheezing out a circus-tent version of "Rock of Ages," bass drum thumping along, an uneven, unreliable heartbeat.

"Klaus," Erin said.

"It's complicated," I told her, prepared to try, but she came back quickly.

"I saw something there, like he was a catalyst of some kind. Like you saw in him something of yourself and finally knew what to do. He inspired you."

"As have you."

"Great," Erin said.

"Well, you're the one who said I should be cooking again. Not lying around. Not just writing about food."

Erin looked at me for several seconds before responding. "So I've inspired you," she said, finally. "Exactly how wonderful is that supposed to make me feel?"

Still, she was connected to me, sitting there. Maybe I didn't quite get it that very second. But when I looked back at Erin, her eyes were in mine. And we were, in that instant, redoing everything we had ever done together up to that moment to create the thing that we had. Voices on the phone. Friendly hands on shoulders. Naked against one another on a sticky black leather couch in the living room of an expensive condominium off Lakeshore Boulevard.

And then, whatever thing it was that we had was gone.

I SPENT A MONTH IN CHICAGO. Cooked almost every night. Learned all that I could learn. And I would have stayed longer but the cold became pneumonia. Francine did not have to press her point.

Klaus didn't talk much more about my mother, he didn't ask questions that would have launched other questions and suggested all the questions I should be asking back. There was a hard web of such questions after thirty years but I was there and we were elbow to elbow much of the time. Connected as possible under the circumstances.

Once he said to me, "Your father died, I think. Is this so?"

And I answered, "That's what I'd come to believe, chef."

Another time he asked when exactly was my birthday.

"Oh, I don't think I can stay that long," I told him. "I'm a fall baby."

And when it did come time to leave, although there were no promises made, he shook my hand slowly, with both hands, as if to seal a deal.

MY MOTHER HAD TAKEN TO sitting in her wheelchair on the terrace. Here were her flowers and the view of English Bay she had always enjoyed. She didn't walk at all any more, Francine told me, the arthritis claiming her, joint by joint. But she did turn in her chair when I came through the terrace doors and reached her arms up to wrap me in a gentle hug.

"Jake. Where have you been?" she whispered.

I pulled up a stool and sat near her. Francine went into the living room and noisily picked up her knitting. "I went to such a beautiful place," I told her.

And her eyes flicked over at the terrace door a second time, as if she thought someone else might be waiting there.

# SILENT CRUISE

Sheedy was a meticulous handicapper. He had a CD-ROM library of past performances and an index of tracks with pictures and layout diagrams. He downloaded race results off the Internet directly to the Palm Pilot he favoured trackside.

Dett was prostrate before the altar of a more impulsive method entirely, the mechanics of which he didn't understand or question and about which Sheedy respectfully did not ask. And yet, they needed each other.

IN THE FAT CHOY LOUNGE at 13:01, Saturday, September 6, 1997, Dett was engaged in the habitual translation of analog detail into digits. It would be impossible for Dett to be in the Fat Choy on a Saturday, or anywhere else on any other day of the week, without yielding to the delicious impulse: the sixth day of the week in a place named with the sixth and third letters of the alphabet, waiting for the third race.

Sixes and threes, two sets.

"What are you getting in the third, Dett?" Sheedy was asking, pecking at the tiny black palm-top. The overhead TV was providing Cantonese analysis of a race that ran at 12:43 in Santa Anita. Around the trackside Fat Choy, Chinese men (twenty-three of them) in patched grey cardigans and battered hats were fanning their forms up and down, beating them silently into their palms, conducting as the timbre of their luck resounded faithfully in the replay.

Dett looked down at his program. The third race at Hastings Park had a post time of 14:23 with twelve horses running. The numbers, the 14, the 23 and the 12, lifted from the page to join the sequence of sixes and threes. Dett visualized this in three dimensions, multicoloured numbers floating in a black void, linking and clustering like molecules, like evolving DNA, each change reconstructing the predictive significance of the strand.

These were Dett's numbers. Spools of digits, a numeric cascade inspired by every ambient detail. A bit-snow, as he came to think of it, that had alarmed him only once. He had played the ponies since high school, betting a combination of handicapped picks and selections made through the sifting of these compulsive numbers. But in second-year university—Dett was studying mathematics—he found himself losing, all at once plunging below the payout of random picks. There were ancillary problems. He was failing his exams.

He couldn't fault the handicapping. His own spill of numbers had increased in manic intensity to the point that they emitted a noise. He was driven to numeric fixations unlike anything he'd seen, calculating the day of the week for any date in Julian or Gregorian history being only the most conspicuous example. This compulsion lasted in full flower for many months, eliminating friendships, disturbing professors whose lectures might be interrupted. And the computation certainly wasn't relevant to any of his courses. The question wasn't on any of his finals.

His professor of non-parametric methods took him aside at the end of second year. A tobacco-stained Irish mathematician whose advice had been compacted in Dett's memory to a single string of words: ". . . the most unusually gifted student does not necessarily succeed . . ."

Indeed, he flunked third year. And although the noise eventually abated, his recent obsession to precisely calendarize everything calmed, he still invested some time researching repetitive word disorders, which he learned were clustered under obsessive-compulsive disorders, themselves a strain of thought disorder. Was he sick?

It was true the numbers tumbled ceaselessly, and his various personal and academic embarrassments satisfied the requirements of the *Diagnostic and Statistical Manual of Mental Disorders,* which stated that obsessions must be "intrusive or inappropriate." But Dett didn't think the American Psychiatric Association's catalogue of disorders captured his mental action in total. On occasion his numbers persisted in sprinkling a pattern of meaning across the situation at hand (mostly at the track, where they had thankfully resumed their function). If bit-snow were a sickness, then he had grown to like the numeric frost on his mental peaks, it was a key feature of his personal topography and screw the APA anyway.

Sheedy never asked about it directly. It was enough that at a crucial moment he sensed a facility soft-wired into Dett's cranial gore, and on that uncharacteristic, unhandicapped hunch had picked Dett to fill a vacant financial analyst's position, for which the advertisement had expressly stated "MBA required."

"You have second sight," Sheedy said during the second interview. Dett remembered that he was wearing a hand-me-down suit of his father's from the Eaton's Pine Room.

Second sight, second interview, second-hand suit. Dett asked Sheedy to repeat himself.

"Second sight," Sheedy said for the second time. "You see shadows behind the numbers, which is rare."

He could never have predicted this. Thirteen months of unemployment, living in a friend's basement next to a thicket of home-grown. Sixty-four applications. Nineteen first interviews. Eighteen polite rejection letters. One lonely second interview and this strutting Vancouver Stock Exchange peacock in a bottle-green suit actually understood his numbers.

"You like the ponies?" Sheedy asked him.

It had been good to get out of that basement on his own terms.

Sheedy sent him on the securities course, basic training for financial analysts, brokers and investment dealers. It had been forty-seven years since anybody scored 100 per cent, you just didn't get everything right in this world.

Dett got everything right.

Sheedy took his new protégé to Hy's Steak House to celebrate. Sent Dett staggering home early with a pound of beef and a half bottle of Chilean cabernet sloshing around his gut. Dett was thinking, 100 per cent every 47 years: 100, 47, 100, 47. Nineteen ninety-seven minus forty-seven makes 1950. Today was January 13, so, back-calculating the day of the week, he established that January 13, 1950, was a Friday.

Friday the thirteenth. He liked that. The last idiot-savant had nailed it on Friday the thirteenth.

FAT CHOY IS CHINESE FOR "good luck."

"Who do you have in the third?" Dett asked back to Sheedy now, sitting across the lino-top table in the smoky trackside lounge.

Sheedy straightened his gold tie against his French blue shirt, shot cuffs out the sleeves of his Prince of Wales double-breasted. He had a distinctly boss-like aura despite being a little man. (He inspired in Dett the auto-thoughts *proportional* and *lifelike*.) Black brush cut. Black eyebrows. Olive skin and a straight nose to match his straight teeth, which were also very white. He walked everywhere like he was pissed off, shoulders hunched, legs and arms straight. The MBAs who worked at Sheedy Mahew Financial called him Bucky Badger after the mascot of his Wisconsin alma mater.

"Got spanked by Bucky this morning," someone would say.

"Yeah, he looked pissed," would come the response.

"A badger is always pissed, you know that, I know that . . ."

So it ran.

"A Little Risk," Sheedy said now, the palm-top having endorsed one of the favourites.

"Ooooh. Ballsy," Dett mocked gently.

They were the only suits in the Fat Choy, ever. This was where Sheedy brought his hot prospects for a couple laughs before signing up a new account. Dett rode data-shotgun from time to time. The two of them would drive out to the track in Sheedy's leased metallic-green Porsche Carrera 4. Dett would run the conventional numbers for the client, establishing base confidence in the firm. But Sheedy also knew Dett could run his stranger numbers and pick a winner on occasion, and if he picked one of Sheedy's hot prospects onto a winner—a placer, a shower, anything that demonstrated Sheedy Mahew was also a *lucky* firm—well then, Sheedy could pitch any woo known to man. Sheedy could wax the sale.

"Who is it?" Dett asked.

"Andrew Xiang for the third race. I need second sight."

"And you like A Little Risk?" Dett asked, scanning the program.

"I do," Sheedy answered, squinting at his six-inch screen.

"Does Andrew know the ponies?" Dett asked, changing tack.

"A little gaming itch, like you or me, nothing big time. You want a drink?" Sheedy produced a money clip and delicately extracted a twenty.

Dett got Sheedy his drink. Southern Comfort and Coke, no ice. "But Andrew isn't a new account," he said as he sat down again.

"Have a drink for Chrissake," Sheedy said, staring at the empty table in front of Dett.

Dett shrugged. "It's only one o'clock."

"Fuck one. We gotta have some fun sometimes. You're not having fun?" This was classic badger, displaying a small wound for emotional leverage. Dett thought all the blood that had cumulatively seeped from Sheedy's wounds over the nine months he'd been at Sheedy Mahew wouldn't moisten the pecker on a Brazilian needle-tip mosquito. But Sheedy was also recently divorced (again) so now he was going to make a little speech on the topic of How Important It Is to Just Have Fun Once in a While, until Dett broke down and had the drink.

"What're you having?" Sheedy said when Dett returned with his glass.

"Southern Comfort and Coke," Dett said. "No ice, boss."

Sheedy laughed, and reaching a manicured hand across the table he gripped Dett tightly by the back of the neck.

"We're having a good year," Sheedy said, and here Dett found himself staring into his mentor's cold brown eyes with a pound of Rolex clicking audibly in his right ear.

"Bre-X," Dett said. He wasn't above reminding Sheedy once in a while that he had counselled selling the infamous gold stock a full month before the geologist went airborne, falling only slightly faster than the share price eventually did.

"You're the best. How much do I pay you?" Sheedy said, releasing him.

"Not nearly enough, but let's not talk about it here," Dett said.

"I'm just asking because you look so raggedy-assed all the time."

"This is Armani," Dett said, touching his lapel and recalling the sticker shock.

"You take your own action I hope, take care of yourself with the things you learn," Sheedy said, between sips.

"I take care of myself," Dett said. It was true. Information trickled through and you didn't need much to beat the house.

"And I facilitate this," Sheedy said.

"You do," Dett said, wishing to move on. "I was asking why we're trotting Andrew Xiang out here when he's already a client. Are we selling something hard?"

Sheedy grimaced slightly and leaned forward again.

"OK," he said, pressing his palms together in front of him. "We have to . . . evacuate somebody."

"Liquidation sale," Dett said.

"Not a liquidation sale," Sheedy said, lowering his voice. "Christ, don't even think that, our seller is still very liquid."

"So who fucked up?" Dett asked, thinking, One of the MBAs.

"The seller is *my* client," Sheedy answered.

Dett regarded his boss, who just briefly pushed a hand through his black hair, straightened his shoulders and gathered himself. Sheedy only had a few clients and they were all guys who lived on very quiet properties in the hills around Whistler and paid commissions in cash.

"Remember Jimmy?" Sheedy asked. "He has to leave the country. It's legal."

Jimmy was one of those clients. When money or signatures were required he flew down from Whistler in a chartered heli-jet. He had an impenetrable sleepy expression and a discordant predilection for angry expletives like "cocksucker" and "whore." On the one occasion they met, in connection with a deal Dett was working on, Jimmy had shaken his hand limply and said only, "Sheedy mentioned you. So let's put this whore to bed then, all right?" He pronounced it hoo-er.

"So sell the stuff," Dett said to Sheedy now. "What's the deal?"

"The shares in concern won't trade openly until the fall, by which time he has to be out of the country. The fall is too late, by then he'll be banned in Vancouver and probably everywhere else."

"A private sale then," Dett said.

"A mandatory sale," Sheedy answered, staring intently at Dett. "He has over four hundred thousand tied up here and he wants his cash."

"Best-efforts," Dett said, shrugging.

"You're not hearing me," Sheedy said. "We sold him these shares and he was more than a little reluctant at the time. But he trusts me, understand? Now he has to do a runner on forty-eight hours' notice and I have to produce his cash."

"Is he threatening you?" Dett asked.

"He doesn't have to," Sheedy said, shaking his head. "We are fucking hooped here, Dett."

"I see it," Dett said, imagining the quiet phone call that Sheedy had received at home last night. It wouldn't have been Jimmy calling either, but some associate nobody had ever heard of before. "It's critical we move on this . . ." Words of elaborate politeness.

"There's an upside, naturally." Sheedy tried to lighten the tone. "Double commission. Undying loyalty of the client's friends. All that shit."

"Fantastic."

"Hey," Sheedy said. "You and I have done this before. Your brains, my good looks."

"So what do we have here?" Dett asked.

"A couple of months ago we took Jimmy deep into two positions. If we unload even one of them he'll be happy," Sheedy said. "You feel like selling some health care or some technology today?"

Dett pretended to look out the window, as if the answer to this question lay somehow in the weather. High, light, blowing cloud, cool and pleasant. It meant nothing.

Sheedy swung his case onto the table, tore open the Velcro side pouch and produced the fax-smeared stock-exchange fact sheets.

"This is all I get?" Dett asked, incredulously. A prospectus was normally six pounds of paper. If Dett was going to do numbers, conventional or otherwise, he preferred more of them. It inspired him, he waded into them and paddled around.

"What do you want?" Sheedy said. "Xiang knows these companies up the ying-yang. We need second sight today, so pick me the winner. Health care or technology.

And a horse in the third. I gotta take a leak." And here he snapped shut the palm-top, slid it into a side pocket of his suit, deperched from his chair and stalked off to the johns.

Dett glanced down at what Sheedy had left for him on the table.

Commerce-Net provided Internet marketing solutions. Yawn. Who didn't? Expected to open at $3.80 in late November. Zero revenue. Zero track record. About the only thing Commerce-Net had were some "channel partners" as they were known, heavy hitters like Microsoft who backed the technology without a direct investment. When Dett had skimmed to the bottom of the sheet he got to the phone numbers. CEO Bertie Perkins could be reached at 1-888-555-0000. Who picked a number like that? Dett closed his eyes: 3.80, 0, 0, 18885550000. It all flattened out and left him in a single void place.

Halox Inc. was developing a bowel-cancer marker which, if it were picked up by one North American hospital in a hundred, would make everyone connected with the company a millionaire—legitimate investors, Sheedy's drug-dealer clients, nieces and nephews of the CFO. Of course, at the moment Halox was hacking and bunting its way through the bush leagues of level-two clinical trials. This would be considered Still a Long Way from the Show. Another zero going public with zero. Pure speculation.

Dett looked around the room, his eyes red from the smoke of the endless collective Fat Choy cigarette, some foul brand these old guys favoured.

Three minutes to the first post here at Hastings Park. Sheedy would be at the window putting down a hundred on whatever horse the palm-top picked to win. Sheedy bet all nine races every time, an indiscriminate strategy that lost him about 20 per cent a year. Dett knew that random bets and the barest trace of luck would get him into the same tax bracket.

Sheedy once said to Dett, "When my old man went to the ponies, the stands were full of honest people and the game was totally crooked. You could actually *play* a game like that."

Exactly. Dett folded up the Halox and Commerce-Net papers and went outside and watched the changing odds on the board across the stretch. Rumsey favoured in the first at lean odds of 8 to 5, which Dett took as emblematic of how the game had diminished. All these hard-core track guys scanning the same numbers, picking the same winners, same losers, with the same information. It was hard to win any money in this environment without second sight, something that could cast a shadow behind the numbers the handicappers had factored down to value zero.

So now Dett looked around at the nearly empty asphalt yard, not yet littered with torn betting slips as it would be over the next hours, and he started spontaneously counting heads. Twenty-six people on the benches. Eighteen people at the fence. He averaged the people in the grandstand with a sweeping glance. One person per ten seats.

Rumsey was at the pole, position number one. The

heavy favourite, according to the form, which said Rumsey "is the one-to-beat." Dett thought, Horse number one, the one to beat, over one and one-sixteenth miles.

He won by one and a half lengths.

"Did you have that action?" Sheedy asked him after Dett had descended again into the Fat Choy Lounge.

"Did you?" Dett asked back.

"You had it, you fucker, why didn't you tell me?"

"You didn't ask."

"I'm slumping," Sheedy said, staring at his little screen, entering the results.

"He was the favourite," Dett said.

"Who picks a favourite? You can't make any money doing that."

"Most people pick the favourite," Dett said. "That's what makes them favourites. You just have to bet a whole lot."

Sheedy made a mental calculation. "I'm thinking at 8 to 5 I would have had to bet about three hundred grand to get us out of our little situation here."

Which brought to mind Jimmy packing crates for the midnight float-plane south of the border. Glued to his cell- phone, waiting for news on the matter of his available cash. "Hey, Eddie, did we get a call from that broker down there?" "Nothing yet." "Well, you phone that cocksucker and rattle his fucking chain."

"Do you want another drink?" Dett asked Sheedy now.

"Naaa," Sheedy said and looked at his watch, which Dett already knew read 1:43 p.m. Ten minutes to the second post. "So what is it, health care or technology? I like technology myself. I met Bertie Perkins at a trade show once. Sharp guy, respected. Xiang will know that."

"Commerce-Net and Halox," Dett said. "They might as well be identical."

"I'm not talking fundamentals, I'm talking gut."

"Either way they're zeroes, Sheedy. Total specs. I would advise a client to buy based on how much long-shot money they had to piss away."

"If I wanted MBA answers at a time like this, I would have brought an MBA to the track with me," Sheedy said.

"Sorry," Dett said. "This is not a fuzzy logic problem."

"Which one can be sold more easily, then?"

"Same answer," Dett said.

Sheedy flopped back in his chair. "Maybe you need the drink," he said. "You need to loosen up."

"You're not listening."

"Talk."

"We sell him both. He knows the companies, so he knows they're both spec zeroes. We tell him it's a hedge, like betting a box, two horses to finish, any order. The Internet breaks up, people will still get colon cancer. The marker tests come up blank, you always have the Net. Technology, health-care. Optimism, pessimism. Shoot him some of that stuff."

Sheedy went up and got the drinks.

"Will this work?" he asked, sitting down.

"Christ, Sheedy, I can't promise. We've done it before, I can say that much."

"Unhoop me, I can say that much. Do you have my horse in the third?" he asked. "We're going to need that horse."

"I'm waiting for it," Dett said. "But I'll get one."

"What about the second race?" Sheedy asked him.

Dett just shook his head. He was going to sip this drink and think about nothing and then go over to the parade ring and have a look at the runners in the third.

"Come on, give me a pick on two," Sheedy said. "I need a win here."

Dett sighed. Outside, he looked across the track up high to the blue mountains opposite and breathed in deeply. Eleven-horse field. Horses six and five were the favourites. Six plus five. Five plus six.

Sometimes he didn't need a big pool of numbers.

He went inside.

"Springhill Billy," he said to Sheedy.

"Horse number one?"

Sheedy bet a hundred and Dett went trackside in time to see the horses pass the grandstand. Grey Lightning by a head on Springhill Billy.

"Interesting," Dett said out loud.

Springhill Billy was holding third at the halfway point.

"Fade, baby," Dett yelled.

Springhill Billy was sixth in the stretch, and seventh at the wire by seven lengths.

"What the fuck was that?" Sheedy said when he sat down. "The thing sprang a leak."

"Sometimes you just bet a hunch."

"Everything you bet is a hunch," Sheedy said, face back over the palm-top. "Number six won."

"And five?" Dett asked.

"Showed," Sheedy said, looking up suddenly. "How are you feeling partner?"

"Don't sweat it," Dett said. "We saved the win for the third race."

"I sincerely hope so," Sheedy said.

ANDREW XIANG WAS STANDING at the top of the steps for several minutes before Dett spotted him.

"Do you guys like this place?" he asked when he'd sat down and had a look around.

Sheedy shot a look over at Dett.

"I like it," Dett said, taking the tag.

"Why not sit upstairs in the clubhouse? Better view. And you can get a sandwich up there," Andrew Xiang said.

Sheedy was on his feet. "That's a good idea. Let's go."

"These guys are the only real betters left," Dett said, looking around as he got up, as if he were seeing the room for the last time.

"Quirky," Andrew said, still seated. "I wonder who'll be betting down here after they all die of lung cancer."

"Hey, it's the Fat Choy room, maybe they won't die," Sheedy said.

Andrew Xiang laughed.

"It has to be the room," Dett said. "You never see the old guys anywhere else."

It turned out they could get sandwiches at the Fat Choy bar.

"Do you wager, Mr. Xiang?" Dett asked. The use of Mr. might have been spreading it a bit thick. Andrew was only a few years older than Dett and although he had a lot of money he didn't have what Sheedy called "a roasted fuck of a lot of money."

"Andrew. Sure I like to bet."

"I'm losing today," Dett said, avoiding Sheedy's curious gaze.

"Too bad, who did you like in the second?" Andrew asked.

"Number one, Springhill Billy," Dett said.

"He faded," Andrew said, wincing sympathetically. "I listened in the car. Long shot though, I can relate. It's hard to make money against your old guys here."

"You're exactly right," Dett said. "The game has changed. More professional and yet harder to play. Bigger house take, narrower odds. It's tough."

"That's business right there, though, isn't it." Sheedy was leaning forward on the table now, picking up Dett's leave. "Bigger house. Competition. You know what I'm saying?"

"It's true," Andrew said.

"I find myself betting the box more," Sheedy said, warming up. "Cover myself off a little."

"How is it going today?" Andrew asked, smiling broadly. He knew the answer already.

"Well, I'd like to be up on the day, if you understand what I'm saying."

Now Andrew was laughing. "I thought you might want that," he said.

Dett excused himself. Sheedy was at stride, talking about three-horse boxes now. Dett figured he might as well go over to the parade circle. Fifteen minutes to the third post, time to listen to those numbers, time to take a slow walk in a flurry of bit-snow.

Crossing in front of the grandstand it occurred to Dett that the scary part was the thought that it might stop snowing all at once. Even when he was researching repetitive word disorders he hadn't actively wished the bits to stop. He always had a sense of how the silence might ring on and he imagined what mental fixations might fill such a void.

With two scratches, there were ten horses running, which suggested immediately three significant numbers: the one, the ten and the difference of nine.

Dett watched the grooms leading the horses out of the paddocks and around the small dirt parade ring. It wasn't his habit to note the beauty of a horse, but Dett couldn't deny that they were all exquisite. A chestnut. A grey. A muscled one, a lithe dancer. Long of body, high of haunch. Was it femininity people saw, Dett wondered, or masculine power? The meekness in the slow step or the wildness in the eye?

Ten horses walking slowly in a circle. Ten glistening coats. Ten horses and one would win. Nine losers. With the scratches, the ninth horse was now Silent Cruise.

He found him in the parade. Silent Cruise was a deep mahogany, muscled and powerful. His head tossed. He appeared impatient. Silent Cruise wore deep purple silks, Dett noticed, a kingly colour.

He glanced at the racing form. Silent Cruise was picked to win and to place by the two race columnists.

He walked back slowly towards the Fat Choy. Pausing briefly in front of the grandstands, he wondered how long the track would survive with nine out of ten seats empty. One seat in ten.

The one in ten. The empty nine. Those numbers again.

Sheedy surprised him.

"Sheedy," Dett said. "Where's Andrew?"

"Still downstairs," Sheedy said. "Pick, please."

One in ten was all he was getting. One in ten and the nine left over. That integer string plus an image of a favoured horse with a rich royal purple silk. Horse number nine.

"Silent Cruise will at least show," Dett said. "Get him to take Silent Cruise."

"Show?" Sheedy asked.

"It's a safe bet and I'm getting it hard," Dett said. "It rings for me. Drop Silent Cruise on the table with absolute confidence like you never thought of another horse. And make a deal about putting down some of your own money."

"I need a winner," Sheedy said.

"No, we don't, Sheedy," Dett said. "We need to show luck, which means we have to be in the money. There's more luck picking a show and showing than there is picking a win and getting beat by a neck."

Sheedy became a very serious badger.

"It's not going well down there," Dett said, interpreting the look.

"He thinks they're both dogs," Sheedy said. "I mean real dogs. He hasn't made his final decision yet, but I don't feel good about this. If we don't show him something amazing in the third, I think he may walk away from both of these stocks."

Sheedy's cellphone bleated.

"Damn," Dett said, looking away.

Sheedy stood adrift on the sloping asphalt.

"You have to take it," Dett said.

"Hello," Sheedy said, and Dett retreated a few yards. Now Sheedy was nodding, cellphone to one ear, left hand up and over his other ear to block out the track noise, to make sure he caught the quiet words, the quiet nonspecific words spoken across the insecure cellular frequencies. Words that Dett imagined stringing themselves along the issues of "our agreement" and "the paper concerned" and "the cashflow aspects of the situation."

One in ten in one in ten.

Sheedy clicked the phone shut, pocketed it and stood for a second with his hand on his lips.

"Our guy?" Dett asked, consciously drowning out his numbers.

"We have to pull something out here," Sheedy said.

"Lower the price."

Tough-looking women on quarter horses were escorting the thoroughbreds down to the gate, the jockeys standing in the stirrups, the wind rippling the silks. The squat working horses and the thoroughbreds, side by side, highlighted the rare beauty of the racers, high-strung creatures prancing and skittering next to their serene companions. As Silent Cruise passed—the deep shining brown, the vivid purple—the thoroughbred laid his head piteously against the neck of the smaller horse, as though seeking a reprieve. It brought to mind how young they were, all of them, the equine equivalent of the fourteen-year-old supermodel backstage with her teddy bears.

Sheedy was saying, ". . . totally wrong signal to lower the price at this point."

Dett flashed on something Sheedy had said earlier. The undying loyalty of the client's network of friends, which suggested the obvious corollary: the downside.

"These really are dogs, aren't they?" he said, as it dawned on him.

Sheedy paused and stroked his small, symmetrical chin. "Commerce-Net lost both its channel partners in some legal dispute this morning. Microsoft is going to sue. Halox is a fucking placebo. The word is that the trials are completely flat."

"Christ, Sheedy," Dett said.

"These puppies are going to sewer on Monday when it hits the street. Jimmy has to be out." Sheedy's speech slowed. "He simply will not take a four-hundred-grand hit the same week he's doing a runner and leaving a dozen houses behind."

"When were you going to tell me this?" Dett asked.

"I wasn't," Sheedy said. "Did you want to be privy?"

He had a point, and he also looked more than a little scared now. "Wax this sale for me, Dett, and your efforts will not be forgotten."

"And him?" Dett asked, nodding his head towards the Fat Choy.

"Fuck Xiang," Sheedy said, the badger was back in an instant. "Don't even ask that question. If it wasn't him it would be some other loser, like on every bet you and I ever made together. You were born knowing this shit. That's why we're a team."

Sheedy stalked off a few yards, hands stiffly at his side. Wounded. Then he stalked back.

"Now give me my winner," he said.

Dett wasn't sure that he had ever used numbers to consciously screw somebody before. On the other hand, he'd never been forced to.

One in ten then, he thought, at the moment of truth

this is all I get? A string of ones and tens, which might be expressed mathematically as 1, 10, 1, 10, 1, 10. . . .

One, ten, one.

January 10, 1901, let's say. Well, January 10, 1901, as it happened, was a Thursday.

Ten, one, ten.

October 1, 1910, was a Saturday.

Thursday to today, Saturday. A three-day spread.

Today, and the holy number three.

Third letter: C.

Saturday and a C.

S. C.

SC.

Silent Cruise.

"This is insane," Dett said, and it seemed to his ears like he was speaking from inside a steel drum.

Sheedy was waiting impatiently.

"There is no rigour in this," Dett said.

"Has there ever been?" Sheedy asked.

"Silent Cruise," Dett said, by way of an answer.

Sheedy was appraising him. "You said he'd show before."

"Silent Cruise is the *one* in *ten,* Sheedy. It's what I'm getting."

Sheedy faced him squarely. "Don't you start guessing on me."

"He's the one," Dett said simply. "The one in ten."

"Who's the jockey?" Sheedy asked, digging in his

pocket for a racing form. Mysticism was one thing, but corroboration never hurt.

Dett gave him the name, having checked.

"Same guy who rode Rumsey to win in the first," Sheedy said, handicapping aloud and liking the result. And with that, the decision made, he turned and marched back towards the Fat Choy room. Ten yards off he stopped and turned. Yelled back, "Are you watching out here?"

"Where else?" Dett said.

Sheedy was back in 145 seconds with Xiang. Dett had counted the seconds: 143, 144, 145. . . .

"This is much better," Andrew Xiang said. "I can actually breathe out here."

Sheedy squinted in the milky sunshine, a little out of breath from trotting in to the windows and making the last-minute bet.

"Did you make your bet?" Dett asked Xiang.

"I got a tip," he said. "You have to bet on a tip."

"Silent Cruise," Sheedy said, leaning in as if to deliver this information to Dett.

There was the gunshot sound of the gates slamming open and in an instant Dett could feel the vibration in his soles.

"Here's to Sheedy's luck," Andrew Xiang said. "Here's to mine."

Dett turned back to the track in time to feel the breeze as the horses hurtled past towards the first turn. Canadian Diamond and Haida Bells, stirrup to stirrup.

New Blazer was third by half a length on Silent Cruise. "Come on now. Come on now," Sheedy was chanting quiet encouragement to the jockey from just over Dett's right shoulder.

Into the back Canadian Diamond and Haida Bells pulled away to one and a half lengths, and the pack squeezed up on New Blazer and Silent Cruise.

"He's flattening out. Don't let him flatten out now. Take him in. Come on, take him in."

Entering the straight the four had again pulled free by a length, and Silent Cruise was moving confidently to the outside on New Blazer.

Thunder to the soles of my feet, thought Dett, his mouth unable to open. Thunder in my empty insides. Thunder, you beautiful, beautiful thing. Thunder home, baby. The One in Ten.

"Ride him home," Sheedy was screaming now. "Ride him home. Come on. Take him in. Take him home." And there was an instant after Sheedy said this that Silent Cruise moved on Canadian Diamond and Haida Bells, in third just half a length off the leaders. But it was only an instant, and then Dett could see that the horse was going down.

"Ride him. Ride him," Sheedy was pouring out his final supplication.

Ten yards off the wire Silent Cruise abruptly fell, half a ton of horse crashing chin first into the dirt. His jockey spilled over his head and into the track, curled already in a defensive ball. Haida Bells ran into the tangle of legs and hooves and also fell, her rider sprawling through the rails and onto the infield turf.

The field surged past. Tulista from fifth to win, followed by Canadian Diamond and A Little Risk.

Haida Bells lunged to her feet, swayed, staggered and cantered away. Eyes spread wide and white froth streaming from her nostrils. Silent Cruise struggled on his side, then rose.

From down the grandstand fence, Dett registered a woman's shout. Disembodied. The words released into a hovering silence: "Don't look, Maggie," she cried. "Don't look."

And Dett did turn away, pushing his back sharply to the track. And from this swivelled position he noted how Sheedy stood defeated. The crumpled basketball leather of his cheeks, the false pearl of his tiny teeth hanging dryly beneath a thin bloodless lip. Andrew Xiang stood blank-faced, wooden, next to him.

DETT TURNED BACK TO THE TRACK. Silent Cruise was standing on three legs, staring slightly upwards without comprehension. His front right leg was shorn off almost cleanly twelve inches above the hoof and from his bloody leg protruded a stump of bone. The hoof and fetlock were still connected by a visible sinew, and the piece flopped brokenly onto the dirt as Silent Cruise looked for footing, weakly finding none, only the emptiness under his right foreleg and what must have been the eclipsing pain of contact between open bone and earth. As the crowd surged to the rail around them, Dett felt a complete silence descend into his insides.

The track horses galloped in, and the track crew circled the damaged thoroughbred, their calm ponies sidling in obediently around the staggering racer. Penning Silent Cruise against the inside rail. A rider dismounted and took Silent Cruise by the bridle, holding his head as he reared tentatively, losing strength, and then he was helped down to his side. Around him rose the wall of ponies and crew, backs to the crowd, shoulders and flanks together. A wall of respect, thought Dett, although through the legs of the horses he could still make out the needle, and the operation that was quickly performed. A tractor pulled a covered trailer onto the track, and the crew held up a blue tarp in front of the dying thoroughbred as he was loaded. A very slight heave of the flank was the final thing Dett saw.

Dett looked around numbly. The two thrown jockeys were on their feet. Fragile as the very elderly, supported by crew. One had made it to the grandstand fence and now stood, muddy circles around the eyes, leaning and shaking. Sheedy and Xiang were gone.

Dett walked back to the Fat Choy in silence.

"NO, I LIKE THAT PICK, SHEEDY," Xiang was saying. "Thanks very much."

"How much did you bet again?" Sheedy was asking, laughing falsely.

"Two hundred and fifty dollars."

"I went down a hundred myself."

Dett watched this jocular exchange, staring at Sheedy and seeing the reanimated fear under his waxy pretence of humour. Even now, Dett knew, Sheedy was trying desperately to find his angles, to return the conversation to Halox. To Commerce-Net. Counting on Dett to assist in realigning the conversation on the axis of the sale.

Dett thought only that Sheedy had walked away from trackside, Silent Cruise down and the results in. And he imagined walking away from Sheedy in the moment of his breakdown, imagined vividly the enraged badger hurling abuse at his retreating back.

"I liked that horse," Dett said.

There was a polite silence as the two men regarded him.

"He was coming on," Xiang said finally. "What can you say? It's racing."

"Running fourth," Sheedy said shaking his head. Disappointed with the dead horse's performance.

"Third," Dett said.

"A Little Risk would have caught him. You could see that, which I mean as no disrespect to your pick," Sheedy said.

Xiang chuckled. "I figured it was Dett's pick," he said. "People are always taking credit for their employees' work."

Sheedy made an insincere face like *Guilty, what can I say?*

"You picked the one to die," Xiang said, looking over at Dett.

"An interesting skill," Sheedy said.

"I thought Silent Cruise would win," Dett said, cutting off Sheedy and returning Andrew's stare.

"You don't handicap at all," Xiang said.

"Nine times out of ten," Dett returned, "handicapping is a crock of shit. The punter is gone and there's no one left to take advantage of."

"In your view."

"In my respectful view, Mr. Xiang, yes."

"And your method instead?"

"I prefer," Dett said, "interpreting the insane pattern of my own numbers."

Sheedy was wincing behind an open palm.

"I am sincerely impressed with that," Andrew Xiang said, nodding slowly as if he had just figured something out. "It's brave and rare."

Sheedy couldn't watch this any more, and leaned forward, palms pressed tightly together. "Could we return to the matter at hand?"

"I can't help you guys," Xiang said quietly.

"Help me?" Sheedy said, flushing and going rigid.

"I'm just not interested in either," Xiang continued calmly.

"Fine," Dett said.

"Fine," Sheedy said, nodding vigorously up and down, his face heating visibly.

Xiang raised his shoulders and smiled. "I suppose there is one way I *could* help you."

Sheedy was beginning to vibrate with escalating badger rage but he stayed in his chair.

Andrew Xiang leaned across the table and whispered. "Get out of Halox. Get out of Commerce-Net."

It was Dett's turn to freeze. He knew.

"Bad news on both," Andrew said. "Obviously I can't say what precisely, but if you have clients long on either, I would back away. Since I won't buy yours, you should know I'm not shitting you. End of help."

And here Andrew Xiang left.

DETT DIDN'T SAY A WORD all the way out to the car. The sale had been dead before it started and Sheedy hadn't seen that at all.

Sheedy ranted on a simple hostile theme, Time and the sexual preferences of Andrew Xiang: "Waste of my fucking time. Faggot wasted my fucking time." All the while walking rigidly, hands in his pockets, jaw thrust out, head jerking from side to side as he scanned his memorized client list for the Plan B sucker.

Dett was flooded with images. Silent Cruise in the stretch, gaining on the leaders, the envelope of his spirit like a sonic boom through the air and soil and echoing off the far hills. Approaching the wire, veins all over the thoroughbred's body had bristled under the mahogany surface, marbling his hide.

"Gilbert Bligh maybe," Sheedy said when they got to the car.

I turned back, Dett thought, standing silently at the passenger door. I turned back to the sight of his break-down, to the sight of his pain. Was there a trace of disrespect in watching Silent Cruise die? In not leaving him with the track crew and work ponies, in the company of his own?

"What do you think of Gil Bligh?" Sheedy repeated, louder.

Or had the fall pushed the duration of the race out beyond its strict borders? Would it then have been disrespectful to turn away, to treat wire results as the entirety of the event itself?

"Answer me!" Sheedy shouted and he thumped his hand on the Porsche's roof, which brought Dett's eyes sharply up from the green surface.

"What's the question?" he asked.

"We are emphatically not out of this yet, you hear me?" Sheedy was yelling at him from what might have been a great distance. His voice came through a kind of static. A static bristling with a thousand digits, rising to the surface of Dett's subconscious. Ones and tens. Nines and other shadowy figures.

"We were punished," Dett said, hardly hearing his own words.

"Give me a freakin' break," Sheedy said, angrily popping the locks.

"I actually got that horse. I *got* it."

"Oh yes," Sheedy said, stepping away from the car, circling with his head lowered, arms rigid and hands balled in fists. And then after two or three circles, when his fury hit some glass-breaking pitch, he looked up and screamed across the car, "I've been meaning to *thank you for that*."

"Those *were* the numbers though. Those were the real numbers."

"Evi-fucking-dently." Sheedy said, spit flying from his lips and speckling the metallic green surface between them.

"The One in Ten," Dett said. "One in Ten."

"Shut—" Sheedy had to back away from the car again and circle. He couldn't complete the sentence.

"One is the full number," Dett went on. "The number that eliminates the other. The One casts its shadow across the remainder."

Dett felt a delicious impulse rise within him as he continued. "The numbers one, nine and ten can give us various dates in the twentieth century," he said. "Like, say, September 10, 1901; October 9, 1901; January 10, 1909; October 1, 1909; January 9, 1910; and September 1, 1910. That's Tuesday, Wednesday, Sunday, Friday, Sunday, Thursday."

Sheedy continued to circle, now making a noise from his throat that sounded like a leaf blower. His arms were still stretched down at his sides but his fingers were tensed and spread as wide as they would go. He might have been psyching up to break bricks with his head.

"But all along it was only the nine I needed," Dett went on, oblivious. "Nine, nine, nine. . . September 9, 1909 was a Thursday! A Thursday, Sheedy. The three-day spread. It corroborates."

This all burst from him in a hail of internal applause. He thought it must have been like this to crack the Wehrmacht encryptions. A room full of jumping, hugging bodies and flying bits of paper.

"The remainder was nine, and I didn't understand it. Nine was the empty set, the left-out number. Nine was the shadow. I was shown the shadow and we used it wrong, we tried to fuck someone over and the numbers fucked us back. It is so beautiful."

Sheedy continued to circle, his samurai cry rising, cresting, then fading off into a plaintive ululation of grief, which itself wound down after a minute or two.

"Get in the car," Sheedy said finally, his face drained. "We have work to do . . ."

"So beautiful . . ." Dett was saying to an audience of billions of digits, which swarmed in appreciation.

". . . phone calls to make, markers to pull in, numbers to run . . ."

"You're wrong about numbers," Dett said, and a brief silence descended in him. "You think numbers are bits and pieces."

Sheedy put his elbows on the roof of the car. Leaned his face into his hands.

"Numbers," he said, his voice muffled. "You see,

Dett, you swim in a sea of friggin' numbers. You float in a data cloud, my young friend."

And here Sheedy lifted his head from his hands, fixed red eyes on his protégé and held up a single quivering finger to emphasize his point.

"And that, Dett, is a *good thing*. That makes all the molecules in your universe the same thing, little snips of data, numbers, digits, bytes. You have the building blocks and you can put them together one way and you have an interest-rate swap. Another way and you have a derivative based on the price of Argentinian Black Angus testicles. A third way and you have the Argentinian Black Angus testicle itself. It's data. *Your* data, *your* world. There isn't an MBA in a fucking thousand who is as stripped clean as you. I hired you because I envy you."

"You're still wrong," Dett said. It was amazing to him how insight, when it arrived, threw a brilliant light across every particle in the universe. "Numbers are perfectly analog," he announced. "Not bits. Not pieces. Perfectly analog."

"We're both going to be bits and pieces if you don't get in the car," Sheedy said. Then he climbed into the Porsche and slammed the door, which in a car of this price and parcelled engineering, produced a sound like *snick*.

But Dett couldn't hear most of this, anyway. The gentle cascade of his numbers had started again and grown to a thunderous noise, the numerals spilling out of him like some kind of anchor chain, screaming and clanking as the linked steel integers fell into the depths—1 in 10 in 1 in 10 in 1 in 10 in 1 in 10 in 1 in 10.

It still had a new car smell, this Porsche 911 Carrera 4, which could do zero to sixty miles per hour in about four and a half seconds flat. But these were meaningless numbers to Dett at the moment, who was busy pondering, musing, smiling, thanking the great host of numerals that arrayed themselves around him on a never-ending, seamless plane.

Nine, nine, nine . . . I would just like to *thank* the number 9.

# NEWSTART 2.0™

## ONE /
## LE RAIFORT

With his dark green mechanic's overalls, the black dial phone he carried around with him and the hand-held air horn he used to punctuate conversation, Dennis Kopak was the only living Dadaist I ever encountered. Irritating as this idea might seem today, at the time I was grateful to him. For the fact that he singled me out. For his obscure yet affecting pronouncements on the topic of my future. For something that was in the order of friendship, even if it anchored itself in an argument and lasted no longer than the sixty minutes it takes to go bell to bell in the standard high school lunch hour.

Fairfield Composite, Prince Albert, Saskatchewan. We were in the dying months of grade twelve and the entire student body found itself in Darwinian contemplation of grades and opportunities, endings and new beginnings. There was a volatile mixture of dread and anticipation in the air, each student affected differently depending on social species and ranked chance of postgraduate survival. A hundred times, a thousand times in conversations in the bleached-out corn yellow hallways and classrooms, on the lawns that emerged pale brown from under the snowdrifts around Fairfield during these months, the question was asked: "So what's up now?" And everybody understood that this was no longer a question concerned with the short term: cutting classes, anticipated visits to the Westmount Mall food court. Or even with the medium term: tree-planting jobs, cottage plans, trips to Australia. Instead *sowhatsupnow?*—chirpy encouragement or nihilistic slur, depending on who was posing the question—was in all cases faceted with longer meaning. Your decisions. Your choices about yourself. Your future. Your capital-P Plans.

I was saved from the worst of this open-air festival of self-analysis by virtue of having no friends. It would be safe to say that I was the only Fairfield student whose declared objective was to be a famous painter and I was left alone for what was surely a mixture of reasons. Fear of

art. Embarrassment on my behalf. I didn't mind. I culti-
vated the distance between me and all things mainstream. I
wore second-hand suits flecked with Gamblin oil colours.
Dented bebop hats. White shirts with French cuffs and
jade links in the shape of the Buddha. I wore a pinkie ring
with the words *Viva Las Vegas* in raised lettering over an
image of the Golden Nugget Casino. I listened to Roxy
Music, Tom Tom Club, Jack Teagarden and the Jam.
Memorized long passages of Leonard Cohen for no reason
other than it occurred to me that some day—long after
high school, presumably—I might be surrounded by people who recited, who quoted, who proved in words that
they drew on a reservoir of remembered profundity.

   I had acquaintances, more or less cordial hallway rela-
tionships. I'd been assigned a locker down in East Wing.
Freak East as it was known, where you might guess the
school administration was implementing a quiet policy to
house students of certain social categories in one ghetto.
We had heads and goths, survivalists and Budd Priest, a
kid in the militia whose widely publicized claim to fame
was having blown up a cow with a hand grenade. Priest
and I spoke once on this topic and he told me that he had
used an adhesive pad intended to affix the explosive to the
side of a tank. And even though the incident had irrevocably chilled his relationship with the Canadian military
establishment, Priest was glad he did it because it enabled
him to have a conversation with Mitzi Mishner. A permanently Oahu-tanned princess from the preppy West Wing,

Mitzi actually stopped Priest in the hall some weeks after his story had ripped through the school. Curiosity swamping the combined forces of her revulsion and social habit.

Mitzi said to Budd Priest, "Did you really blow up a cow?"

To which Priest responded, "Yes." Thus enabling him to say with grim-faced irony for the next two years at Fairfield that he and he alone in Freak East had had a *social* conversation with Mitzi Mishner.

Social conversations were rare for me, no doubt in part because I spent all my free time in the art lab surrounded by crumpled tubes of Gamblin oil paint, my chosen brand, with which I identified in the same convoluted way people identify with a particular brand of cigarette. There is no smell in the world, to this day, with a more strongly placed memory for me. One heady whiff—the ineffable scent of undiluted colour itself—and I'm back at the black Arborite bench, my lunch spread open next to a smeared palette and a Squirrel Peanut Butter jar full of brushes. There I would churn out my baby Pollocks and my rip-off Curnoe collages, my slabs of paletted colour in the mode of Paul-Émile Borduas or Jean-Paul Riopelle or Jock Macdonald or Braque or any of a long list of painters that I would read about, admire, then worship, then imitate. When a slightly warped variety of representational work gained popularity in the big art-scene cities around this time, I too began doing hacked-up, half-erased portraits with the eyes scratched out. I splashed up these heads by the dozen, stood back and admired them, then painted the canvases over white and started again. I was a kid consumed, spinning without friction in the vacuum of my social sphere. Nobody was pulling me aside and asking me "So what's up now?" because they had reasonably concluded that they already knew what was up with me now and that no vision I had of the future could conceivably be relevant to the consideration of their own.

It's possible, although not certain, that Louise Dupres was the one exception to this rule. She and I were assigned to the same bench for the art section on charcoal and pencil drawing techniques. Louise was captain of both the women's volleyball and baseball teams. She was lead international conflict negotiator at the Students' United Nations. Her boyfriend, Rory Peterson, was a dead ringer for Seth Justman of the J. Geils Band. He had a dirty blond mane, a Baha Bug and well-placed relatives in all of the key Prince Albert institutions of power: mayor's office, school board, Junior A hockey franchise and the cop shop. Louise could jump high, throw hard, think laterally and score cute influential guys. I dressed her up like Cleopatra in my mind. But with her designer jeans and her Italian loafers and her out-of-style silver peasant jewellery that she told me had been given to her by an aunt who lived in Avignon, I had observed Louise to mix her aristocratic West Wing attitude with a small measure of the inchoate impulse to be elsewhere, to see a broader horizon, rich with new experience. This last bit intrigued me.

She phoned me at home one night. I had never previously (nor have I ever since) seen my father look as pleased with me as he did when passing over the receiver. He and I were sitting at the table in the kitchen of our apartment. Kraft Dinner remains hardening in our chipped bowls as we bore down over the only life lesson my father ever wanted to teach me: Texas Hold'em. Night after night of freeze-out tournaments. Dad playing with money Mom sent him from Scottsdale. Me with my busboy gravel. There was no ethical, moral or philosophical dilemma possible in a lifetime, my father would have me believe, that could not be best analysed using the rubric of this seven-card poker game.

I had just pulled a triplet on the river and was going all in, which wouldn't earn me any praise. Dad would chastise me later for playing a lousy pair of eights when they weren't improved at the turn. But the breaking china sound of the old dial phone ringing, the sweet and husky voice of a 'burb girl, these things got his attention.

One of his delicate, under-used jazz-piano-player hands went softly around the mouthpiece and he broke his own poker code by looking me straight in the eyes. No hiding the pride as he whispered the word, *"Pussy."*

Louise wanted to talk about art class or, at least, that was the thin cover under which crept her vague and itchy curiosity about me, about Dad. She was working on gesture drawings of her Jack Russell terrier, she said. We talked about the work—mood and line, composition, my gentle reservations about the pet as subject—until she stuttered to silence. I felt it looming in the unsaid, but still it surprised me: "So what's up now, Shane?"

Vancouver, I told her. Pacific College of Art. My dad was nodding and smiling and shaking his head all at once over there at the table, our hand still live, my stack of quarters shifted forward for him to call or raise or fold on. And although he wasn't looking at me any more, I knew he was listening and processing clues like the gambler he was. The likelihood of me having that triplet to beat his two pair against the likelihood of Scottsdale coming up with art school money against the likelihood of me making a go of it following my heart of all goddamn things.

"Are you going to, like, make paintings?" Louise asked me, breathy.

To which, without a quiver of irony, I responded, "I'm going to make beauty." Blocking out a chortle from the Hold'em table and listening only to the silver sound of my words as they slipped up the phone line and into her ear.

Next morning, I quoted from *Beautiful Losers* around the corner of her locker door. She was bent over getting a history text off the bottom shelf. I spoke to the small of her back, to a patch of tan skin and a bare silvering of hair that peeked out between her Jean Michel jeans and the tail of her pink Lacoste.

"'The telephone, hitherto so foreboding and powerful, was our friend!'"

She straightened up sharply, startled. Her Melmacgreen eyes took a precautionary, flickering look over my shoulder before settling on my face.

Out behind the bleachers, 4 p.m., same day, all along the top row of seats above Rory Peterson and me, there were eager faces. I removed my paint-flecked suit jacket slowly, faking calm as I looked around for a place to hang it.

The crowd jeered. Peterson snorted.

He swung a right hand at me. Lazy. I don't recall choosing to do what I did next. But as his weight came off his back foot and he leaned in, as his right hand came over hard but slow, I stepped to one side and tagged him on the corner of his right eyebrow with a loose-fisted left-hand punch. A flick. A fluttering delay of the inevitable, had not the Golden Nugget Casino gone with me, *Viva Las Vegas* twisting into the corner of Peterson's pale blue eye, exploding a two-inch cut on his eyelid and puncturing his eyeball. He bled instantly, copiously. His eye drained warm fluid, a drop of which came back on my hand.

Peterson was on the ground. There were many, many people there. He was wrapped in a pearl-white blanket with a cobalt-blue border and put into an ambulance. I was in the back seat of a different car, then in a room. I was talking to a man who took notes on a flip pad and chewed on the cadmium-yellow stalk of his pencil. My father was there, smelling bad. Talking loud. He disappeared and came back a few hours later with Downstairs Mo, his attorney friend from Saskatoon who specialized in suing doctors, but still managed to put the whammy on the Peterson cousin working the RCMP detachment. I walked away without a court date.

Dad found it in himself to scream at me down in the parking lot, "Is this the beauty you had in mind?"

I was back in school. Days later. Weeks later. I can't remember the precise timing, but there did come a time, a fullness of time, when I was standing with my back to a locker and Rory Peterson came around a corner with a black eye patch. He was surrounded by all his friends. A healing cocoon of social upward mobility, long-term life certainty, the physical guarantees of their joint success and health. Mitzi Mishner. Louise, of course. I can still see Venetian coral beads bouncing in the hollow above her breastbone. The silver jangle on a thin wrist, two tiny charms the shape of alpha and omega. She didn't meet my gaze. Mitzi did not swing aside from the Eau Sauvage- and Polo-perfumed mass of them to ask, *Did you really try to blind Rory Peterson?* Not because she didn't think I had tried—on this point the collective student consciousness seemed to have agreed—but because nothing as physical as a glance from any of them would now pass my way. I had passed out of registered colour zones. The planes and surfaces of my being now shimmering, transparent. They floated past and I was staring after them. A question that had been asked of me only once now receding completely into the mineral-spirit silence.

*So what's up now, Shane?*

I mouthed the words.

SOMETIMES YOU HAVE TO STRIP down your approach to things.

"In the middle of a game I'll start bluffing," my dad said, fiddling with his pipe, packing in the little muff of herb he smoked nightly. "I might have played tight the entire game, then I tear up the book and do it a different way. Screws them right up."

Dennis Kopak came to Fairfield in the last semester of grade twelve, transferring in from a boys' school down east. He wore his private school uniform on the first day. Hunt red blazer, smoke grey flannels, cap with piping. If anybody in the school outside of the Freak East hard core had still been speaking to me I might have noticed that the tide went out on me and ebbed immediately into Kopak's cove. There was something dangerously gravitational about this kid whose eyes glinted irony behind round wire specs and whose premature pot belly pushed out the open front of his crested school blazer. His stride was confident and rolling. His laughter ready and sarcastic even as he was surrounded and roughed up at the edge of the football field his second day at the school. I watched from the art lab window, paintbrush drying in my hand. He was getting pushed from one kid to another. I heard him laugh. A delighted, absurd shriek just as one of them stepped forward and nailed him. He collapsed to the grass, blood running from one nostril down to the lapel of his blazer and disappearing into the wool.

"Vive le raifort!" Kopak yelled. Laughing and bleeding.

The kid who landed the punch stood over him, frowning. And eventually they left him there, dispersed in confusion, unsure of the procedure under these circumstances.

"Vive le raifort libre!" Kopak screamed after them.

The next day he left the uniform at home and came in what he widely announced were his street clothes. An oversize pair of zip-front, dark green mechanic's overalls with the word *Raifort* embroidered in silver thread on the right chest pocket. Cherry red Converse All Star hightops. He wore a workman's tool belt around his waist, in which he slung an old black dial phone—rigged to ring despite the dangling, frayed cord—and a little $CO_2$-powered air horn, the kind used by yachtsmen to start a regatta. He eventually agreed with the principal that the air horn was not for indoor use—it blistered eardrums at fifteen yards—but he still answered the phone periodically, barking at imaginary callers.

"Pronto. Yeah. Interesting. I'll pass it along."

Click.

Nobody beat him up any more. And after a calculus quiz he was suddenly out of the regular class and taking one-on-one tutoring from Mr. Algonquin, our purposefully loony math teacher.

"What happened to the Kopak freak?" someone eventually asked. Algonquin turned, pulled his beard. When he had settled on an explanation that he thought we would understand he turned to the chalkboard and drew a horizontal line, pulling his pale stick of chalk from left to right.

"This is a graph plotting the average mental horse-power of all the students I have ever taught," Algonquin told the kid who'd asked the question. "Because you're an above-average, although insolent, student, let us plot your horsepower as follows."

Algonquin drew another line, above the first. It started at the same point but extended a few inches further right. The class rippled, laughing.

"Now, here's your freak," Algonquin said. And he planted his chalk at the same starting point and began drawing it to the right again, all the way across the board this time. And when he reached the end of the green surface, he let his chalk jump the wooden border and he continued drawing across the bulletin board and out the door. Somebody followed him and reported that he was drawing his line all the way down the hallway, bumping and skipping across lockers and classroom doors.

Algonquin didn't come back that day. The math class dismissed itself and carried the story from that classroom outward, thirty branching lines leading to various places within the sprawling school. Kopak was met with faintly frightened silence in the hallways from that point on, with complicated stares.

I told my dad. I had looked it up in the French-English dictionary, so I was able to answer the question when he asked, staring at me with curious intensity over the edge of his cards.

*Raifort* meant horseradish.

I WAS WORKING IN NEW DIRECTIONS. I had discovered that if you reduce a photocopy over and over again, you can compact a regular photograph to a grain of itself. It takes repeated reductions, hours at the photocopier, the light slapping back and forth, stripping away the meaning. It takes indulgence from the school librarian as you grind down your yearbook photograph again and again until you have achieved a distillation of all of the data it once contained. Reduced it to an incomprehensible singularity.

I made a hundred such copies on clear sheets of overhead plastic. A hundred discs of black that I scissored out into a hundred snips of acetate the size of match heads. I kept these in a Ziploc bag, static electricity pasting them to one another and to the plastic around them like they were alive and trying to get out.

In the lab, I stared down a six-by-four-foot canvas for a week, sitting five entire lunch hours before I understood the idea that was sounding within me. I went to Revelstoke Hardware that weekend and bought half a gallon of high-gloss snow-white exterior latex and a roller. I laid down a coat a day from Monday to Wednesday until the canvas had acquired a built-up, uneven, shining base. My micro-portraits could now be affixed to this surface with the touch of a finger, the static holding the acetate onto the latex surface. I spent the balance of the week silently rearranging these. Distributing a hundred black discs in patterns. Squares. Circles. Polygons of various dimensions. At one point I threw a handful of them

against the surface and the ones that stuck ended up looking quite remarkably like the Big Dipper.

Not right, I decided. Not the solution. Of course,
I didn't know what solution I was looking for. Nor
even what problem needed solving. But I bushwhacked
onward through the incomprehensible jungle of the
idea. I began to work with smaller groups of the discs.
A dozen. Three. Even one. Silence falling deeper and
deeper within me as I tried to find an arrangement that
I assumed would reveal itself in a cascading instant. A
pattern that would be manifest when the canvas itself suddenly fixed the placement of my images and held them
where they were correct. And so it was with a shuddering
release of breath that on a Friday—the prairie sun bak-
ing up June outside the windows, the shouts of a crowd
watching senior track and field not reaching me—I found
my fingers arranging six discs in a simple line set into a
lower corner of the canvas and leaning just slightly left at
the top. A six-word sentence rising and evaporating on
the infinite field of white.

I left the painting overnight. The next day I struggled through two periods of History of Human Conflict
and one period of Utopian Literature, trying not to think
about it. Trying to set aside my sense that the canvas had
whispered a coded secret to me that must now be deci-
phered. At lunch I took two risers at a time up the east
stairs, heart beating hard. I burst into the art lab to find
everything as I had left it. Stool, workbench, painting

against the far wall. My six inspired, ascending marks float-ing on the surface just as they had the day before.

Only today, Dennis Kopak was sitting on the work-bench, legs swinging. A Pop Tart in one hand, a can of Mountain Dew in the other. His black dial phone on the desk next to him. His eyes locked on what I had made.

He turned his head when he heard the door. We exchanged a nod.

"What does the year 1916 mean to you?" he said, eyes back on the canvas. At conversational range, he presented the image of being prematurely aged. His hair was thin-ning, middle brown flecked with grey. His body softening into his forties right out of high school. But he also had cunning eyes and a prominent nose that hooked down towards curling lips. His forehead was high and lined, and seemed to pulse slightly from the activity within.

"Easter uprising in Dublin?" I tried.

Kopak smirked. "Battle of the Somme. Battle of Verdun. Year of the first German air raid on London."

Kopak's phone rang and he snatched the receiver from the cradle with a practised snap of his wrist. "Pronto. Speaking. In a meeting. Call you back." Kopak smacked the receiver down. "Anything else?"

Not that I could think of.

"Clue," Kopak said. "Which of the following state-ments would date to the same year?"

Here his phone rang again. I thought he must do it with a trigger in his pocket, but both of his hands were visible, fingertips locked in front of him. A combination t'aichi/Catholic prayer pose.

"Number one," Kopak said, ignoring the phone. "I heighten my tone values and transpose into an orchestration of pure colour every single thing I feel. I am a tender-hearted savage, filled with violence."

No glimmer of response or recognition from me. The phone stopped ringing.

"Number two: my task as a contemporary artist is to amplify the voices of those who might not otherwise be heard."

There was a surge of noise in the hallway while Kopak waited for a decision on this one. Ghetto blaster, basketball on lino, body against the lockers, catcalls. Returning silence.

"Or three. I have broken the blue boundary of colour limits. I have emerged into white. Beside me, comrade pilots, swim in this infinity. Swim!"

Kopak swivelled around. Eyes wide.

"Swim! The free white sea, infinity, lies before you!"

I had to admit the words were evocative. The six marks suggested a continuum. The white surface an infinity across which this continuum might stretch. "I guess I'll take door three," I said to Kopak.

"You and Kasimir Malevich."

The name meant nothing to me.

"Russian," he said, as if my blank expression were primarily the result of confusion about the man's nationality. He hopped off the bench, approached the canvas. Leaned in close, examining.

I told him what they were. He liked that. "And the line?"

"Seemed like the solution."

Kopak picked up my Ziploc bag. "May I?"

I memorized the position of the marks and Kopak stepped up to the canvas.

"Did you think of constellations?" he asked me.

I told him how one had unexpectedly appeared.

"Ursa Major," Kopak said, hands moving over the white surface until his Big Dipper was complete. He shuffled the marks again, leaving a sideways V-shape. "Capricornus, the Sea Goat."

Kopak's hands were flying now. Perseus the Hero. Taurus the Bull. Sagittarius the Archer. He seemed to dial these patterns up, working the painting as if it had levers that set spinning the cogs of an internal mechanism.

"A trapezium to the north of Hydra," Kopak explained, hands briefly still over a compact cluster that he called Corvus, the Crow. "Found at the end of the curve made by Bootes, Virgo and the North Star."

"Wow," I said. I was impressed by his galactic capacity to remember celestial bodies, but even more by the idea that so many of them might be contained within the canvas. So many solutions possible.

"And, my personal favourite," Kopak said, in the manner of a magician who's performance is at its climax, "Pegasus."

Kopak swept clean the markings of Corvus and dealt out this final constellation in thirteen precise movements. I stood over his shoulder and admired the result. Four of the thirteen stars formed a rough square. The remainder scattered and diffused to the right with no discernible pattern at all. And although I could no more see a horse in it than a horseradish at the moment, it still struck me as throat-tighteningly beautiful that someone lying on the grassy shoulder of the Aventine Hill, or wherever it had been, gazing up at this same shape, had seen, sweeping and powerful and sudden, the head and front hooves of a prancing, flying horse.

"Do you believe in astrology?" I asked him.

Kopak considered the question. "You mean, can the stars help us make decisions? Can they help us understand ourselves or the future?"

I shrugged. "I guess."

"I don't know," Kopak answered. "Although I have always wondered if maybe the stars were an enormous machine. A working inference engine that might be used for all the purposes that astrologers claim, only we've misplaced the instruction manual and lost all clue of how it works."

He reached out slowly, regretfully, erasing Pegasus and restoring my six-point line. He didn't say anything for several seconds, staring at this result instead. I could hear him breathing loudly, raspy cycles of air through his mouth, as if breathing were not always easy for him. It was the most childlike sound I'd heard him produce since I met him.

"What else happened in 1916?" I asked him, thinking just then of where this had started.

Kopak went over to the chalkboard. "Here's what some crazy Russian unleashed on the art world the same year the British invented tanks."

He drew a vertical rectangle on the board, the outline of a canvas. Then dropped a six-point line into the lower corner, leaning just left at the top. Identical to my own.

"Kasimir Malevich," I said.

Born in 1878, died in 1935. Russian founder of a movement called Suprematism. A man who went on to produce a series of near-blank canvases with elemental geometric forms and metallic-sounding names like *Basic Suprematist Element: The Square* and *Suprematist Composition: White on White*.

"All this thirty years before that plagiarist Rauschenberg," Kopak said, eyes cocked in accusation.

I tried to defend myself. He was intimidating—how did he know so much about art without being in any art classes?—but he was also standing in front of a canvas that had announced itself to me. It seemed only fair that I get credit for having duplicated an obscure modernist masterpiece without having known anything about Malevich beforehand. Surely that proved something in itself.

"Like what?" Kopak asked me. "That you're an artist by fortunate accident?"

"That wasn't an accident," I protested. "Maybe subconscious, but there's a difference."

"So what about you half-blinding that guy? Accidental or subconscious?" Kopak had his hand on his chin. He appeared genuinely consumed with this question.

"It's unrelated," I sputtered, picking up a brush. It came to me that I should begin painting. That I needed to demonstrate to Kopak that he had nothing to say about my work, my future, my art. That these were matters on which I was well and truly centred.

"Unrelated?" Kopak went on. "Tell me then, after you poked out one of Rory Peterson's eyeballs, did you or did you not come up here and sit for a month of lunch hours without social contact because you were waiting for that canvas to arrest your portraits in a pattern that could not be improved?"

The paintbrush was idle in my hands. I *had* used the word solution.

"And were you not building this thing in the faint hope that it might make a telling statement about you, to yourself?"

Kopak was staring at me. I can't say that I knew precisely what the hell he was talking about, but still he threatened me. His falsely benign expression. His insinuation that—in the absence of a social group, a social life, even a social self—I had been reduced to carrying on conversations about myself with a canvas. Defensive anger was gurgling up the back of my throat.

"Oh, yeah?" I yelled at him. "Well, what the hell is with horseradish anyway?"

Our seconds were dwindling. The clock was ticking audibly towards the bell. I could see the rise and fall of Kopak's asthmatic lungs behind the word *raifort* on his left chest pocket.

"It's a good question," Kopak said, at last. "And I don't know the answer. All I know is that I really like horses. That's it. Maybe it's a Dada thing."

Another comment that might have been worth exploring, but I was already gone. Out the lab door. Down the stairs. Straight to the library. Of course he hadn't made it up. There it was in *Concepts of Modern Art*. The Malevich I had knocked off was called *Suprematist Composition Conveying a Feeling of Universal Space*.

I returned to the art lab but Kopak was gone. I considered my line again. My Malevich line. Did it reassure me about myself? Did it explain to me how I had become who I was? I didn't know. I didn't know how Kopak even thought to imagine such things. All I knew for sure was that my line did not look right to me as it had before. It was no longer the solution to the canvas. And this was not merely because Kasimir Malevich had conceived of his line before me. The dots themselves seemed less arrested. My micro-portraits less irrevocably placed. And the only reason I could think of for this change was that Dennis Kopak had lifted me clear of the room. Shown me what I'd done from far above.

SCOTTSDALE CAME THROUGH with the money and I did go to PCA. In my Foundation year I studied colour, two-dimensional language, materials, Form and Space. The human figure. Observation and description. I immersed and swam in the tropical warmth of those creative seas, surrounded for the first time by a school of fish with essentially similar genetic architecture.

The only notable divide in the school lay between students in the visual arts and those in commercial design. Design studios were neat, the student aesthetic situating itself at the corner of origami and New Wave. My visual-arts colleagues and I, whether painters, sculptors or the then-new devotees of video, lived in worlds of deliberate chaos. Studios were disaster zones. Punk ruled. And while the whimsy of commercial design was always framed by the function of an object, uselessness was our code, our ongoing celebration. But the clearest of the many ways the schism could be appreciated lay in the presumption of postgraduate employment in your field. Design students had an industry day. They put together presentations, using overhead projectors and 3D models, and spoke confidently to a PCA auditorium full of software and gaming company HR people who came by to scout the talent.

My friends were people who painted with their own blood. Students who did buggy kinetic sculpture and video installations. A girl who spat up ink in the middle of her performance pieces, geysers of black onto the blank paper over which she traced her fragile steps. A student who wore a suit covered in bananas to his interview for the second-year sculpting program.

"It's an interview," he told me. "You want to dress up."

I worked for three months on the piece that I hoped would earn me passage from Foundation into the painting program. It was in the vein of what we then called "hard representationalism." Polaroids and opaque projectors. Gridded canvases and perfectly matched pigments. Our debt to the reverent compositions of Caravaggio so clear that we could only secretly hope that what we did somehow turned around on itself and became ironic.

I called the piece *Sowhatsupnow? The Illuminated Manuscript*. Half a dozen diptychs, student portraits on one side, a square canvas with text on the other: the subjects' words on themselves and where they were, auto-text blurb quotes about the personal future as it could be known.

*I'm moving to New York on August 17th*
*I'd really like to get some more sleep*
*I haven't a clue what I'm going to do next*

The diptychs were to be arranged in checkerboard style. Quotes and portraits framing one another in what I hoped would be a wall-width suggestion of the sound made, the motion described as the future swept over you, pooled around you and carried you away. I remember I was working on the portrait of a friend of mine, also a painter. She had wrinkled her brow at the moment I snapped the Polaroid, creasing a small omega-shaped loop into the skin between her eyebrows. I was struggling with the shades created by this tight folding, working fleshtone into deep yellow and rich gold. My friend's quote hung on the corkboard nearby. *I have a job at Starbucks; I'm learning to make a cappuccino.* These words to be painted in foamed-milk white over a latte field. And it occurred to me, in a cascading instant of the kind I had earlier longed for, that I had been in this position before. That I had once before built a painting hoping that it would solve itself. That my wall of portraits and quotes of friends contemplating an uncertain future—in a common pattern to be discerned or in the space left between them—was a project designed to suggest my own image and words. To adumbrate a self-portrait that I could not otherwise contemplate.

And the smell of horseradish was suddenly very strong in the air.

I tried to track him down. There were six Kopaks in the book and I eventually got a cousin. He gave me another number, disconnected. He was less patient on my second call, but he did produce a contact name in Montreal. I got an answering machine there, a tired male voice. Not Kopak but someone who'd been getting a lot of messages for Kopak

*. . . and if this message is for Dennis, he's moved to California. I don't have the number, try directory assistance. Thanks. Bye.*

I tried Los Angeles, San Francisco and San Diego before realizing that I couldn't search the entire state.

I phoned Montreal and got an answer, the same tired voice that went even flatter with fatigue when I asked after Dennis Kopak.

"Man, he is gone," the guy said. "I don't know where. Try the United States of America. Try Brazil. Try Europe. Maybe if you go up in the space shuttle you'll be able to make sense outta what pattern Kopak is tracing across this world."

I remember looking out the window after I hung up. There was a crow doing his little pharaoh's strut across the pavement outside the PCA front doors. Making his way calmly out into traffic to pick at the mat of guts and feathers left over after a delivery van had run down a starling earlier that morning.

I was breathing heavily. At one point in the dwindling seconds of this awakening, I remember trying to assure myself that at least I had not inadvertently copied someone. At least the work I'd started was original. But in those moments—as awakening became merely wakefulness—I realized that even so, I had done something worse than copying. I wasn't just struggling with my Malevich line, hoping against hope that the canvas would freeze me at the moment of perfection. I was going further than demanding of the work that it speak to me on the topic of myself and asking that it confirm a future for me as well. Make decisions for me. Like the thinking machine, the machine of the stars that Dennis Kopak felt was impervious to understanding.

And given—as Dennis Kopak *had* understood—that the impenetrability of the stars was due to our lack of an instruction manual, well then, this whole endeavour was simply hopeless. Wasn't it?

What's an original idea? Does it merely lack resemblance to any idea that has come before? Or does an idea become original over time if it proves itself by spawning offspring ideas, each of which then bear testimony by a degree of resemblance?

I caught myself in the mirrors just inside the arrival gates. A tall man in a black linen blazer pushing a hand through strawberry-blond hair and working free of the crowd. Off in strides towards the moving walkway, carry-on suit bag humped over the left shoulder. Computer bag swinging from the right: notebook, cell, digital camera with mini-printer, disc recorder for interviews. Deck of cards. *The Guide to Giuseppe Vasi's Rome.*

Beyond cathedral-high walls of smoky glass the sun was hot over Fiumicino.

How original was a once-new idea that nobody could remember? You had to wonder. A person comes up with something they think is original, but maybe they can't know right away. Maybe the quality has nothing to do with past and is all about the future. Less about the idea being unique and more about it demonstrating fecundity upon release.

I could feel my phone ring, so I stopped and swung my bags to the ground, unzipped the computer case at which point the sampled mechanical dial-phone ring jangled out through Arrivals.

Mia.

"Everything OK? I'm just off the plane."

We were behind already, it seemed. The photographer was running late. "I'll have them page you at the Alitalia Lounge," Mia said. "Sorry about this, I know you're raring to go."

It was true. I was ready. "Not your fault," I told her. "I'll wait. What's her name again?"

The photographer's name was Fontana.

Right, right. In a very high-concept move for the *Phrate Magazine* art department, they had not retained a fashion or even a portrait photographer for this assignment but a photojournalist who specialized in war zones. Somalia. Sarajevo. Kosovo. Chechnya. The rumour flying around *Phrate* was that Fontana had once taken a Serb sniper bullet through her right bicep.

"So the plan is, once I'm set, I'm going to take a couple of days just to look at the Talloni paintings," I said, walking again. "Then I'll go to work getting the interview."

Mia made an assenting noise. Distracted. I could tell she wanted to talk about something else. Here we were on the topic of the commissioned piece and my managing editor wasn't really tracking along with the discussion.

The silver doors of the lounge sighed open. The woman behind the counter looked over my boarding pass and waved me up the black marble stairs.

"Whatever you think," Mia said, letting go the tiniest breath of a sigh. "The capsize profiles have made a really good series. A good idea of yours. Now go nail this one and come back to me."

I gave her a kiss through the phone. Corny. So unlike what I imagined she would like when we were first together. But here I am, a year later, blowing smooch.

Upstairs, I poured myself an orange juice and went to find a quiet desk. Plugged in the notebook and waited for power-up.

She was right about the series of capsize profiles, each one examining an artistic life at some point of critical change. It had been a good idea. Spontaneous and yet, once articulated, it seemed predestined. Two o'clock in the morning. An unplanned encounter with *Phrate Magazine*'s founder and executive publisher, Abbot Freightling. Everybody had worked crazy hours in the beginning at *Phrate,* but two o'clock was notable. And here was Freightling—a month after circulation of the thick, square art/design/technology periodical had topped a cool hundred thousand—snooping around the back. Looking specifically for me.

We went upstairs to the publisher's office and drank Scotch, smoked a chain of his clove cigarettes, standing by an open window in the middle of an Afghani war carpet. Looking down over the container port, enormous cranes in silhouette, ladders spidering up their sides. The water stretching black to the even blacker mountains opposite.

"Why 'capsize'?" Freightling had asked me, when the idea came out.

"Because in this one case we don't care about trends. We don't care about what's hip or 'the shit.' We just care about the moment of aesthetic upheaval. What came before and what followed."

"So who would be an example?"

Well, there was a photographer who had developed total colourblindness and had to reinvent himself. I produced five thousand words and the photographer provided a series of garish black-and-white self-portraits, his own face bleached, wrinkles glowing. Behind him an eerily blackened sunset.

I called him when I first saw the prints.

"Describe them to me," said the photographer in a voice like hourglass sand. And when I sketched in words what I was looking at, the photographer answered, "That's what I see."

Three months later we profiled a sculptor whose kid was shot in a Memphis convenience store and went from Moore-ish modernism and a day job to doing enormous aluminum and glass installation pieces, one of which ended up in the MoMA. I got the cover. *Phrate* got letters from around the world.

Those pieces, covering those kinds of artists, had been one of my better ideas.

Power was up. The e-mail gates opened and in they flew. Zip zip zip. A note from Mia, sent while I was in the air. Subject line: Miss you.

The current profile subject, Piero Talloni, however— much as I would have liked to take the credit—could not technically be considered my idea. In fact, I'd passed on the story before Freightling reassigned it. Freightling the un-bosslike boss. The Luddite double agent who managed to time the market and make everybody an ass-load selling off 49 per cent of *Phrate* just before the NASDAQ and the WIRX went vertical down. I will never lose my image of Freightling with his brown brogues on the sill of the boardroom window saying to me, *I'm liking Talloni. I like that he's in Rome. The Eternal City. Eternal ever since last May. I like that his capsize point is the same as his point of discovery.*

Freightling had a cup of tea covered in a saucer balanced on one knee. Waiting for my answer, even though we all knew that once he decided, I was going. I was on the plane to Rome and profiling this late-discovered talent even if there wasn't a single other thing to know about the man.

Simple truth about life not accommodated in the framework provided by Texas Hold'em: e-mail. The flow was unstoppable. A dozen when I logged in. Here were five more. How do you play a game when there's no final card?

THERE WERE TIMES DURING my run from freelancer all the way up to the editorial board that I found myself wishing I had started earlier. Not wasted so many years after PCA. Other times my life seemed like the kind that had to be explored a little. Cul-de-sacs required. Aimlessness for a time after all that early direction, all that first-quarter certainty. After PCA I did half an undergraduate degree in history, then another half in poli-sci. Took acting courses through Continuing Education and scored a shaving cream commercial. Taught myself HTML and web page design when that was the thing. And I travelled, significantly. It turned out I was good at this, something you can't know about yourself until you try. I had a batting average pushing a thousand when it came to hitting spots the instant before they were anointed hip by travel scenesters. And, in perplexing contrast to high school, I was suddenly able to meet women without scaring them away. Or maybe they met me. I have no ideas, no theories why this suddenly became the case. But, true fact: during those unplugged travel years when I belonged to no particular idea or place, I couldn't stay single for more than a month. I was in Prague forty-eight hours before meeting Inga. She was in the theatre and got me a job working sets. My Barcelona bachelorhood lasted a week. Then I met Amy—on extended leave from Columbia Journalism—who was running an alternative English-language arts newspaper and hired me. I didn't work for all of them. But I acknowledge that I was rarely without a girlfriend during this time who wasn't busily engaged with me on the topic of myself in some way, much as a manager might be with a key employee. And I have an unclear memory of not minding this terribly. They got their teeth into you, which could be pleasant enough. But one thing I remember very clearly is that in the summer of 1995 I found myself in Dublin (a perfectly timed twelve months ahead of the Celtic Tiger), running a gallery off Grafton Street and sleeping with the owner, a married woman named Fiona; and it was then that I scored my first gig with *Phrate*.

Being on the ground in Ireland was no doubt a factor—they were specifically looking for an arts-in-Eire type piece—but they liked my approach too. I pitched a double profile to a deputy editor named Mia Noonan. The first man was a much-loved poet in his late seventies who lived in a stone house in West Cork and only came up to the capital for those quintessentially Irish national events where living poetic legends are in demand. The second was a database engineer and much-vaunted rave sponsor. Young, newly rich, the owner of a Ducati and a house in the city that had once been a Church of Ireland. Two people who together might be thought to capture—in their oppositions and in their surprising similarities—the emerging soul of the New Ireland. The story had art. It had technology. It had intergenerational friction and admiration, complexly twinned, cutting both ways. Plus it came out of a place with pre-hip travel cred. It was made for *Phrate*.

Mia bit. They ran my first freelance assignment as a cover story. Two head shots, side by side. The poet was looking up over a pint of Murphy's. The d-base guy was wearing a T-shirt that said "star@porn.com." Freightling liked the piece. Word trickled down.

"I love playing out that whole art-commerce dichotomy bullshit," Freightling apparently told Mia, capturing in this quip all of the ambivalence, the cultural shape-shifting that made *Phrate* popular. They were an art magazine. They were a design magazine. They covered the then high-flying dotcoms and were politically ambiguous. Ask ten *Phrate* subscribers what the magazine was about and you'd get ten versions of the story with the only common point being that the book looked great. Wacky layout. A little hard to follow the text sometimes. But very cool.

The piece went up for a National Magazine Award later that year, *Phrate*'s first nomination. Mia tracked me down and offered to fly me back to the gala. And as a direct result of her doing so, I ended up moving home. I had a grandfather-clause Irish passport with built-in access to every economy in the EU. I would happily have stayed in Europe for as many more years as finances would allow. But Freightling didn't come out to the awards dinner—honourable mention in the "One of a Kind" category—and I ended up being entertained by Mia Noonan. Five years older than me, a slim woman with high cheekbones, blue eyes, red hair and a faint constellation of freckles across the top of her chest. She had a henna wristlet and an emerald ring that had been her grandmother's. She was, in short, every bit my image of the post-Riverdance, globalized Celtic beauty. And *Phrate*'s managing editor by this time, to boot. A heartbeat away from Freightling.

A heartbeat away from me, sitting there at dinner. We were our own conversation at the periphery of group talk: Dublin real estate, good hotels in Temple Bar, why there were so many European call centres in Cork. Fewer and fewer people linked over to our discussion. I sensed things were going well by the time dinner was served. I had to think we were dealing with mutual physical attraction by around dessert. I turned to say something to her in one of the few moments the man sitting on her far side had managed to engage her attention. She put a thin hand on the man's arm, like touching the pause button. Turned back to me, glancing upwards into my face from the tops of her eyes, chin down.

"Just a sec," she whispered.

And my brain cavity was suddenly a very well-lit place, the truth illuminated: we were both thinking about something other than Irish socio-economic trends.

I extended my stay. Mia set up a room at the Hilton on the *Phrate* tab. She had me in the office working on assignments by about the third day. This was a time of complete, although creative, chaos at the magazine. Print subscription numbers were storming upwards at a rate almost faster than *Phrate*'s production staff (not to mention their bankers) could handle. Freightling had just splashed out big coin launching www.phratemagazine.com and there were rumours flying that he was courting big-money partners. Mia had me doing odd editorial jobs—arts calendars, announcements, errata—before she had her first big idea about our future.

We were spending a rare night off eating dinner over at her place. (When I think back to this period I remember most of our time together being spent at work, in bed or in transit between the two.) But that evening we were just eating and talking. Personal history. The various things we'd done. And when I told her I could write HTML, Mia was instantly and irrevocably decided. I would help run the new web team.

Of course I protested. And, equally obvious now, in retrospect, she prevailed.

"What do I know about running . . . well, anything?" I asked her.

"Nothing, you're an artist," she told me.

"Was."

She looked at me, eyes intense in my own.

"At the very least, dormant," I said. "Deep undercover. A double agent."

"Abbot will *love* that you put it that way," she answered.

This was week four of my triumphant return home. I had phoned Fiona in Dublin precisely once, fibbing about an assignment. I liked the attention, to be sure. I liked the implied confidence, the feeling that Mia's glance produced on my skin when she looked across the granite countertop in her open kitchen. I liked the sense that with this glance, Mia had the power to change things. To move my life sharply forward.

So it was that I became part of what was referred to as the *Phrate* "Backside," the online part of the magazine. It differed most strikingly from the Frontside—where the print publication was produced—in having been decorated by geeks. Every physical thing was new, was being installed or tested or debugged, and chaos was written on the surface of things. Cubicles were crammed, without visible order. Miles of cable and phone lines, black servers in stacks, blinking routers, papers and manuals, teetering CD towers and a more or less constant game of inter-office Doom going on. I was parachuted into this scene. With Mia's oversight, and Freightling's above hers, I was given a single authority and objective: ramp up site traffic.

Everybody knew I had no experience but this didn't seem to matter much. The fact was we were *all* making it up as we went along. It was a feature of the work, in those early days. No frame, no idea how far you could push it. That was exactly what had drawn most of these people to coding and networks in the first place. And sure I had only a fraction of their technical skill. Boasting about knowing HTML to these guys was like telling a group of astronomers that black holes absorb light, what might be called a superficial appreciation of the matter at hand. Still, it could be said that we were all there with the same essential enthusiasms. First thing I did was hang a hit counter high on one wall. It took data live off the Net, the numbers ticking up with every set of eyeballs that crossed the site. And when the employee share-purchase plan came in and someone suggested we track the then-hot NASDAQ and WIRX stock indices, well, up those went too. There was no arguing with the rise and fall of that barometer.

I still hadn't met Freightling at this point. I saw him from a distance once, across the lobby, from which I gleaned that *Phrate*'s founder was a regally thin, hawk-nosed, youngish-looking man who wore one of those British small-check sports jackets over jeans and old-fashioned shoes. Mia told me he was a Cambridge grad. Economics, although apparently the story wavered on the point. Freightling also spoke of having studied literature and art history. But it did seem clear that he had attended King's College, following in the footsteps of his father, a peer of the minor, not deep-pocketed variety, and that his family had once been involved in the noble sport of horse racing in a big way. Down one long wall in his office, Freightling had hung dozens of yellowed photographs of past champions and cup winners, studs of apparent renown, all in chipped black frames. The only other decoration was provided by an aluminum work table and an enormous carpet depicting the AK-47s and grenades and Hind gunships of the Afghani-Soviet war. No computer, I noted.

Typical Freightling. A man who founded a major web site and still refused to use e-mail. A man whose strategic directives landed on my desk hand-written on antique quadruplicate memorandum forms. *To, From, Re, Date.* The story circulated like wildfire through the back when one of the coders found Freightling in the air-conditioned CPU room late one night. He was holding a cable in his hand, staring down its length to where it disappeared into a sheath of others and up into the guts of the server. There was a fold of concentration and bemusement running the length of his high, white forehead. He looked exactly—the coder described later, mouth full of pizza—like an archae-ologist who'd excavated the lowest stratum of an Egyptian dig and turned up the same object. Stark incomprehension and not a little bit of concern.

*From: AF*
*To: All Staff*
*Re: New Phrate Vision Statement*
*We are not an Art Magazine. We are not a Design Magazine. We are not a magazine and we are not a web site. Phrate is an all-media content generator distributing information about and analysis of global aesthetic weather systems.*

At our next weekly meeting, one of the site administrators suggested we whip up a global aesthetic weather map. It was supposed to be a joke but, as these things sometimes do, it turned into a theoretical discussion about how the swirls and eddies of global trends in art and design might actually be plotted on a map. How the Winnipeg Art Lodge could be assigned a temperature. How the high- pressure front of graffiti might be shown to influence other weather systems.

"What about mocking up an aesthetic Beaufort scale?" somebody asked.

Sir Francis Beaufort, it turned out, invented the concept of "sea state." Thirteen stages by which a rising storm might be defined. Zero is "calm": no wind and the sea is like a mirror. Seven is a "near gale": wind speed rises, waves break and foam blows off the water in streaks. Beaufort twelve is a hurricane: wind tops seventy-five miles an hour, waves are "tremendous," the air fills with spray and the surface of the sea turns white with foam. Visibility at sea-state twelve is nil.

It didn't take long before our engineer was at the white board and the collective brain was hacking together a practical idea. Sea state could be expressed as a function of two values: wind speed and water conditions. As a proxy for wind speed, a numeric value could be assigned to an artist's media profile using clipping services, web searches, maybe a LexisNexis tie-in. A proxy for water conditions, on the other hand, might be derived from an aesthetic "event report," which anyone with a Net connection could submit by e-mail. These reports would compile such things as trend news, artist sightings, what's hot, what's not.

"Crunch your two proxy values into a sea state," the engineer said.

"Rip off some weather-data-plotting code," someone added.

"Bingo," the engineer was looking over at me. "You got your weather map."

It might never have come to anything. But not only did one of the kids knock out the necessary code in a couple of days, but when we went live the event reports flooded in. You couldn't predict these things, but somewhere out there in the psychological machinery of the thing, the place, the idea of the Net, the aesthetic weather map caught on. The code was shareware, the result being that anyone could build the map into their own site, collect input and forward it to *Phrate*. It was showing up at art and design colleges around the world. By the end of the second week, if you popped up the weather map in a browser window, it had fluxes and steady colour changes highly evocative of a satellite weather photograph. Colours from blue calm through the green mid-ranges and right up to the red fury of a sea-state twelve, shifting and patterning across the map, forming and breaking in fronts. The red zones predictably clustered over the big cities of the globalized west, but these too would splash out and surprise, based on the steady flow of information and ideas sweeping in through the e-mail gates. When the soft blue calm over the Korean peninsula started to shift and swirl, and then steeped up hard to the oranges and pinks and hot reds of a rising storm, I must admit I felt a palpable sense of excitement.

*What's with Seoul?* I e-mailed our engineer.

Apparently quite a lot. He got a list of items pulled off the event reports on Korea. Bold new directions in Korean cinema. The Seoul bar scene breaking in New York—Scotch bottles on the table and open very, very late. And, not incidentally, a poll of linen designers conducted by Martha Stewart's in-house research team had recently determined that colours in the so-called "kimchi spectrum" were exceedingly of the moment. Light cabbage green, a washed-out warmer lime. Radish white, translucent almost to silvery. Worked well in kitchens. Chili red. Frank and hot, bold and casual.

"Did you know Korean film is very popular in Vietnam at the moment?" I asked Mia in bed later.

"I know that site traffic is up 25 per cent over thirty days," Mia said, rolling on top of me. Straddling my hips, hands squarely in the middle of my chest, about to commence a very vigorous CPR-type sexual manoeuvre she favoured. "It's all Abbot wants to talk about these days."

It was all anyone wanted to talk about: watching the WIRX numbers climbing next to the spiralling hit counter. I was in a meeting with the engineers talking about a massive upscaling of our servers at the same moment the big word came down. *Phrate* was sold. An Internet portal company won the bidding war. Nobody even knew there had been a bidding war.

*Is this a gale?* E-mail from Mia.

*Hurricane,* I wrote back. Cheques had been written. Virtually everyone in the office had shares, however few, and when this money was distributed there followed a period during which the air seemed to ring with surprise. A kind of mild corporate tinnitus the result of which was not anxiety but a zoned-out, semi-stoned optimism that permeated every exchanged pleasantry, every corridor greeting.

"Zzup?" "Yo." Low five.

Life was good.


"MR. DONALD?"

Another simple truth that resisted the stratagems of Texas Hold'em: upon being addressed as *Mister* Donald, my internal poker face cracks a wide grin and I fulfil every cliché by thinking immediately of my father.

"Your car is waiting at arrivals. No check bags?"

I approached the sliding doors, still some thirty yards off, and imagined that only upon exiting through the skin of the airport would I enter Rome. The Alitalia Lounge at Fiumicino International Airport was, quite clearly, not in the Eternal City. Not on the dusty, ancient surface of this countryside at all, but unplugged. Twenty degrees cooler.

"Shane Donald? I'm Fontana."

She was dressed in soccer warm-ups. Black nylon with white flashing. Black hair, eyes obscured behind aviator frames. She made me think of an ocelot. Edgy feline sexuality, sure. But rapier-quick decisions too. Compact speed.

"It's about forty minutes into the city," Fontana informed me. "You need any information, please ask."

We climbed in. There were things I could ask, of course. But I found myself thinking about the bullet. I couldn't help it. A 7.62mm Dragunov round, somebody said. It had entered the arm (*her* arm, *this* arm right next to me) on the inside, a few inches below the armpit. Exited on the outside just above the elbow. Navigating a very fluky, translateral path that intersected neither bone nor artery. How all this was known by the art department, with details of such un-*Phrate*-like goriness, I had no idea.

Fontana was now running down a short and specific list of things on which she might be profitably quizzed. Number one, real Roman food. Number two, Roman street addresses and the fastest routes between any two points in the city.

"Former taxi driver?" I asked, trying out a smile.

"Former bodyguard," Fontana replied, looking at me evenly through enormous sunglasses.

Number three, the Sistine Chapel.

"What about Piero Talloni?" I asked.

"*Il Tempo, Giornale de Sicilia. In Rome Today* photo spread. CNN, BBC World Service. Now, *Phrate Magazine.* I can tell you that he must be a very great artist."

I listened to her tone of voice as she rhymed off the media outlets that had covered the story before me, then decided this was not irony. I didn't think she had the gene. "You've seen his work," I asked her. "What did you think?"

"Very beautiful. Very moving. The butcher shop in Via del Vaccaro is around the corner from my studio. Everyone in the neighbourhood went to see the painting there."

I turned to look at her. Physiognomically speaking, she was a halfway morph from Aphrodite to Hades. There was quite a lot of "pretty" about her. But all of it was hardened by dark lips that were sharply formed at the edges. By hair that was dense, with forked locks. Her eyebrows and nose-line moody.

"What else?"

"Very sad," Fontana said. "This is what else."

"The years of isolation?"

"Yes," she said, staring forward out the windscreen. "Partly also that it is sad to be directed to a single future without hope of another."

I thought this one over. "Talloni didn't have to quit."

Fontana's lips pursed and she shrugged. "Even so," she said. "Now he wishes to be left alone and this cannot be. People have his work. His work has value. They will now sell this work and it will grow in value. I don't think this is the future that Piero Talloni would have painted for himself. But it is the one to which he was assigned."

I resettled in my seat. Fontana had a point. I was well aware how the old man was now hiding from the attention his own story had attracted in the press. Talloni had politely declined my own request for an interview, once by phone and once in elegant handwriting on a piece of thick, personalized stationery. And yes, Talloni probably now regretted making himself available to the Italian papers when his story first broke. He probably wished CNN and BBC hadn't covered it. But Talloni had to realize that he didn't control what his work meant to people. There was a point after which it didn't wholly belong to him, and he was obliged to share what part of his work had been claimed by others. But I didn't bother presenting these arguments. Fontana gave off a very strong vibe of being someone not easily convinced. Plus, more pressingly, I felt my body clock all at once assert itself. Was it midnight for my spleen while Fontana's enormous Seiko Sport just now ticked up into the Roman midmorning?

"Well, what about the Sistine Chapel then?" I said finally.

Fontana nodded, gripped the steering wheel as if to aim the car, and we exploded away from the curb. She cut shallow arcs through traffic, sliding the Fiat gear shift with the thumb and first two fingers of her right hand. I didn't feel any fear for my own safety. Not only did she manifestly know what she was doing behind the wheel, Fontana's voice was enveloping. Soothing and authoritative.

"There are thirty-three panels on the ceiling. I will start with the creation of the sun and moon. Here, his brow dark and forehead furrowed with the great strength of his endeavour, God the Creator points his finger and commands the sun to shed its light upon the earth."

I settled back into the seat, dusty green countryside pouring past. Hard earth. Rich foliage. Cellphone towers on the ridge line and at the horizon ahead, a rosy ring of smog. I let my head touch the seat back, come to rest. We passed a truck hauling a bright orange shipping container. Swung smoothly back into our lane some fifty yards on.

HOW IS IT YOU AND *I have never actually met?*

I started. Swivelled sharply in my chair and found the Man Himself, backlit by the Pepsi machine, hand up on the top of his cubicle divider. Check jacket. Jeans. Brogues. Upstairs, he offered me an Indonesian cigarette from a crumpled pack. Then another. A glass of Scotch from a bottle in his drawer. Then another of those too. The conversation went this way and that as we stood on the war carpet and surveyed the container port. Freightling asked questions and listened with interest to the details of my background. He had pretty fair knowledge of Texas Hold'em, as it happened. We sat on either side of his aluminum desk and Freightling produced a deck of shot cards from an American casino. He re-enacted a particularly good hand he remembered, enthusiastically describing the raising and reraising through the flop and the turn, the river where he pulled the third part of a triplet.

I listened and admired the wall behind the publisher's desk, which was covered from floor to ceiling with horse photographs. Noble equine heads, shining coats, broad-chested tweedy trainers and the flint-hard, small-bodied jockeys with their leathery, oddly troubled expressions. I could make out some of the horses' names, hand-written on the prints. Bendalot and Kingsilver. Amontillado Tuesday and Chateau Bound.

I asked Freightling if he was a rider himself, accepting another drink and leaning back in my chair, gazing down the length of this impressive gallery. But Freightling didn't hear the question, or chose not to answer. He was looking right at me, the first such direct and unguarded glance. There was actually something he wanted to ask.

The publisher sketched his idea slowly, stammering a little, although I knew this was verbal effect. Maybe he wanted the idea to appear of that moment. Of our sitting there together. Scotch and beedi fumes pleasantly commingled. But the idea had been crafted beforehand. I felt the sense of eyes on skin. Change in-rushing.

Freightling wanted me back on the print side. He said special assignments. Compensation. Flexibility. Travel. Editorial board. It was a promotion, the publisher averred. Although something I might like to help design myself. They were interested, he said, in my ideas.

Somewhere in the back of my mind, I had been angling to mention our success at the site, to quip about our own profitably rising storm. But as Freightling's interest became clear, I found myself thinking instead about what followed the gale. After the changing event has happened, the altering comment is made. After red swirls faded to green, then to blue. Cooling and calming. How is it for the person in question once the storm has passed?

*I'm interested in the moment of capsize and what follows,* I heard myself saying. The break point in a creative life that separated someone from a past way of thinking about things. Sweeping alterations in creative outlook; aesthetic upheaval. Whatever the cause—geographic dislocation, personal tragedy, spiritual reawakening, sexual rebirth, calamitous physical decline. Change of heart. *I'm interested in how the person's art, their work, their life are irrevocably changed.*

FREIGHTLING FAVOURED A 3 P.M. START time for editorial meetings, an hour that assured a changing backdrop of daylight, dusk, sunset and finally blackness outside the windows. There was an idea captured in this timing. The world revolving while we spoke, the curve of change leading us, the core six. Freightling and Mia. Bell Dali and Finnegan Lear, both senior editors. Huey de Saint, the *Phrate* design director. And most recently, Shane Donald, special features editor.

The first time Piero Talloni came up, we had been fishing around for a story to follow up the photographer. Ideas had come and gone. The Talloni story blipped into the press and I seriously considered it. Here was an artist—a painter in his late seventies—whose work would never have been widely known had he not undertaken to destroy it all. As far as they went, I remember musing as I read the clippings file, it was a pretty good capsize point.

"Fire in Via Polacchi" ran the headline in the original story that appeared in *Italy Daily*. Secondary headline: "Entire Oeuvre Slain."

On May 23, 2000, the fire department in Rome was called to deal with a blaze behind an apartment building on a narrow street in Campo de'Fiori. Responding to the alarm, firefighters found the flames contained in several large oil drums, releasing a pungent and potentially toxic black cloud up the side of the building. They doused the fire, only to determine that the barrels contained over two hundred burned canvas sheets, rolled and most likely soaked in kerosene. A very few of these could still be cracked open to reveal the colours of what had been oil paintings. Neighbourhood enquiries led directly to a suspect, an elderly, reclusive painter who lived in a nearby building: Piero Talloni. He confessed immediately, and told police with some pride that he had never sold a painting in his life. He went on to explain that in quiet preparation for his own end, he was now destroying the canvases that had consumed his life. In the photos *Italy Daily* ran with its piece, Talloni is seen wearing an AS Roma scarf—I could pick out the wolf suckling Romulus and Remus—a watch cap and a corduroy jacket. The outfit was jaunty, but his eyes were distant, sorrowful and yet unclouded by any doubt about what he had done.

The original arson charges were eventually dropped. Another few weeks went by and a mischief charge was likewise dismissed. I leafed through three more articles that appeared in the Roman papers over this period. There was sympathy evident in the prose, although not exactly a sense of civic loss. It was entirely possible, the columnist for *Il Tempo* implied, that the quality of the work was not terribly high (although, he allowed, two hundred paintings, even mediocre ones, was a large number to destroy). Nor did Talloni particularly court the press, I noted, reading his unflaggingly polite but bemused answers to the questions he was asked. Yes, he had worked in his studio in Via Giulia for over fifty years. No, he had never sold one painting in all of that time. Why?

"I am not an alchemist," Talloni told *Il Manifesto*. "My business is not to turn the paint into lire."

Sixty days after the fire, the old man ended up getting a stiff but not onerous fine for disposing of garbage by fire within city limits. And that would have been the quiet end of Talloni's newsworthiness, I imagined, had not the old man's paintings starting showing up in other parts of Rome.

A florist in the Via d'Aracoeli, just down the steps from the Musei Capitolini, reported the first one. She remembered buying the piece from Talloni several years before. *Il Giornale* described the unassuming work (*Flower Sellers in the Piazza,* oil on canvas, 60 by 80 cm) as "a very lovely example of post-war social realism with evident cubist inspiration." Having praised the art, *Il Giornale* then went on to gently rebuke Talloni for being a capitalist after all.

Anybody who hadn't been in self-imposed artistic hiding for the past five decades would have understood this to be an affectionate joke. But Talloni was not amused. He wrote a letter to the editors of the paper acknowledging the work as his own, but stating that the painting had been a gift. *Il Giornale* declined to print a retraction when it learned that, while she had not technically purchased the work, the florist had traded several dozen roses for it.

"Surely barter counts as commerce," wrote an editor at *Il Giornale* the following week, then hastened to add, for those who did not understand this to be implicit, "But who could impugn Mr. Talloni for putting flowers, if not bread, on his own table?"

Piero Talloni was far from done. He took the matter to his lawyers. They sent a letter to *Il Giornale* threatening to sue and one to the florist insisting that the painting not be sold. On which grounds it was not at all clear, as they did not deny that Talloni had painted or bartered the work in question. But it was an ineffective strategy anyway. Talloni's missive only prompted *Italy Daily* to re-enter the fray, trying and failing to get an interview, but succeeding in flushing out two other Talloni owners. There was a butcher in Via del Vaccaro, a tiny street running into the Piazza della Pilotta, who had a Talloni hanging behind the counter. It depicted, fittingly enough, people buying sausages. And then an antique shop down Via dei Coronari discovered another, wrapped in brown paper and stacked in the back of the store. This was an exterior street scene with bustling crowds and a very worried-looking woman in the foreground. From her dress, it was dated to the late 1940s. Talloni had fallen to sullen silence by this point, but the three paintings were quite clearly by the same hand.

The last clipping in my file was a long piece for *Il Giornale* wherein an art historian from the Galleria Communale d'Arte Moderna e Contemporanea was quoted. On the three pieces, he offered words of unalloyed praise with more than a little bit of excitement ringing through.

> *Talloni's eye and his heart are identified with the common people he depicts. The flower sellers are full of joy. The butcher and his customers are working class, round-limbed. And the woman in the foreground here—I would guess this is Via dei Coronari itself—her distress is etched with his intricate sympathies. I think of the work of Il Fronte Nuovo della Arti from around this same time. Birolli. Ennio Morlotti. Even Giuseppe Santomaso's more realist work. I consider it fortunate that Talloni did not succeed in destroying these pieces, but I must say I find it heartbreaking that he has worked in darkness all these years and that, we must conclude, this is where he wishes to remain.*

Interesting enough. I made some calls.

The reporter at *Italy Daily* was blunt. "You'll never get him to talk. And frankly, I'm not sure it's such a big story anyway. The piece from the florist shop is as good as a minor Renato Guttuso, no more. I do not believe we have discovered a modern master living in our midst, exciting as that would be. We have discovered a recluse who lost control of his own solitude."

"Who is Renato Guttuso?" I asked.

Italy's pre-eminent artist in the vein of post-war social realism, as it happened. "Born in Palermo, 1912. Moved to Rome in the thirties. Part of a pre-war anti-fascist outfit called Corrente. Expressionist, political activist. Artist of the people. Died in 1987. Style-wise, Talloni and Guttuso would have been contemporaries."

I said I wanted to call Talloni anyway and the reporter gave me the contact information. When I finally got through, Talloni was polite but brittle.

"If I have chosen to give someone a painting," he said, in hesitating English. "Why can this not be left so? Left as I have placed it? Do you wish to take one?"

I was pretty sure I got the general drift here and tried a different tack. "But those works are no longer your own. Even if you gave them away, they've been seen and enjoyed by others. Doesn't the artist work his entire life to have something like this happen? I'm only interested in how that change must feel. To have your work recognized and desired."

To which Talloni responded simply, "The ring of the cash register will not be the final note in the song of my life or my work." And then he hung up.

The letter was a formality. I was surprised even to get

an answer back. But Talloni did write. And again, his tone was polite despite evident unhappiness with the attention. *I have done all that I wish to do. I do not wish to do more. I do not wish to speak of what is done.*

So there it was. The desire to create in private. To destroy all of one's work. Billows of black oily smoke disappearing up into the rosy light of a Roman morning. A flood of amused attention that turns slowly to appreciation, even awe. Angry and ill-fated legal threats and an artistic life capsized, most certainly. But it would be pure speculation to try and guess how the artist had been affected as Talloni was devout in his commitment to silence on the matter.

"He feels that his work is finished. That there is nothing more to discuss," I told the editorial board after reading them the letter.

Of course, I also had another idea to pitch. And so off I went to New York, where I met the sculptor. I wrote the piece. It ran on the cover to great response. We sifted and discussed other profile ideas for three months, Talloni drifting well and truly clear of consideration, before Freightling's assistant Heddy raised him from the dead.

We were running late. The sunset had flattened to black outside the boardroom windows. Mia had shifted twice on her stool in the past half-hour, sloping and reshaping her shoulders in a dissatisfied way that I recognized. Impatience and anxiety cross-fertilizing. And just as Freightling appeared to be acknowledging these cues—his foot up on the window sill, teacup balanced on his bony denim-clad knee—he stutter-stepped.

"Heddy, you had something?"

Freightling's assistant, to her credit, did not hesitate. No attempt to dramatize. "Piero Talloni," she announced. "One of his paintings just sold on eBay for 330 million lire."

The antique shop in Via dei Coronari had been the one to sell, apparently, not the florist. The winning bidder was a gallery in Los Angeles. There was a second of silence while everyone caught up.

"How much did you say?" gasped Finnegan Lear.

It was about $150,000 US, still a lot of money for an artist nobody had heard of three months before. And whatever we thought of Piero Talloni, he very much existed now, Heddy said. "CNN and BBC World Service have both done bits."

What bits, I wanted to know.

Short bits, Heddy assured me. Shot in various Roman locations but no interviews.

I sat forward, elbows on the boardroom table. "They've found more paintings," I said.

Two. One in a café near the Pantheon. The other in a tailor's shop. Talloni was a patron of both places and the handwriting people were able to confirm the signature.

"I'm liking Talloni," Freightling said, looking over at me. "I like that he's in Rome. The Eternal City. Eternal ever since last May. I like that his capsize point is the same as his point of discovery." He took another sip of tea, returned the saucer to the top of the cup. The cup to his knee.

"I like the story too," I agreed. "I'm just not sure how to get the guy."

"Well . . ." Heddy said, elaborately arriving at her point. "We might try convincing his new business agent."

Collins. David Collins. Palo Alto big shot. Software mogul.

"Ah," Freightling said.

That would be enthusiasm for the art-commerce-dichotomy-bullshit coming through, I thought. "Are we supposed to know that name?" I asked Heddy.

Maybe not, but he was an early-generation Silicon Valley success story. Made some kind of corporate planning software called NewStart. Heddy thought it had something to do with artificial intelligence. In any case, Collins made his money, then got out and became an art collector. Nobody was quite sure how he linked up with Talloni, but in the press releases he immediately began firing around, Collins betrayed no experience in the publicity business. Instead of making his client accessible, he actively rebuffed the media. His client had been exploited, Collins said. His client's right to privacy had been consistently violated. His story had been distorted. And henceforth, Collins pledged, his requirement for a peaceful environment in which to be creative would be rigorously protected.

"In which to be creative?" I said.

"As in, he might start painting again," Heddy agreed.

"Maybe they'll sell rights to Talloni's life story," Mia suggested.

I sat back in my chair. "Maybe he had this agent all along."

"He sandbagged for half a century to make the big score?" Freightling said. "That would be interesting too, don't you think?"

Conversation in the room had broken free of turn-taking. I judged from the quality of the babble that everyone was rapidly arriving at the conclusion we had to do this story.

"This business agent," I asked finally. "Software guy. One final question: what was the company name?"

Mia rolled her eyes. Freightling had the courtesy to acquire a look of curiosity about where we might be heading with this line of questions.

Heddy went into her papers again, sifting to a particular point where this piece of information had been high-lighted. She read the name aloud, challenging me with her tone of voice to find something of significance in this bit of commercial nonsense.

David Collins, it seemed, was the founder of Raifort Management Systems Incorporated.

WE WERE SPINNING INTO the heart of the city. Were I paying for this lift by the kilometre I might have questioned the serpentine route. Hadn't we just circled this piazza a moment before?

The geography of the place was slowly returning to me. Inga and I had come up from Prague. And although that summer with her seemed an impossibly long time ago, still the place names were returning to the surface, the remembered texture of streets rising into my consciousness. This is the Piazza di Venezia. Those white steps run up to the Musei Capitolini. And those faintly dangerous-looking policemen sprawled in a squad car, all four doors ajar? Well, they were everywhere.

I felt in the outside pocket of my computer bag for the Giuseppe Vasi guide. A gift from Mia, the book offered walks through the city illustrated with the etchings and maps of the eighteenth-century master. I cracked it open, rubbing my eyes.

"Via Battisti," Fontana said as we swung left with a swarm of Vespas into a major street. Cathedrals crowded in on either side, browning stone walls climbing away from the narrow sidewalks. "You think you'll find us before we have moved on to another street? Well, hello, here we are in Via Plebiscito already."

She laughed, but did not share a smile with me.

I let the book drop to my lap and drowsily turned to the window. At a light, Fontana nosed the Fiat up into the crowd of scooters. To my right, at close range, a woman in dark glasses sat with her long legs planted on the ground on either side of a Piaggio. She was talking on a cellphone, smoking. She wore a blue cashmere scarf. When she felt my eyes on the smooth length of her left calf, the woman glanced over and found me instantly. I was sufficiently awake to give her a smile.

Simple truth about having strawberry-blond hair, approaching thirty-five and smiling at women: they always smile back at you. You're safe. You remind them of a Scottish cousin. You do not appear to be four-flushing. Unless you happen to be in Italy.

The woman on the Piaggio snapped her eyes back to the road ahead. Discarded the cigarette and pocketed the cell. Fontana hit the gas at the same moment and we disappeared in different directions through a diesel-tinted cloud.

## THREE /
## PIERO TALLONI

Albergo Pomezia is in a street called Via Chiavari, which I read on an online hotel-booking site and thought of Michigan Avenue. Who knows why? But Via Chiavari—I thought it would be the grand boulevard.

In fact, I can almost reach out of my second-floor window and touch the wall of the building across the street. Grey-orange plaster scaling off. Red brick coming through. When I pulled in there was a woman in the suite opposite who was playing the cello and seemed unconcerned by my proximity.

I went to bed far too early. Simply couldn't keep myself up. This decision came after eating around the corner at Ignazio, a place that faked being good with nice furniture. My server dug deep to come up with a wine recommendation. For the tortellini? "Rosso," he said, looking over my shoulder and out into the street. "Secco."

The prosciutto turned out to be luncheon ham. Did they see me coming? Who were *they*?

David Collins. When is changing your name not about messing with people? What did the guy in Montreal say?

*Try the United States of America.*

Makes me wonder how Kopak burned up his welcome in Montreal. Maybe he had tried to be someone's business agent.

*Try Europe.* How long had he been here? Still meddling in the lives of those around him. Still uttering his obscure pronouncements. I wonder how long it took him to convince the old guy that quitting was in his best interest. Not just quitting either, but torching a lifetime's worth of paintings. All so they could hype a sale on eBay?

What do you bet Kopak owns the antique shop?

I could phone and ask him these questions directly. I could identify myself. Maybe he'd remember me fondly, a prototype project for whatever he was trying to do with Piero Talloni. Maybe he'd get me that interview. Of course, maybe he'd go to ground too. Maybe he would deny he ever knew me.

Nearly delirious with fatigue, I wrote down a bullet list of things to do. Unable to finish my pasta. I see this note to myself on the nightstand first thing when I open my eyes. The Ignazio napkin and the rollerball scrawl.

- Get to the antique shop on Coronari
- Directions to Talloni's studio? *Italy Daily* guy.

I don't remember how I left things with Fontana. It occurs to me she has nothing to shoot until I find Piero Talloni. Maybe I'll give her a couple of days. Something about the woman makes me sure she'll track me down if she needs me. Pad up soundlessly and tap me my shoulder on a crowded street corner. Or, I suppose, it's possible I'm only hoping that she'll do so.

Had a terrible sleep. Woke up at four in the morning to the sound of trucks, scooters, formula one race cars. I went to the window and found out that Chiavari, narrow as it may be, serves as some kind of critical short cut from somewhere to somewhere else. A truck went past at sixty miles an hour, mirrors finding only centimetres of clearance on either side. I shook my head, standing there naked at the window. My cellist was nowhere to be seen.

How does someone with what I imagine to be extraordinarily delicate hands sleep through this?

After the truck came seven scooters. One at a time. Wasps falling down a well. These are the early-morning delivery scooters, battered, boxes on the back. Hard leather gauntlets built into the handlebars to protect the fingers of those who drive every day, all day. The walls were ringing with them. I started to laugh.

Hotel Pomezia is, not unpleasantly, humble. There's a lumpy bed and a tiny bathroom. One wall is covered in cork sound tiles. There's a mirror opposite, where I keep catching glimpses of myself about to launch into the unknown.

Pomezia itself was my idea. One of Freightling's assistants had me booked into Hotel Raphael, up top of Piazza Navona. Matt Damon stayed there, or so said *Details* last month. Pricey. Gorgeous. Stuffed with antiques. But not in Campo de' Fiori. I have a two-bullet list of things to accomplish. I have thirty-seven e-mails this morning. There is one from Mia that I sense without opening should be read and answered later. No idea what it contains, but I envision shoulders sloping and resloping, and set it aside. But all this notwithstanding, I know with certainty—have known from the beginning of all this—that I must be in the neighbourhood where Piero Talloni did his work.

Campo de' Fiori. Field of flowers. This is old bohemian Rome. There were palazzos here. Renaissance families like the Farneses and the Spadas built houses so they'd be near the papal processions. But this is where the old Jewish ghetto was too. Restaurants sell marinated artichokes and battered deep-fried zucchini blossoms. The squares are plugged with markets every day of the week. Flowers, fruits, vegetables, cheese. I've read all this in my Vasi book.

Six o'clock, I walk out to get papers. Down through the tight cobblestone streets. Yellow buildings leaning in, green shutters pulled tight. Scooter traffic has died off. We're going to have an hour-long lull here before the day's real madness begins.

On my way out the guy at the front desk suppressed a smile. Same as yesterday. "Tredici," I said then, asking for my key. He pinched off a grin.

"Buon giorno," I tried this morning. There it was again.

I pick up the *Herald* and *USA Today* at a newsstand on Vittorio Emanuele. I find myself reading sports when I'm travelling. I have little time to indulge the interest at home and it doesn't come up easily around the *Phrate* water cooler. But abroad, busy or not, my appetite for the box score, the gridiron anecdote, the latest premiership trades, these consume me. Now I'm reading an AP wire story on a bout between two Mexican bantamweights I've never heard of but you'd guess I had money on the fight from the way I'm holding the paper, hunkered over, following the line of type with my finger. The woman behind the Nuova Simonelli is watching me. She thinks I must be very rich and very idle to come all this way to read American sports.

VIA DEI CORONARI USED TO be called the Via Recta in the Middle Ages. The straight road, the route of choice if you were a medieval pilgrim heading to St. Peter's via the Ponte Sant'Angelo. This was the centre of the rosary trade. This was where two hundred pilgrims were crushed to death in their exuberance to cross these cobbles, to get to that bridge and across. The holy year of 1450.

Vasali Antiquario is down on the left past the Piazza San Salvatore in Lauro. On the terrace up top of San

Salvatore itself there are nuns, habits dazzling in the sun, an arch of blue vaulting over their prayers.

I take the snapshots that I will use later to jog my memory while writing. Coronari to the west, to the east. Vasali Antiquario from across the street. I cross over and go inside.

I admire some prints in the front of the small, crammed shop. Eerie pieces of work these. A monkey hiding behind a still life of roebuck haunch and fruit. Two marmosets sitting on a pineapple. One hundred and twenty-five thousand lire a pop.

He comes up out of the back, elegant in his deep blue tailored suit and bespoke calfskin shoes.

"Dennis Kopak?" I say to him. I see at once that it's not him, but I'm leaving every other conceivable door open with my intonation, with the light glance I give him. If he knows the name, if he has ever heard the name, if there is a Kopak anywhere in the Venn diagram of the man's life, well then, my question will provoke a response.

He has no idea what I'm talking about. English minimal, he signs to me.

"David Collins," I try.

Now his eyes hood. He thinks. He looks at me, then over at the marmosets. He turns and goes into the back, leaving me to believe that he is fetching the man—I am now imagining Kopak/Collins in the back of the shop, his Dell notebook open on a messy workbench, browser window open, with a single spare Italian light fixture hovering. My heartbeat is rising—but my man returns and looks distinctly surprised to see me still there. Not surprised in a good way.

I hack at meaning with my bad Italian. "You sold a painting a few weeks ago."

Much laughter at this. We sell paintings every week, he tells me. It's what we do for a living around here.

"But . . ." I can only think to say the name. "Piero Talloni."

I provoke an exaggerated sigh. What of it? He shrugs and steps behind the counter at the rear of the shop. Yes, he sold it. Was it not his to sell? Must he keep every painting for all of his days? "I am a *businessman*."

"Sir," I start. Mollification mode. "I'm sorry. I'm just a . . ."

And here I make a scribbling motion with my right hand, lines being written. A page completed. A page turned and another commenced.

I produce a copy of *Phrate*. My cover story.

He softens marginally. He motions me into the back. We walk together out of the cluttered elegance of the front room and into the very ancient, very unplanned clutter of his storage area. There are wrapped paintings here stacked against every other wall, choking the walking area down to narrow paths, just enough for one to pass comfortably. Two must squeeze.

He's talking Italian quickly now. We have both forgotten the fact that we do not really share this tongue.

Instead volume, intonation and body language will communicate what may be communicated. All else is up for grabs, meaning-wise.

I'm pretty sure I understand what *pittura* means. He describes the Talloni work with his hands. It was a bold work. Here he opens wide his arms as if to encompass a much larger canvas. The colour is aggressive. The lines are strong. There is no fear in the technique, in the way the paint is applied. And it was valuable, yes. His fingers sift coins for me. His facial expression, his shoulders, the pantomime of a man apologizing for his own good fortune. And yet it was a delicate work too. Just so big. I am judging from his hand motions that much significance is attributed to the simultaneous largeness and smallness that Piero Talloni has achieved.

With this artistic point having been made, I see that rhetorical gears are being changed. The man turns to me. He is asking now that a standard of reasonability be applied. The painting had been in the store for many years. It was wrapped in many layers of paper. (He pulls some free of a nearby object to show me. Heavy waxy paper.) And it was hidden too, back here. (He moves down the pathway carefully, pointing.) Back there was where he found it. It was something of a mystery even to him.

"Ah . . . ah!" he says, remembering something he thinks now is obvious. He smacks his forehead. He disappears into the little office. He returns with a beige slip of paper. It is the size of a playing card, a page torn from a receipt book. The writing is illegible, it's smudged. It's in a shade of light blue ink that I take to be very old.

"HE BOUGHT IT," I TELL FREIGHTLING, who broke with convention sufficiently to e-mail me, but only in order to ask that I phone. "Probably years ago, given the receipt he showed me. Maybe it was a family purchase. In any case, he didn't even know he had it. Seems he discovered it one day doing inventory."

"You believe him?"

"Yes, I believe him. He's not a guy who has to scam. Maybe he *would*, but his situation doesn't require it."

Judged how, Freightling wants to know.

Dress. The man was wearing bespoke shoes. Plus, very nice stuff in that Vasali Antiquario. A couple of Bellottos. A Canaletto view painting with its capricious, nostalgic depiction of Roman ruins: three columns from the Forum are set in what appears to be English countryside with the Colosse in the distance.

"Any word from the business agent?" Freightling's voice sounds like it's coming through water for a moment. Then through a hollow wall.

"I've tried him half a dozen times." I watch myself lie, my image a night reflection in the window of the café Haiti Sud. I haven't phoned at all, yet. I want to speak to Kopak if and when he is to be found. But there is still a lot to learn about Piero Talloni. A great deal of information still needed to prepare myself.

"No voice mail at Raifort Management either," I tell Freightling.

I'm in Rome, just around the corner from Pomezia. I am launching an untruth across eleven time zones.

Freightling offers to get someone working on it from his end. I decline.

"When he realizes I'm sniffing around, he'll come to me. Just watch. We'll be in a better position then."

I tell him about tracking down the studio. *Italy Daily* came through for me here again. The writer directed me down to Via Giulia, not far from my hotel. You approached the house down an alley of furniture restorers. Disassembled tables and chairs stacked on the cobblestones, the air fumy with turpentine and shellac. Where the alley meets Via Giulia—a sixteenth-century thoroughfare, now just an ordinary street off the banks of the Tiber—the alley flares out into a mini-piazza. Here a furniture shop sells the product of the neighbourhood and, to the left, a leaning black door leads up to an apartment. No buzzer. No sign or number.

Freightling asks how I got in.

"He wasn't home," I tell him. "I bribed the housekeeper."

She accepted five thousand lire and my assurances that I was not a journalist. When I told her I had come all the way from North America to see Talloni's work, she nodded and told me in excellent English, "I'm glad to hear it. I don't need this money. But I am worried for Mr. Talloni, who is both a genius and a fool."

She tapped the side of her head knowingly, then disappeared into the kitchen to make coffee.

"And where is he now?" I called out a moment later. I'd taken half a dozen snapshots in the main room, but there wasn't really much to see beyond the evidence of a recognizably messy artistic personality and the sudden cessation of its artistic activity. His palettes and paint tubes, his brushes and soiled clothes, all these were piled into open cardboard boxes and stacked against a wall under a large mirror that made the room seem bigger than it was. There were unmarked canvases leaning against one another in a closet filled with a surprising number of suits in the Italian businessman portion of the fabric spectrum. Charcoal to steel blue. Near a dented futon folded roughly back against the wall there were several large plastic Orangina bottles. Full, although not with carbonated OJ as far as I could tell. I leaned over to examine them more closely.

The housekeeper returned with coffee, professing to know nothing of his whereabouts. "He comes, he goes. He pushes an envelope with cash under my door," she said, handing me a cup. "I wouldn't touch those if I were you."

"What is it? Thinner?"

She made a face to suggest they smelled very foul. "Late at night," she said. "He will not make it to the toilet."

"Fascinating," Freightling says, when I tell him this detail. "He pisses into bottles. Sounds like an old boozer. How'd you make out finding his other paintings?"

The woman who runs the Haiti Sud brings another

Kronenbourg to my table. It has taken me three nights in a row but she'll now bring them outside without me flagging her through the window. Now she glances down at me talking into the little dangling mouthpiece of my hands-free cell apparatus. My tourist map and my Giuseppe Vasi etching depicting the city core of Baroque Rome are both spread out on the table under the empties. She laughs. She's wiping out my ashtray, chuckling, looking me over.

"Grazie," I tell her. Then back to Freightling: "I've seen the five we know about."

I'd made a dark pencil mark on my tourist map where each of them had been found. Then traced my way through the swarming streets to find them, looping up through the fountained grandiosity of Piazza Navona to find Vasali's. East to the Via della Stelletta, where the sun wouldn't reach the ground except for a slice at highest noon, and the walls are greened with thin moss towards the base. There, tucked up an alley too narrow even for scooters, I found the tailor shop. Bolts of fine Milanese wool were unfurled in the small window across the shoulder of a wooden fitting mannequin. Inside it smelled of felt and hair oil, brandy and pine. The tailor took me proudly by the arm into the panelled corridor that led to his workroom. Halfway down hung a tiny portrait, poorly lit, the size of a large postcard. Oil paint on a wooden shingle as far as I could tell. Bright colours, a shade off primary, applied with a palette knife in slabs, making a fractured modern backdrop for the upper body of the man depicted.

Is it you? I tried asking the tailor with gestures. There were no specific features to be discerned in the face, I thought, only qualities. Was the man tense with commitment? Was the hand curled into a fist?

Not me, the tailor mimed, and smiled. Pleased with this, but more so with what he next communicated. "Talloni!" he said. He painted the air for me to understand just who this was. But he would not understand my questions on how he had acquired this rare object of mounting value.

The florist and the butcher were tiring of the traffic. Both demanded I make a purchase before they permitted me to see the paintings that now hung well out of sight in the back of each of their shops. The florist had perhaps the more valuable piece, I thought, looking at the happier and more colourful of the two. The square was splashed with the sun's colours, golds, reds, straw yellow. In the background the white steps running up to the Capitolini might have been disappearing up to heaven itself. Although, to be fair, there were collectors who would prefer the more serious, more social themes of the butcher shop. The faces of the customers evincing hunger and strength.

I took a salami campagnolo and a clutch of blue-and-white hydrangeas back to Albergo Pomezia. When the sky was finally deepening in colour and the air was cooler, I ventured out again. This time up into Piazza della Rotonda. Scooters lined the streets outside of apartment buildings and the first wave of evening café activity was beginning. As I came up Via dei Cestari the great back of the Pantheon appeared to the north, its enormous half sphere rising into the dusty sky. I found the café Il Argentine on the west side of the square opposite the obelisk. I sat at a high aluminum table just under the arched doorway, a position from which I could survey the terrace, the piazza and the long interior of the café. And there, at last, I found him. Hanging above the service bar, above the plates of artichokes and olives, marinated octopus and a dozen kinds of crostini. The closest to abstract of any of the Tallonis I had seen. Beautiful angling shafts of colour, a bar most certainly, with the currents and flow lines and concentrated splashing of café action into the foreground. Swirling into darkness at the back of the canvas. Creating a powerful visual suction, a vortex for the eyes.

The woman behind the counter spoke English. She gave her assessment of Talloni in the time it took to plate a serving of bucatini all'Amatriciana and pour a pinot bianco so cold it beaded instantly on the outside of the heavy tumbler.

"He is a great painter because he draws no attention to himself. He cares nothing for the money, I think. This is Talloni's money here, this paint. This one here and the others. The owner here does not even remember receiving it, so long ago was it. But we each have known it to hang here for some time."

Freightling is silent after I finish this description.

"Everybody has their own explanation for the thing," I say.

"And what exactly have you decided is *the thing*?"

Something with a start and a finish. "Like a hand," I suggest. "Like cards being rolled."

I can hear Freightling rise from his desk, approach the windows of his office. He is standing now on his favourite carpet.

"Is it valuable?" I remember asking him that first night we had drinks together in his office.

"Vulnerable value," he told me. And when I betrayed with a half nod that I didn't understand what this meant, he explained. "After the war with the Soviets, Afghani makers moved on to other themes, so these woven Hinds and Kalashnikovs have become increasingly rare. But if this scarcity were to manifest itself in higher prices, I can assure you Afghani carpet-makers would re-embrace the depiction of war."

Good paradox that, I remember thinking. It is valuable because it has no value. Were it to acquire value, it would no longer be valuable.

Now I hear him crack the window and take in the morning sea breeze. Freightling is looking out over a quilt of colour. Dawn at the terminal. Aquamarine mountains rising to his north. The light streaking down the valley to meet the ocean.

"Well," he says finally. "We know it's not a seven-card game."

He's heard of three more, Freightling tells me. "Making eight. Word came in via one of our event reports. Anonymous."

From Rome, no surprise. The boys in the Back ran down the bang path as far as an anonymous remailer somewhere in the eternal city.

"They tell me it might originate at one of the universities," Freightling says. "Or an Internet café."

"Read it to me." I know he had the e-mail printed out for him. It's been sitting on that brushed aluminum surface since he heard about it. Waiting for my call. He goes to get it, and in the slice of night sky visible at the top of Via Chiavari, I can see stars. I crane my neck back, stretching, looking high up out of the little café, up past the folded Pellegrino umbrella. Up, up to the stars.

Freightling is back with the e-mail, paper rustling. "Whoever it is writes, *I don't want to make this too easy for you, but allow me to point out three more.*"

One is minutes from where I'm sitting, a few blocks away in Vittorio Emanuele. Freightling reads out this address, and two others northeast of the old city core near the Palazzo del Quirinale. Via di Santa Maria. Via della Dataria.

"Collins," Freightling says.

"No doubt," I answer, darkening pencil marks over three more locations on my map. I look at them for an instant, trying to imagine if they yet compose a whole thing. Eight blackened circles over the chaotic street grid of a strange city.

We say goodbye and I click shut the phone. I pay my bill and pack up my things, folding my map so I can navigate up through the night streets, reading it as I walk.

I know that the places in question might be closed. But if I stand outside and stare in through the glass, I think I'll know if he is there. If he would choose to be there.

Vittorio Emanuele turns out to be a souvenir shop, open late. Inside a seventeenth-century building with towering, regal façades I find racks of postcards, endless shelves of plaster statuettes. Columns of Marcus Aurelius. Heads of Hadrian. Discus throwers. Venus de Milo in three different sizes: desktop, garden gnome and grotto.

The woman working the shop at this hour turns out to be Australian. She doesn't know anything about Talloni. But when she takes me back to have a look in the manager's office, with his tidy desk and shelves of catalogues, my eye is drawn immediately to an enormous black floor safe.

I'm still thinking about that safe as I charge up through the streets towards Santa Maria. Romans are spilling out of their houses and apartments on their way to dinner. A parade of soft pleats and fabric with good hand. Gathered silk at fine throats. Many pant legs breaking perfectly over tan leather insteps. Approaching Santa Maria from the west, I find myself crossing the swirling flagstones of Piazza Colonna, the Chigi Palace rising grandly at the north end of the square. Cafés running out of themselves, full and noisy. There are wine and water bottles, plates of olives, bowls of spaghetti carbonara on the tables. Gypsies are hawking fans. The Internet café NetPoint is garishly lit and streaming with people.

I consult my map again, confirm street numbers. But just

as that safe was enough to suggest Talloni's hidden presence, so now does the correspondence between the address and this darkened scooter repair shop very nearly convince me. I stand with my hands cupped around my eyes, leaning into the front window, staring. There is a cluttered and suitably oily front counter. There are the obligatory calendars from Piaggio and Elf. There is a portion of the room that stretches into blackness on its way back towards the garage. Here there are shapes on the walls. Perhaps. Perhaps.

In Via della Dataria I find a Tuscan restaurant. Open. Not overly busy. Here, I decide, the answer for all three of my new locations will be given.

I sit at a table offering a good view of three walls covered with paintings in the hodge-podge tiled fashion of the long-time collector. Dozens of works. I have time for a long and considered inventory, before the waiter returns with my appetizer of grilled eggplant and zucchini, toasts with a coarse liver pâté.

"Mi scusi."

"Signore?" he answers, cracked over a degree at the waist. He will spring into action upon apprehending my next requirement.

I wave a hand towards the walls, up them, across them. I don't have any other words except the name. "Talloni?" My tone apologetic.

The servile tension comes out of him. He unbends. His eyes close slightly, his face elongates between the high rounding of his shoulders. His own elaborately physical apology.

"Mi dispiace, Signore."

I resolve to eat and think of nothing else. The map will wait. The eggplant has a trace of heat that sings just lightly on the lip. The pâté is garlicky and washes down well with the glass of white that he has recommended. Risotto and a roasted rabbit leg follow, served with truffle sauce, simultaneously intense and fine. Espresso sharply revives me. Biscotti and vino santo bring things gently to a close. I have a short walk back into Campo de' Fiori. I have a deep sleep ahead of me and tomorrow morning we will start this project all over again.

You may hide behind Piero Talloni, I think, addressing my thoughts through the glittering night to wherever Kopak may be. But I have all the time in the world. I have time to walk a full 360 degrees around this man and his art. Eventually, through him, I'll find you.

While my Diner's Club is authorizing I walk back towards the rest rooms. Here I pause, hand on the brass fitting. There is a sound that restaurants make at the end of the evening that I have always admired. Envied even. Dishwashers. Jibes exchanged. Muffled, upbeat shouts. The clink of cutlery being filed for another day. It's the sound of certainty. Or it is to me; I have never worked in a restaurant. Certainty that what had to be done has now in fact been done and nothing remains but the emotional release, the coast down from the summit. A few drinks. A friendly argument. A bite to eat. Sex maybe. Sleep.

The hall continues, elbowing around a corner and back

towards that sound. I follow it, stepping quietly. I find a narrower hallway with two doors, through the portholes of which the steamy kitchen may now be seen. The shapes of the people I have imagined. There is a man drying his hands on a white towel, calling out to someone across the room. There is another man holding a rack of dishes and staring at the first, laughing aloud. I turn to leave.

On the wall opposite the kitchen doors, I find the back room of the owner's collection. Art for personal consumption. There's a series of very early daguerreotypes. The bawdy variety, nipples and the darkening of pubic areas suggested through sheer silk. Crimped hair pulled free of ruddy faces, willing, open. Contemporary photos of the chef with famous guests. Roberto Benigni. Catherine Deneuve. Roman Polanski. I am standing quite still, looking at these. Something in the second before I notice Talloni makes me imagine that I have seen somebody just before I have been seen.

It's a football player, mid-strike. Roma, most certainly. A leaping volley. A one-time on-the-fly eighty-ninth-minute goal, who knows? The explosion is manifest in a splash of focused orange on the eternal pitch of green.

I move over to it slowly, sidestepping down the wall. P. Talloni, a scribbly, warbly, inexpert signature. Like one not used in a long time, then used often. Scribbled with the tip of a number seven brush. And this one has a name too, I see. It's bolted to the frame on a tiny plaque.

It reads simply: "Roma!"

"TREDICI, PER FAVORE."

Apartment number thirteen at the Albergo Pomezia is becoming something of a war room. I've bought myself another map of the city and pinned it to the cork wall. I've marked my Talloni locations with coloured thumbtacks. I've mounted my snapshots in clusters connected by yellow thread to the tack marking the corresponding location.

After much cajoling, the front desk has produced two white boards from a local office supply house. Here I have made my lists, many lists. Hoping something pops free. Willing a key to be suggested.

Locations:

| | |
|---|---|
| 1. Antique store | 5. Scooter shop |
| 2. Tailor | 6. Restaurant |
| 3. Café | 7. Florist |
| 4. Butcher | 8. Souvenir shop |

I have another list for the painting subjects I know— street scene, self-portrait, café patrons, people buying meat, football player, flowers. On still another page I have tried to make sense of it by considering their geographical distribution.

West of Piazza Navona there is one painting. East of del Corso, there are three.

These analytic schemes are leading me nowhere, of course. I find theories spooling and unspooling more quickly than I can write them down. They come almost quicker than I can reasonably reject them.

Does every location correspond to a Giuseppe Vasi view? Well, Giuseppe Vasi sketched his views of Rome from just about every bridge and intersection in the city, as it turns out.

It's getting late on my fifth night in the city. I've run down Chiavari and out into the Piazza Campo de' Fiori itself. Found a coveted table on the terrace outside Taverna del Campo. Sipped my way through two glasses of Proseco, thinking, staring into the night. Listening to the music pumping out of the Irish theme bar next door: Run-D.M.C. and Aerosmith, "Walk This Way." In the piazza young Romans parade on foot, on scooters. They consider one another, faces alight with caffeine and hormone-fuelled enthusiasm. A more or less constant cellphone bleat fills the air. A thousand toads croaking over a tiny pond, the sound scattering, concentrating, sharpening, reaching a crazed scherzando as midnight approaches. I pay my bill, but before leaving I lean back in my chair to look again at the stars. See none. Lights out in Chiavari and only the dim glow of Haiti Sud to compete, the heavens had been faintly visible. For those of us out here in the square, they are hidden.

Now it's very late and I'm sipping from a bottle of even cheaper *frizzante* I picked up at the delicatessen down the way, staring at my map. I have my feet kicked up on the lumpy bed, lounging in the chair provided. I'm done throwing Hold'em hands out on the bedspread for amusement.

Ten deals and nothing to beat Jakes and eights. There is a pad of graph paper across my knees, on which I have made a rough grid of the city. I plot my locations again and again. There are eight dots on the paper in front of me. I tear a sheet off the pad and hold it up against the light, my marks suspended. And as my eyes move across the page, the points may be seen to concentrate, starting as a diffuse scatter on the right margin and hardening to a point on the left. They may be seen to have a direction. A flow.

I'm on my feet. I'm walking the paper over to the map and holding it up against the profile of the city. Those points scattered to the right of the page are now superimposed over the easterly parts of Rome's city centre. My scooter shop, check. The football player in the Tuscan restaurant. Got it. The butcher. The tailor. The florist and the Piazza della Rotonda café. All find their places in a triangular pattern that tightens, thins, and finally sharpens to the single hard point over Vitali Antiquario on Coronari street. Looked at this way, the whole thing, the sum of the parts, is like an arrowhead directing the eye of the viewer to sweep westward across the city. Down Coronari to the Tiber. Across the Ponte Sant'Angelo and following the pilgrims who had crushed in their thousands down this route before, westward to the Vatican itself. Not once to this point had I thought about visiting this famous place. No time. Not a lot of interest, to be frank. And now, halfway down a bottle of sweet, fizzy, headache-inducing wine, I am standing, swaying, feeling a distinct magnetic pull.

This is ludicrous, of course. But then haven't I been waiting for the iron filings to stand on end, to align? How many more times can I reasonably expect this to happen? So they have scattered his paintings through the city in such a way as to point the viewer towards the Vatican? Maybe this was their way of drawing the eye off the subject and away to some greater beyond. Maybe—and here an idea is born as I push through morning crowds and up the Straight Street towards the Tiber—this was an emblem of some kind of late-life religious capsize. Was Piero Talloni in the spiritual water?

Last thing I had done the night before was e-mail Mia, excited. She would have been in the core of her workday, involved in the transactions of a less fanciful hour. Her e-mail back read, *You're thinking maybe Talloni is hanging in the Vatican Museum?*

*Isn't it very late over there?*

I left early this morning and assumed I'd beat the crowds. But things are already tight in the old Via Recta. A shop door opens out onto the narrow street and I dodge to miss it. At the Ponte Sant'Angelo I am held up by a rank of people taking photographs. Six, eight simultaneously inspired shots of the dome of St. Peter's viewed looking westward from the bridge. The green riot of Tiber-side vegetation overwhelming the far river wall, leaning down as if to touch the water. The cameras whirr like insect legs. I shoulder through, across the bridge, crowded with African and Sri Lankan faux-gear merchants. Nike, Pepsi,

Ford Motor Company and the Chicago Bulls. For a song, one may purchase an indulgence from each of the world's foremost commercial denominations. All under the watchful eye of the Archangel Michael, perched on the tip of the Castel Sant'Angelo. And of the statues mounted on Bernini's balustrade. Peter, Paul and ten angels holding elements of the Passion: the scourge, the throne, the crown of thorns, the vestment, the dice, the nails, the vinegar, the lance, the cross itself and its derogatory inscription, INRI.

Westward into Via di Conciliazione. From the long mall St. Peter's may be observed to hover, shimmering white in the low-lying smog that colours the horizon. I join a river flooding up towards the square. Traffic moves in sluggish bursts. A delivery van sounds its horn. Yellow school buses grind into the side streets and disgorge passengers.

By the time I enter Piazza San Pietro, I realize I'm in a crowd of thousands. Not quite moving of my own accord, more in keeping with what this flow will allow me. I angle northwards, trying for a spot against the colonnade. Trying not to be pulled to the centre of the perfect and enormous ellipse. Resisting the centripetal forces that seem to radiate from Caligula's obelisk. I am breathing heavily with the effort when I finally find my place. Back secure against marble wall, staring out over the teeming square and trying to understand what this is, who they are.

Mostly children, it's suddenly clear. In large groups. Colour-coded into teams with scarves of gold, blue, red and lime green, worn as a cravat or a kerchief, tied to a belt loop or waved in the air. There are a few young adults per group, in jeans and fine wool sweaters, with ball caps and cellphones. Teachers. The religious equivalent of soccer parents. Shepherds to the tens of thousands swarming here outside the Seat of God on earth. And at the top of the square, surely St. Peter's is the largest thing any of us have ever seen. It whites out the sky beyond itself.

"Per favore," I ask a Swiss Guard standing nearby, gesturing at the square, the crowds. The children. "Non capisco."

"I speak English," he tells me, without a smile. It's a holiday for the Catholic Youth Organization. A papal audience is expected.

Crowds continue to spill in from Conciliazione, packing the area between the colonnades. The scarves combine in shifting bands of colour, concentrating, swirling across the piazza. When the children choose to wave their scarves together, there is a ripple of texture as if electricity has charged a corner of this living canvas.

The Swiss Guard are now carving a walkway through the crowds. A fenced-off boulevard beginning at the broad steps of St. Peter's, cutting through the crowd in an enormous square. Returning to the same steps.

What is about to happen is now beginning to happen.

You see the crowds move long before you see anything yourself. You see the electricity flow and arc. The scarves flurry, they become a hurricane of colour, passing the storm from one section of the crowd to another. It's three hundred yards away, across the square, barely visible. Then it's a hundred and fifty, a hundred. Then fifty yards away and closing. The scarves signalling the pressure of this weather system, pushing it towards you, driving whatever excitement is held within to the out-side of everyone around you. People's hands are in the air. A man is holding a camera up, firing blind shots of what he can only hope and trust is in fact approaching. The scarves are now flying. The hurricane sweeps over you, the sky is briefly hidden. There are Swiss Guards now quite close by, lining the barricades. There are other men in black suits and square sunglasses. A slight sheen to the hair and a feline way of moving to reposition them-selves along the route. Standing, staring into the crowd. Padding on just before his arrival. He surprises you, slip-ping in behind them. Emerging from the frenzied field of colour. He is there all at once. He passes very slowly by, standing in the back of his white golf cart. You have many seconds to consider him.

His hand is outstretched. He is stooped, very pink.

Then he's gone.

Sweat is streaming from my hair and down my back. I've forgotten my sunglasses at the hotel and my eyes are burning. The sky is a dome of forbidding, other-worldly white. But I'm seeing coloured rings. Cadmium yellow, hunt red, burnt orange. Dancing on my retina.

IT'S OVER AND THE CROWD is slackening in the square. Tidal tension reversed, the coherence of the current gone. This sea of bodies begins to rip unpredictably at the edges, finding escape routes, channelling in and back on itself, funnelling away between the fences and back into the top of Conciliazione. Down the sombre boulevard to find the buses hidden on the side streets. I release myself into the current and let myself be carried out of the square. I find slack water at the edge of the street and stop to consider the souvenirs on sale. I buy a snow globe, the Pope blessing the masses from the centre of a flurry of white flakes.

"Come stai, signore?"

So much closer to Aphrodite than to Hades today. Her hair is pulled free of her face and tied in a manganese violet band. She has a loaded bag over her shoulder. A camera with a long lens pinched under her strong right arm.

"Molto bene, grazie, Fontana." Did she come to find me?

Of course she doesn't believe me when I say that I am well. "You look terrible," she says. "Cigarette?"

"I'm hung over," I tell her, declining.

"For an audience with the Holy Father. What disrespect." She tosses a match to the gutter, exhales a plume of smoke.

"Mi dispiace," I say. When I ask her what she's doing here she tells me she has an unrivalled collection of close-up shots of the Pope. Her eyes are laughing.

"Everyone needs a hobby. And you? You're here, so I take it we still have a story?"

I start to tell her how busy I've been tracking down the paintings. Talloni popping up all over the place. Me in my hotel room trying to sort out what exactly we have here.

Fontana nods slowly. Looks away down the boulevard. "Are you eating well?" she asks me, changing the topic abruptly. Moving us onward to a point I imagine she had been planning to raise.

She's not impressed with my Tuscan restaurant or with the Taverna Campo de' Fiori. I tell her about another place, osso buco and saltimboca, pricey. Where the waiter offered to grate fresh truffle over my green salad.

Fontana smiles at me for the first time. She takes great pleasure from this story even before it's told. "You didn't ask how much, did you?"

Of course, no, I hadn't.

Her smile broadens, expectant.

"A hundred and twenty thousand lira," I say, sheepish.

Fontana laughs hard. She removes her sunglasses and wipes the corner of her eye with a thin finger. "Very good," she says. "Sixty-dollar salad. That must have been very tasty."

I agree to eat real Roman food.

"Then we can discuss this story," she says.

"Yes, of course," I say to her. "The story."

And so I cross the river again later, this time walking south and into Trastevere. There's laundry on lines between the windows and overflowing garbage cans in the main street. Kids on black mini-bikes are throwing up pebbles, running loops around the octagonal fountain at the centre of Piazza di Santa Maria.

I find La Lucia in one of the tight, curling streets beyond the square, guided to the spot by the snip of a map Fontana has drawn on the back of one of her business cards. Capri Fontana and a cellphone number. No company name. No job description. I had no idea I was calling her by her last name.

"This is nice," I tell her. La Lucia is a kitchen in an alley, really. The folding tables and chairs are mostly outside. Above us are the lit windows of apartments. Quiet music comes from various sources at once, mingling pleasantly with the bubble of conversation in the alley. She orders us house pasta and the daughter of the owner brings over wine. An unlabelled litre bottle of the perfectly quaffable vin d'ordinaire variety. Fontana pushes the bread in my direction.

"Cheap and essential," she tells me. "Roman food has little in common with the Vatican. Or your Il Cardinale truffle, for that matter."

She speaks as if there is no hesitation between thought and word.

When she arrived—just a few minutes after me, I hadn't yet been seated—I saw her enter the top of the alley and stroke a hand across the front of her sweater. Smoothing a wrinkle. Wiping away an imaginary speck of lint. Unconscious of the motion entirely, I imagine. But her hand flattened the wool across her stomach, touching the top of her thigh on the downstroke. She was wearing khakis. From the Gap off Piazza di Spagna, no doubt. And I saw myself all at once in Rome. A person whose connections lay elsewhere but who was nevertheless nervous with anticipation at meeting this woman. This forceful, unhesitating stranger.

Simple salads have arrived. I lay out my map for her and she leans forward to examine. Every street must be familiar to her. She traces a pattern between my eight marks with the index finger of a long hand, her veins standing clearly in relief.

"What did you say was in the e-mail?" she asks, without lifting her head.

Two key points. First, the writer did not wish to make it too easy for us. "Second, he asks that we allow him to point out three more."

Capri spears a forkful of salad. She looks up, chewing. "I'm sorry, so?"

"He doesn't want to make *it* too easy. *It*. So there is some specific thing Talloni is doing here."

She shakes her head and swallows. "You didn't even go into the scooter shop. Maybe there's nothing there. Or the souvenir shop."

I sit back in my chair, both exasperated and distracted by her. I lean forward again, focusing. "I was in the restaurant. Piero Talloni had been there. I saw the signature. Now why would someone lie about one location and tell the truth about another? They'd have to know we'd check."

She waggles her head back and forth, noncommittal. "What else?"

"They wrote 'three more.' As in, these are not the final three." I turn to my own salad, radicchio and romaine lettuce, as far as I can tell, but it is salty, lemony, crispy. Perfect.

Capri is back over the map. She looks for a moment more and then sighs. "How can I help you with this? I'm ready to take pictures when you are."

"We can photograph the paintings any day of the week," I tell her. "But I want to understand this first. 'Allow me to point out three more. Don't want to make it too easy.' I want to know what Talloni is trying to tell us."

Capri Fontana is visibly unconvinced Piero Talloni is trying to tell us anything. She continues to eat, using her bread now to mop up oil and vinegar left in the dish. She looks up to find me staring at her. She holds my gaze for only a second before making a gesture to bring me back to the topic.

"You know Rome," I say to her.

"I know Rome. Yes."

Perhaps better than even she realizes. This woman from the war zones. I imagine she is used to interpreting geography, topography, the physical lay of things in the world right around her, in terms of their flow and their possible resistance. Here is a clear path. Here our way is blocked or will soon become dangerous. This road will take us more quickly from here to there. This route is impossible.

"We have these eight points. We believe there are more. Now, can you imagine these as a route of some kind? And if so, where does it lead?"

"Perhaps to the Vatican," she says to me, deadpan.

I lean back. Does she find me funny? Odd? Are the other men in her life very unlike me?

She looks at me steadily, waiting for me to tell her the truth.

All right. I tell her that, staring at the map on my wall in the middle of the night, I thought I saw something. An indication of what direction my attention should be shifting on the map. Maybe even some kind of spiritual epiphany? "It's speculation. I don't claim to actually know anything."

Capri raises her eyebrows. "That's just as well." Then she turns back to the map, her hand falling back to her own throat, where she very lightly strokes the underside of her chin with the back of her fingers. Her other hand spreads over the map, not touching the paper, but gliding above the surface. Above my pencil marks.

Pasta arrives. We eat in silence for several minutes.

"I don't believe Talloni is trying to tell you anything with this," Capri says, finally. "I think it more likely that all his life he didn't understand how good he was and now he is surprised that so many people have held on to things he gave them."

I'm disappointed, but I say nothing. If she believes what she has just told me, I'm calculating that she also believes some contrary thing is possible. I wait for her to tell me that part. And sure enough, in only a few seconds her eyes reveal a light chop rising on internal seas. She flicks a glance down the alley and to the rooftops. Seeking the horizon. She returns her gaze only slowly to the table. Starts eating again. Savouring her simple food of Rome.

"It's good, yes?" Capri says.

La Lucia house spaghetti is very good. Dressed simply with bacon, black pepper and pecorino cheese. I take a mouthful and nod.

"OK," she says. "Let's say Talloni is trying to tell us something. Even if this were so, it would not be directions to the Vatican."

"No?"

"No," she says. "Because he's a social realist. And in Italy during this time, unless he was a Fascist, which I doubt, that means he was probably a socialist."

I nod. It makes sense.

"And even socialists, in those days, were not so willing to use the Holy Father as a figure of ridicule. You understand? To have him on a map. To have an arrow pointing at him. No. I don't believe it."

I start to object. It could be a tribute, could it not? But Capri is unswerving in her commitment to completing this point without interruption.

"And quite aside from that . . ."

I put down my fork and listen.

". . . if an artist were to create a legend about himself using his own city as a canvas—a city where he had lived and worked in isolation, painting away the decades towards his own demise—I doubt he would draw a picture that did not include the studio where he had completed this enormous, unlikely project."

She reaches across the table and takes a pencil from my shirt pocket. Tracing its tip slowly down Via Giulia.

I show her the right intersection. Capri makes the mark. It's a few blocks due south of Coronari, the antique shop that had been formerly the point of my westward-pointing arrow.

"So?" she says. "Now you have nine points. Better? Worse?"

I stare at the map, transfixed. She has destroyed anything directional about the distribution of Talloni's marks. But I am already trying to spin this development forward. Treat Via Giulia as a ninth data point. As another upturned card in this mystery game I am playing with a painter born before my father.

"Maybe you should just think about your food," Capri says, dipping a chunk of bread in her wine. "For me this food is Rome. Hot and simple. It has a few ingredients, but the right ones. You cannot imagine this pasta having any *less* on it but you wouldn't want to disturb the plate by adding anything more."

I agree.

"But if you were missing one ingredient in this dish, I think you might guess which one it was. So simple is the combination of flavours that the absent one might be suggested. Am I right?"

I have no idea. Maybe if you're Roman, I want to say. Maybe if you know this food from childhood. Which I don't. Which I can't.

But I don't say anything. Capri is staring at me. Her hand is tented on the map in front of her plate. Middle finger planted on the Via Coronari antique shop. Index finger an inch south on Talloni's studio in Via Giulia. Thumb an inch east of the studio over the souvenir shop in Vittorio Emanuele. Three points at a rough right angle. Three points seeking a fourth to make the square.

Capri's naked ring finger waggles uncertainly in the air somewhere up over the top of Piazza Navona. I watch it, briefly hypnotized by its movement. Waiting for it to come to rest. I recognize what she is encouraging me to think. But when her finger does not come to rest, does not touch down on the paper but lifts away instead, her hand returning to her fork, I am quite suddenly filled with completely unrelated questions that I would like to ask her. Maybe I've just had the right amount of wine. Perhaps the evening temperature has dropped to some perfect will-changing dew point. But now I want to know where she is from. Was she born in Rome? I want to know about her travels. How did she get into her line of work? What happened after she was shot?

But when I try to ask these things, to generally redirect our conversation to some warmer, more personal place,

I don't get far. She was born in Spoleto, in Umbria. She came to Rome as a girl. She doesn't remember the bullet striking her or many of the hours that immediately followed. I run out of questions quickly, flushing. She has a small, amused smile on her face. She's looking at me. Now it's me turning away, eyes to the horizon.

She insists on paying for dinner, dismissing my protest with the wave of a hand. Peels off three twenty-thousand-lire notes and has enough left over to tip handsomely. Dinner for two with wine for less than my truffle salad.

We shake hands. I have a sliding, foolish sense of not knowing what comes next. And Capri, of course, homes in directly on this thought.

"We know what we must do now, yes?" she says, letting go of my hand. "You get me somebody to take a picture of."

I cross the Tiber at the Isola Tiberina, a little boat-shaped island linked by bridges to shore on either side. At St. Gregorio, the church on the island, there are inscriptions in Latin and Hebrew, which I trace with my fingers. I cross Ponte Quattro Capi leading north and back to Campo de' Fiori. The night vaults up, Prussian blue. Below, there isn't much water in the river, but it sounds distinctly under the high arches of the bridge. Echoing up. The amplified sound of very distant voices. I stop on the bridge to listen.

Part of me wants to head up to the top of Piazza Navona immediately. But even with the feeling that I could predict where Talloni will next appear, I know it's foolish to go now. Even Capri Fontana's thin finger hovered over several city blocks. How long am I prepared to wander around the north end of the Piazza Navona waiting for the exact location to announce itself?

South is the ruined Ponte Rotto, the last of several unsuccessful antique attempts to bridge the river at this bend. One surviving arch is now crumbling into the river, a stone at a time. Beyond, the Aventine Hill rises darkly, a deep olive and wine-coloured mass reaching up from the river. The silhouette of the Santa Sabina church tower visible at the top just over the trees.

I climb down off the bridge and burst back into the more typical energy of Rome. Traffic is howling along Lungotevere Aventino, the boulevard that flanks the river. To my north, all the way from here back to my hotel, there will be tight streets with overflowing cafés and restaurants still seating diners. The aluminum tables at Taverno de Campo will be packed, cellphones croaking in the night. The Irish bar will be advertising its hardwired connection to the global culture grid with a shifting soundtrack of rap and metal and punk.

I head south, no destination. I'm aware only faintly of the Aventine towering up as I approach it. Rising in the darkness until eventually, one or two hundred yards down the road, I finally come to a stone arch that leads into a steep, flagstoned alley. And seeing it rake upwards to my left, I am forced to stop and consider where such a trail might lead. I look up. The silhouettes of the churches can't be seen from here, but it reminds me that up above is a vantage point from which, as Giuseppe Vasi has illustrated, spectacular views may be had. And it occurs to me further that with a week now gone and little accomplished, I might benefit from another look down over the whole thing that has had me perplexed.

The little walkway is arched over with heavy trees and within a minute I am climbing in darkness. Out of breath, hands on the top of my knees as I pump up the stones, one long step at a time. At the top of the rise there is a high red brick wall, grown over with ivy. A gate too, a few inches ajar. I pull it aside and enter a long, narrow garden. The grass is trimmed tidily. There are benches lining the gravel walkways. Earthen pots as tall as myself, growing over with palm plants. High orange trees have littered the ground with their fruit and the fragrance is that of something very sweet at the earliest stages of decay. Orange perfume and the whiff of citrus rot. I can make out a square church tower at the top of the garden. The other way, back towards the river, there is a wide opening in the trees and a swath of Roman night sky.

There's a deck here, where tourists flock during the day to take panoramic photographs. To either side, the hill shoulders away, bare for a few dozen metres before the slopes become forested. I find a spot in the longer grass and sit, Rome spreading out below me. But not in the modern fashion of North American cities. Those views draw my eye to the skeleton of the power grid on which the tissue of city life grows. It's actually quite dark up here, even though I've punched through the trees. I can see the glint of what little water is in the river. I can see the ochre and mercury glow of street lights on the bridges crossing into Trastevere. Traffic coursing down the boulevards on either side of the Tiber, lights shining silver and chrome. There are spots that glow within the city and the dome of St. Peter's is a blazing titanium-white beacon to the northwest. But the activity of Rome below its canopy of trees is otherwise hidden. I try to pick out the spots where my map is marked for Talloni but I quickly lose track. Would those be the lights of Vittorio Emanuele there? Have I traced my eyes as far east as the Rotonda?

Nothing on the surface of the city below makes any sense, although I'm not disappointed by this particularly. I'm glad I came for the darkness. For the relative cool. I'm glad I came for the quiet, since from this height and distance the city also holds its sounds to itself. I have to smile there in the darkness imagining the phone call that I will go ahead and make in the morning. Break down and dial the Raifort Management number.

Maybe I'll start with, "Is it just me or is it starting to smell like horseradish around here?"

He'll struggle to remember me and then it will come flooding back.

"Business agent? Is it rare for business agents to advise their clients to quit? To destroy their own work?" I feel at liberty to be direct with a guy who once toted around an old black dial phone in a tool belt.

He used to say *pronto* into that phone of his, didn't he? Funny thing. At some point in my life—presumably when I came here for the first time, all those years ago—I would have learned that this is the standard phone salutation in Italy. But I don't recall connecting this knowledge to Kopak at the time.

We'll strike a bargain after that. After the link is forged. I'll explain the capsize profile. He'll understand what it means to have a client covered in the very well-read pages of *Phrate Magazine*. And then I'll simply say, "Take me to him. No more subterfuge. Not with me. There was a time . . ."

I'm imagining every minute of this conversation, sitting on the grass up there on the Aventine Hill. And right at this moment, I'm imagining a theatrical pause on my part. I'll breathe in deeply. Stare at him. Because we're going back now. Moving back, back in time. I'm carrying him with me. Dennis Kopak may be a guy who made a fortune in software before this was an obvious thing to do and against what anybody could possibly have expected of him. He may be a guy who went on to change his name, thereby repudiating any connection to a personal past. Still. So long has been the time since he and I last spoke. So many light years from here to Prince Albert, Saskatchewan. And so clearly did he seek me out at that time. I'm certain he will ride back with me over the years during this pause.

"There was a time," I'll continue, "when you tried to change the life of another artist. Do you remember that, Dennis? Funny thing about that though . . . look at us both now."

Two Freak East alumni flying business class.

I realize I've been angry about this in the past. In the recent past. I've pictured a reunion with Kopak, imagined engineering it to the point where key questions can be asked and answered. Did you intend for me to be diverted? But I'm flush full of La Lucia pasta and up on the Aventine Hill. Part of me is still thinking about Capri. Yes, I am imagining her. And I am unexpectedly pleased with life. More pleased than I have been in some time. I'm proud, come to think of it, to be sitting up here on a hill above the city of Rome and having this internal discussion. And my imagining of an encounter with Dennis Kopak has been suitably softened. Made more cordial. The idea is not to assign guilt but to establish that lives will fork off in their strange directions. Mine did and may soon again. Kopak's did. Seems like maybe this is what Piero Talloni wants as well. And if a life decides that it will do so, whose right is it to interfere?

"Take me to Piero Talloni." That's what I'll say to turn the matter back to him. "It's time for him to tell his story."

Settling on this strategy, I lean back slowly into the Aventine grass. Cool, rushing up to cup my head, to make the sound of rustling paper in my ears.

It occurs to me, lying there more or less happily, that my own life might branch off again in various ways. Maybe it will have something to do with Mia. I haven't thought about her much since landing, I realize. I've been saving her e-mails for the right moment. A moment when I will have the mental space necessary to respond. Now I'm feeling like maybe I'll do that when I get back to the hotel. There's no doubt some shoulder sloping and resloping has been going on over there. She has had thoughts. We've been together what? A year and some. But these were intense months. Living, working together. We connected ourselves to one another very quickly on meeting. Not without any parallel to other fast-forged links that I have made over the years, I acknowledge. But intense, nevertheless. Mutual needs and capacities being complexly paired between us. And if this were the moment of change that I felt approaching, she would have to be somehow wrapped up in it.

She would marry me, if I asked her. I find myself thinking about this unexpected idea, all at once.

Decisions, decisions.

Many stars visible tonight from this point in the city. Were Kopak here, I suppose he might still be able to identify them all for me. Each of the animals and the hunters in that jungle of lights peering out and making eye contact with him. Making their faces plain.

There was a crow, as I recall. A bull.

It brings to mind a memory. Kopak standing at my Malevich rip-off canvas, rearranging the tiny black discs, my micro-self-portraits. Of course, even he didn't pretend to know what the shapes meant. What they might tell us about the future. Some kind of galactic machine, he said.

Only we'd lost the instruction manual. All the while shuffling those discs around, moving them into the shapes of
different constellations.

Somewhere down on Lungotevere Aventino, a truck
is honking its horn. Long, angry bursts. The two-tone
warble of a distant siren begins. Rising, rising.

I remember that he showed me a particular constellation and I wondered how anyone could have gazed up
into the night sky, found this pattern—a lopsided square
with a number of outrigger stars to the east—and taken
the pattern for the prancing, galloping horse, Pegasus.

Sometime after the siren began, I stood up. I don't
remember doing it, but here I am, standing on the
Aventine Hill. I'm up on my feet, head back. Scanning
the heavens. Across the city another siren has joined the
first, and now they're both galloping down on me.

He threw them up there in a few seconds, so familiar
was the shape to him. I remember his hands flitting across
the white surface that I had painted over the week before.
My emphatically blank slate, to be perfected with this pattern.

Kopak said, very nonchalant, "And my personal
favourite . . ."

Thirteen stars. I stood at his shoulder and admired
how quickly this was done. Thirteen black dots dealt onto
the canvas without hesitation. Each dropped into its right-
ful place.

## FOUR /
## NEWSTART 2.0™

"Where's your camera?"

Capri produced a mini Rollei SLR from the leg pocket of her cargo pants. The camera was about the size of a cigarette package.

"You realize we may only get this one interview."

"I shot most of Sarajevo with this camera. What are you worried about?"

I was looking down the bank of PCs and iMacs towards the front door. Out in the Piazza Colonna the cafés were being torn down from the lunch service. Businessmen were passing in groups heading back to their offices and trading houses. It was overcast, humidity rising by the hour. I'd had my one week of sunny Rome, and now weather systems were changing.

Capri sighed elaborately. "If we get a sit-down with the guy? Time to set up and light? My Hasselblad is in the car."

While she was talking, Capri was clicking through the *Phrate* web site. I glanced over to see what she'd found.

"Where is this thing exactly?"

I took the mouse from her and clicked up the navigation bar, then selected the icon for the aesthetic weather map. It opened up in a separate window.

"Well, well," Capri said, as the window swirled with colour.

I used the nav-bar to select Europe, then panned down over Italy. Left-clicked on Rome to pull up the submenu, one item of which offered details of the weather system in question. Two hundred and seventy Talloni-related submissions that month alone, the most for any single artist in the country.

"We're making the weather," she said, amused by this idea.

"Not us. People who submit comments or reports on him are creating the system."

"So, Collins, then."

"He probably is doing some of it. God knows he manipulated Talloni—no reason he wouldn't try the same on us."

"And he was using an anonymous remailer. So you wouldn't have known," Capri said.

I held up my hands, plead guilty. "Sure. All 270 event

reports could be his. But I highly doubt it. There are fil-
ters. We can sniff out same-source postings at our end."

"Ah," Capri said.

"And you can't argue with what we've seen, either.
The paintings are real. The reaction to them is real. You
have your photos of the work."

"I have my photos of the work," she said, closing the
weather map window.

"Now we get to Talloni through this Collins guy, and
you get your photos of the man himself."

"That easy?"

"Trust me," I told her. "I'll get you Talloni."

"You know where to find me," Capri said, laying her
head down on the desk across folded arms.

Indeed I did. Everything was in its place now. I put
Kopak's favourite constellation on an overhead transpar-
ency and projected it over his map on the hotel room wall.
The rough square of Pegasus's body to the west. To the east,
three branches of three stars each, which, in the diorama,
were his head and the two rearing front feet. In the quivering metallic light, the thirteen stars of the constellation
settled down over the city. Nine fell perfectly over my
thumbtacks, confirming the known Tallonis. Four more
fell on unmarked locations in the city, which Kopak would
have chosen. There was a carbonated fizz of excitement at
the top of my stomach as I approached the map. Nine con-
firmations. Four clear predictions of what we would find in
the future. Kopak's use of Talloni made clear.

I began scribbling notes to myself. There was one around the Piazza Colonna. Another in the streets off the Piazza Venezia. One east of the Area Sacra, not far from my hotel. And the fourth I found off the top of the Piazza Navona just as Capri had suggested at La Lucia. Only this one—falling right into the Convent of Sant'Agostino—gave me a moment of doubt. There was no arguing with the projection. The constellation map was downloaded from the US Astronomical Society. It was right. But a convent?

Sometimes the place on the map, viewed from street level, seemed to have been selected perfectly for its special status. Talloni will *be* in this place, I would find myself thinking. Outside the scooter shop I had instantly known. When I went back there, the day after my dinner with Capri, all I said to the man at the front was, *Please, may I see the painting?* They took me back into the garage to show me a watercolour bound with cling wrap to a piece of stiff cardboard. It might have been done by a child. A formula-one Ferrari from the mid-seventies. Simple lines rendered the car in motion. Primitive. Emotional.

"Lauda?" I asked.

"Si si," was the excited response. And great amusement all around that I knew of either Piero Talloni or Niki Lauda. Nobody was reading the English-language *Italy Daily* around here, apparently. Or watching CNN for that matter. Still, after only a short period of amusement, the proprietor grew serious. Is he famous, came the inevitable, nervous question, while I examined the painting from close. Holding it back, then up to the light. The signature was real.

"Famous?" he asked again, pointing at the painting.

Not really, I tried to convey. I held fingers a few millimetres apart. "A little." We both laughed.

It was the same thing in two other locations that the constellation had predicted. Running southwest from the souvenir shop on Vittorio Emanuele, through and past the florist in the Aracoeli, was the horse's head line. Capri and I went hunting separately for the two missing spots, armed with new printouts. I was standing with a smile on my face opposite a watchmaker's shop in Via Fornari, a dusty quiet side street just off the Piazza Venezia, when my cell jangled.

"I'm starting to like this Talloni," Capri said. "Decent painter. Good taste in food."

"What have you found?"

"Jewish restaurant just east of the Area Sacra here. I've been to this place. Most excellent *fiori di zucca*."

"What else?"

"Nice *carciofi fritti*. You have this? Lightly battered, deep- fried artichokes."

"Capri."

"Your man painted a rather large canvas of a group of people eating *coda alla vaccinara*. Braised oxtail. What's happening over in Fornari?"

Well, the jeweller told me, it seemed Talloni couldn't pay the repair bills on the old watch he favoured. A jump hour direct-read mechanical digital watch from the fifties.

"Very impractical," said the watchmaker, without looking up from the Rolex he was cleaning. "Broken half the time."

"So you fix it half a dozen times and he gives you that," I said, gesturing towards the cubist collage of watch faces that sat propped against the wall on top of a file cabinet.

"I told him: last time," the jeweller said.

"What did he look like?" I asked.

The jeweller waved a dismissive hand. But for that hand, which fluttered up and back to the workbench, his physical focus on the Rolex was unwavering. When he needed a particular tool, his fingers whispered aside to the spot where it lay, found the tweezers or the swab or the tiny cog in question. Grasped it with hardly a glance.

"You never looked closely?"

Never looked. Never cared. Wouldn't tell if he had or did.

"I'm an artist myself," I told him. At the moment the words came out, I felt that the simple arch of the statement could still bear the weight of the truth. But I blushed, my cells, synapses, animal instincts, my whole physiology telling me, telling anyone who was watching, that this was a lie.

The watchmaker noticed nothing of this internal conflict. But he put down a tiny screwdriver at this point and sat back in his chair. His eyes rested still on the project in front of him—as if to avert his eyes would finally destroy the bubble of concentration that shimmered around him—but he did speak to me directly.

"Do you think a great artist comes himself to have his watch repaired?"

I said I had no idea what Talloni might have done.

"Let me tell you then. He sends his housekeeper. This is what a great man does. This is what a great man does when he needs something in my little, my very *busy,* shop."

I withdrew before the man picked up his tools again. Point taken. But it was at least confirmed that I was in the right spot. One of the right spots.

Outside the convent, by contrast, I knew just as simply that I was in the wrong spot. I walked north to the corner, to St. Apollinaire, where Gregorian chants are still heard every Sunday. Back down into the tiny Piazza delle Cinque Lune. East to the Via della Scrofa. And completing that simple three-point turn, I found myself staring across the street at a delicatessen and sandwich counter. One of a hundred narrow shops in Rome that from twelve to three are bursting with people trying to navigate to the counter, order something, find elbow room at the standing counters along the walls. I crossed the street and looked hungrily in the window. Pyramids of cheese. Cacio de Roma, rustico, Montegrappa and Gorgonzola. Stacks of little blue-and-red cardboard boxes, each holding a one-ounce tube of black truffle paste. Tubs of green olives ranging in colour from purple black to khaki and right on up to a very bright, limy green. And in the back, rank after rank of bottles. Frascati. Colli Albani. Pellegrino. Orangina.

I felt unexpectedly nervous about going in. But did. And when I worked my way to the front of the crowd at the sandwich counter and ordered a prosciutto and basil panini, I finally saw what I was looking for. Its style not quite like any of the others. Garish colours combined—maroons and light greens, straw yellow against blood red. Colours disconnected from the subject, which still could not be missed for what it was. The sow for which della Scrofa was named. This one enormous, stretched full length on the ground. Asleep? Dead? Waiting for a suckling brood?

Back in the war room, I checked the position of the deli. It plotted a few hundred metres east and north of the actual spot where the star fell. So, a very good but not perfect match was made. I phoned my engineer buddy at *Phrate* for an opinion on the mathematics of the situation.

"The pattern is not random," the engineer told me. "That is simple mathematical truth. So while the distribution could conceivably have occurred by chance, without the agency of the human hand, the likelihood of this being the explanation is really, really small."

Like how small?

"Let's say 225 to the power of ten," the engineer said.

"Meaning what exactly?"

"Meaning you'd know the feeling if you were playing Hold'em and got two aces in the hole ten times in a row."

Which left one location. Pegasus would have us believe it lay somewhere to the west of the Palazzo Chigi on the Piazza Colonna, a place I had passed on my way to find the scooter shop. Capri and I went up together, circling the streets around the square. There were tea shops and tourist boutiques in the Via della Colonna Antonina. There was another, smaller, square called Piazza di Pietra opposite Hadrian's Temple, where the Roman bourse now resided. Capri poked her head into half a dozen shops and restaurants in the Via dei Bergamaschi before we found ourselves in Piazza Colonna itself.

"He wouldn't hang out here," I said, dubious, looking at the chichi cafés on the square. The polish of the clientele just now arriving for late lunches.

Capri was scanning the area. There was a shop selling expensive pens and knives. There was a high-end wine store.

"He likes to drink, you say?" she asked.

"I see him as more of a cheap *frizzante* man, myself," I answered, part of me convinced by this reasoning. Would a man who pisses into empty Orangina bottles be buying expensive Brunello di Montalcino in the square opposite the Chigi Palace? Would a wine store like that have a dotty old painter on the client list and be prepared to take his art as credit?

All that was persuasive before I spotted the Internet café. Still quiet at this hour. The neon front signs cold. But inside there was a man walking up and down the banks of PCs, powering them up. Preparing for the trickle and then the flow and then the high tide of users. Whoever had by whatever means become familiar with the technology of connection. Come to know it. To need it. And in they would come to send their e-mails. To harvest data across the spaceless nodes of that great constellation.

"What?" Capri said, as I stepped off the curb and into the square, responding immediately to the impulse by plotting my shortest possible route to the Café NetPoint. "You're telling me some eighty-year-old painter is surfing porn sites? Flashing off anonymous e-mails?"

Not Talloni. I was nodding with satisfaction before we got to the door. And I was still satisfied even when we didn't find a painting. When we didn't shine enough light on the situation to get a glimmer of reflected recognition from the young man behind the counter. The owner and only employee of the café.

"I don't know names," he said. "You come in, give me 10,000 lire and away you go."

Yes, they offered a remailer service. Sometimes people wanted to send e-mails that couldn't be traced.

"I know what an anonymous remailer is," I told him.

"So? Are you police?"

I gave him a copy of *Phrate* and he calmed down. "I like this magazine," he allowed. "Quite a lot of people in Rome like this magazine. But all day long, they come. They go. Students. Other young people. People from the university. Travellers. I don't see who they all are."

He agreed we could wait there. I told Capri to go be inconspicuous at the back of the room.

"No painting," she pointed out, looking around the room.

Didn't matter. There hadn't been a Talloni painting in his own studio on Via Giulia either. That was where the whole thing started, the entry point. This was the exit. The point from which Kopak broadcast Talloni's message to the world. We wouldn't find the artist here, I knew. But if we waited, we would eventually find his spokesperson.

Capri sat down at a computer in the raised section against the back wall. I went down and sat a little closer to the door. Outside, the sky was darkening. Computers were humming all around. Here I was, sitting bang on the last of thirteen points plotted across the Eternal City. First Kopak, then Talloni. An article about the two of them would write itself.

"What's he look like?" she put her hand on my shoulder. She was whispering, just a few inches from my ear. "I never asked you this."

I swivelled. I'd been staring out into the square. It had just begun to rain. The flagstones of the piazza blackening, then shining. The Chigi Palace disappearing behind a gently lowering bank of grey. Earlier in the week, in the late afternoon of one of the drifting days when nothing appeared to be connected to anything else, I had wandered up to the Piazza del Popolo for a breather. Up to the square at the North Gate of the old city, where they used to execute people by hammering their temples with a stick, this to great crowd approval, long after the invention of the guillotine. In the church at the gate, Santa Maria del Popolo, there are the Cerasi Caravaggios. *The Crucifixion of*

*St. Peter* most notably, in front of which I stood for a long time considering the saint's face: a mélange of devotion, fixation, bravery, certainty and no small amount of fear and physical pain. Moving along the north wall, I came to the Chigi Chapel, where the noble family would have offered up their private and aristocratic solicitations to the beyond. Here on the floor, the Chigi family crest was laid out in an elaborate and colourful mosaic, perfectly preserved. A grinning skeleton hiding behind the Chigi shield. A mischievous image of death, I found myself thinking now in the NetPoint, looking around and finding Capri very close—an image that had established its fecundity, spinning down over the ages, reseeding itself over five centuries and surviving to the present day in Grateful Dead imagery and biker tattoo art.

Links and links.

She was waiting for my answer.

"I have no idea what he'll look like," I admitted. "I'm thinking I'll just know."

"Maybe it's him?" Capri said, her eyes gesturing for me to look to the front counter. It was a man wearing a dark cape and a hat with a broad brim. Fiftyish. The cape came open as he extracted a long billfold with gold clasps, and a silk foulard tumbled free of his throat.

Capri was laughing quietly, pretending to be convinced. Her fingers sliding down the outside of her thigh, finding the button that held shut the pocket on the side of her pants.

"Very funny," I said. But now I was no longer looking at Capri or the man at the counter. I was looking at the front door instead, where Dennis Kopak had just walked in.

TWENTY-ODD YEARS SINCE OUR last meeting, and I knew him immediately. My first thought was that he didn't look particularly well. Like he had a flu or a cold. Hard to say. He was pale and unshaven. Loose skin hung around his eyes, which were revealed to be red, and flickering nervously, when he removed the large Gauthier sunglasses. But still, even across the gulf of time since high school, instantly recognizable. Not because he was unchanged, but for the many ways that he was the physical outcome of what he had been, or what I remembered. I thought I saw the end point of many trend lines first observed years before in the art lab. There was still evidence of unstoppable calculation in the expression, although now his forehead creased deeply with the computation and manipulation going on within. What had been a youthful pot belly—something Kopak would have construed as anti-mainstream in his youth—was now a hardened gut. A stomach that told you, in its rigid convexity, the depth of its hang over the belt buckle, that it had been vested by the years. Hair fully grey now, strands of it slicked back and kept in place by the rapid, unconscious movement of a thick hand.

He was talking to the man at the front now. Negotiating, coming to some settlement. Capri was whispering again but I ignored her.

His clothes were certainly expensive, or had been when he bought them. The leather-trimmed, green hunting jacket (Rizzi? I wondered) was frayed with years of use. Threads dangled from tears in the sleeves. The shoulders were soaked where the gabardine had not been water-proofed in a long time. He was wearing a crumpled cotton dress shirt, tiny yellow checks with French cuffs. Thomas Pink, or Turnbull & Asser. A cobalt-blue suit, long in need of the dry cleaner, but tailored. No doubt here. I knew it from the soft roll of the lapel, the gentle collapse of the fabric to the laces of fine calfskin shoes.

If there was any single message delivered in all of this—the simultaneous evidence of money, of carelessness, of personal neglect and disrepair—it was the clear sense that over the years Dennis Kopak would have had not just one, but many pressing occasions on which another name would be desirable. I wondered how he had chosen Collins. Although I wondered only briefly; it didn't matter.

"Are we going or not?" Capri was at my elbow.

I turned back to the computer on my desk. "Hang on," I said.

"For what?"

I was trying to breathe slowly and deeply through my nose. Here he was. Nothing left to do but rise from my chair, cross the room, say the words. And all would then be set in motion. We would talk about Piero Talloni and his project. About the role that Kopak had played. Maybe even some of how it was that I, Shane Donald, had come to be here.

Capri threatened me with a quarter-rise from her chair.

"Wait," I said.

"The Pope never goes around twice. What's the matter with you?"

Nothing. Nothing. I pressed fingers to my eyes, plunging briefly behind the grainy black safety of my eyelids.

"OK," I said.

NO CLEVER COMMENT. No simple key of words to unlock what was closed tight, to collapse all the time between us. I caught him on the sidewalk outside. Capri was behind me, finding her position. And in the instant that he turned to face me, startled, wary, his blank expression revealed how far beneath the surface of his memories I was submerged.

"Yes," he said, sharply. An overtly discouraging tone.

I was a stranger to him.

I revised my tactics in mid-breath, and led with a lie. Maybe it wasn't something anyone would confess by saying, Father, I told a lie. Perhaps it was only something about which a person might say, Father, I contributed to deceit by failing to speak the full truth myself.

"Mr. Collins?" I said.

I told him I was from *Phrate Magazine*. I did not introduce myself further.

"No photos," Kopak snapped, turning a shoulder and covering the side of his face.

I held up a hand and Capri lowered the camera. I encouraged her with a glance and she pocketed the Rollei.

"Mr. Collins, I'm only interested in your client, Piero Talloni." Again, the multifaceted untruth.

"You're not alone in that," Kopak said, irritable. "Only problem for all of you people is we don't give interviews."

"Off the record," I blurted.

Capri turned to stare at me. She didn't have to say a word to communicate how foolish she considered this strategy.

"We talk for a bit about Talloni, about you," I continued. "Then we decide whether to proceed. You decide."

This was well played. He had, of course, encouraged *Phrate*'s interest with his anonymous e-mail. Maybe he'd done the same with other art magazines he favoured. The trick, it would seem, was to project ignorance of this. To encourage him in the overvaluation of his hand.

We walked over towards the Piazza della Rotonda in the rain. Kopak directed us up a narrow alley and into a closed square. Here he stopped, fumbled his cellphone free of a deep jacket pocket. Turned his back on us and, after waiting a long time for someone to pick up, engaged in a short, harsh conversation.

When he was finished, Kopak turned back to us and announced, "I won't promise anything. He's getting on in years but he still lives large, if you know what I'm saying. Two o'clock in the afternoon is very early in the day for Piero."

Kopak stood on the slick stones in the middle of the street, the rain straightening downward in the windless square. Splashing up off the soaked cloth on his shoulders. He smelled fairly strongly of last night's liquor at this range.

"We have nothing but time, Mr. Collins," I said.

Kopak looked us both over. The gold braided arms of his sunglasses beaded water as he cracked a look over at Capri, then back to me.

"How about a drink?" he said, turning and heading towards a small restaurant at the end of the square. "David," he said then, trudging ahead of us. "David is fine."

The restaurant wasn't open, but Kopak pushed on in through the front door, crossed the room in a way that suggested he had many times before. Selected a favourite table for us against the far wall under an enormous rack of antlers. The room was dark-timbered, with a red-tiled floor and heavy wood furniture. It appeared to be some kind of hunting club. There were shotguns over the mantelpiece of an enormous, arched fireplace. A man came through some swinging doors at the back and greeted Kopak across the room with middling warmth. Kopak spoke loudly back to him, gesturing towards the table. Capri interrupted, declining a drink.

The man was back in a few moments with a cold bottle of *frizzante* and two glasses. An espresso for Capri.

"Grazie," I said to the man, who poured for both of us and retreated to the quiet clatter of his kitchen without another word.

"Best restaurant in the city," Kopak said.

Capri sipped. Made no comment. She knew not to take the Rollei out, but was instinctively looking around the room, framing shots. Itemizing what in this place was worthy to record on film.

"Hungry?" Kopak asked me. "I feel like a burger."

I looked around for a chalkboard. "They serve hamburgers here?"

"The Pope'll serve you poutine if you pay enough," Kopak said, then hollered back towards the kitchen.

This comment sat rather poorly with Capri, who glanced sharply towards the front window. When her tide was turning, I had the complicated pleasure to observe, she sought the horizon for reassurance.

The long-suffering chef came out and Kopak ordered his burger with a side order of nachos. The chef nodded wearily, then leaned over and refilled Kopak's glass right to the brim.

I watched the man make his way slowly back through the tables to the kitchen.

Kopak shrugged. "You eat somewhere five times a week they should cook what you ask. Only had to train him not to put ricotta on my nachos. Otherwise he's crack."

"Do you own the place, by any chance?" Capri asked.

"No. Not that he hasn't asked. But maybe someday I bring Talloni here and he gets a painting out of the deal."

"And why would Talloni give a man one of his paintings for cooking you burgers?" Capri asked.

Kopak sipped his wine and looked a little dreamy. "*Phrate* is Canadian? American?" he asked me.

Capri excused herself to go to the ladies' room although I thought she might be wandering farther than that. I looked up, caught her eye. She would be back in a while, Capri said with an angry gesture of her head towards the door.

I said *Phrate* liked to think of itself as North American.

"What about you?"

I waited a half beat. "Canadian," I said.

Kopak sipped his wine. Lit a cigarette. If there was a glimmer of recognition in this line of questioning, if something had stirred deep in Kopak's highly self-absorbed consciousness, it was passed over and once again forgotten with his next words. "Sorry to hear that," he said. "And now you want the story of Piero Talloni. Off the record. Scout's honour."

"Tell me your version," I said.

Kopak exhaled smoke. "There is no other version." And then he was off, suddenly quite happy to sip his way through a hangover, to smoke, to spin the yarn of the old man's life.

Piero Talloni. Born in Palermo, Sicily, in 1912. A simple beginning in a difficult place. A place where the people—his own family and the community around them—had a close acquaintance with hardship. With the oppression of forces larger than themselves. The Mafia, the Church and the relentless, sun-beaten realities of trying to make a living in that place and time.

"But these are hard people. Very tough," Kopak said. He was leaning into the table, his *frizzante* in constant motion between his lips and a holding position just to the side of his face.

Talloni moved to Rome in 1931.

"He's nineteen. He has professional ideas. Wants to make something out of himself," Kopak told me. "So he starts out life by studying law."

He did this for a time. But slowly and inexorably there grew an interest in art, in artistic expression, in painting, in the paint and canvas and brush and turpentine fumes of the project itself. And, in due course, these things came to swamp everything else in his life.

"But how?" I interrupted. "Or rather, why? Why does he change his mind?"

"Part of what I like about Talloni is that he has never tried to answer that question," Kopak said.

"Nobody influenced him," I pressed. "Nobody intercepted him while he was a young man with an aptitude for and an interest in the law? Diverted him from his original goal?"

Kopak considered this, sipping slowly. He shook his head. "There were a lot of factors at play. He met people in legal studies that he couldn't respect. They bored him. He was young, excited by the city. By the opportunities. Transgression was possible. And art, of course. He met artists and admired them. They had given themselves over to the style of the day, exaggeration in colour and shape, and they encouraged him to do the same. But who can say what might have been inspired by his memories of dusty, hardworking Sicily against the backdrop of the splendid, gaudy, eternal Rome?"

Talloni apparently taught himself to paint, Kopak went on. Had some early success. Even got a piece into the first Quadriennale exhibition.

"I thought he'd never shown a painting before," I interrupted.

Kopak shrugged. "He's getting on. He forgets things."

In 1935, Talloni went to Milan, where he stayed for two years. Here he developed a network of socially and politically active friends. In 1937, he returned to Rome, where he became part of the anti-fascist, anti-Mafia association of artists known as Corrente.

I sat back in my chair. Corrente rang a bell.

"The point being that all of his work came to draw on the social and political reality he experienced around this time," Kopak said, talking through a mouthful of the burger that had just arrived. "The sense that power was unjust. That living for ordinary people would be necessarily hard. All this swirls in the paint itself. It's like an added ingredient, as I'm sure you've observed."

"The butcher shop. The people buying flowers," I said.

"All of them," Kopak said, chewing. "And there was something more than his sympathies in this. Talloni found art. He was set free. But he knew that other people were not similarly liberated. And so he painted with compassion and identification. But more than any other thing, there was direction in the young man at this point in his life. Having turned aside from another pursuit, having taken up the brush, there was nothing else in his future but painting. No options. No alternatives."

The nachos arrived, heaped with cheese and accompanied by the condiment tri-colour of guacamole, sour cream and salsa.

"This is actually crème fraiche, believe it or not," Kopak said, scooping out a dollop of the white stuff on a chip. "My heart could go at any minute."

I sipped my *frizzante*. Then took another larger sip and topped myself up. Maybe it'd help things to ride a little way along the intoxication curve with Kopak. We were getting somewhere. "Go on," I said.

Kopak's tired face contorted as he cleared a fragment of tortilla chip from a molar. "Second World War," he said, finally.

"What about it?"

"Invasion of Sicily. Summer 1943. Corrente has come apart. Mussolini is chased from office. The Allies are landing. Italian troops are routed. Germany is fighting backward towards the Strait of Messina, where the Allies—God knows why—are letting them cross back to the mainland. Meanwhile, Hitler has pulled his Sturmgrenadiere off the Russian front and has them goose-stepping into the country from the north. Every conceivable political current is ripping at the same time. Nobody knows what the fuck is going on."

Kopak ate another nacho. Took a slug of *frizzante,* finishing the bottle. Here he raised his hand to the back of the room where a waiter I had not previously noticed had taken up a station near the cash register.

More cold wine. While we waited for the waiter to open it, to refill our glasses, I listened to the rain picking up. Pelting the front window. Singing in the square.

"You might think the early choices of an idealistic young man would be cemented under these circumstances," Kopak continued, when the waiter was gone. "That the crush of these forces would change the internal chemistry, make the will hard as a diamond. Maybe this would have happened with Talloni, but we'll never know. Because on the 28th of July, 1943, Piero Talloni was forever changed. The town of Agira on Sicily was assaulted by the Allies and the man's entire family was killed. Mother, father. Grandparents. Two kid sisters. Mortar shell through the roof. It punched down two floors and exploded in the kitchen where they were all huddled next to the stove. And in my experience, if you obliterate the main floor of a stone farm house, the upper stories will most certainly descend."

It had the desired effect, this detail. Its specificity. The way it suggested that Kopak was intimate with such matters—ballistics, ordnance—that he knew many more troubling details about the event than could be politely shared. I found myself appropriately frozen, hand across my mouth, rerunning the details of Talloni's life up to the concussion of this event. I even thought that maybe I felt a shadow of the feeling, the gravitational shift, the sudden slew of outlook that must have completely reordered the young man's sense of self, his self of personal future in the moment after hearing the terrible news. But even as I thought these things, I was myself capsized. Everything that was wrong with this version of Talloni's life story was suddenly laid bare. Every contrivance. Every falsity. Corrente. Arriving in Rome in the thirties. Familiar data points these. Tells, you might say.

"I thought Talloni was from Palermo," I said to Kopak.

He coughed, knocking a cigarette out of the pack. "Maybe they were visiting Agira. Maybe they moved after the kid went up to the big city."

No. Not at all true. The delivery was far too practised. Phrasing written on the surface of the words. The pauses finely calibrated. The cough. The slow lighting of the cigarette. The exhaled plume. And then the name finally swamped back into my mind. The name I needed.

"Interesting," I said.

Kopak nodded, taking another long drag.

"But utterly untrue."

Kopak cocked his head to one side in surprise. Blew smoke towards the ceiling out of the side of his mouth. "Does it lack the ring, counsellor?"

"Oh, it rings true," I said. "It just isn't true. There's a difference."

Kopak's turn to sit back. Not enough to make him stop drinking, of course, but as he tipped his glass and finished it, slow swallow by slow swallow, he managed to keep his eyes firmly on me. He was growing curious and you might have guessed that, by his own calculation, only more wine was required to understand what needed understanding.

He set his glass down empty on the table. "Well, do tell."

The problem was that Talloni's story already belonged to someone else.

"Guttuso," I told Kopak. "Renato Guttuso. Born in Palermo in 1912. Moved to Rome in the 1930s. Founded Corrente. Except for the mortar shell, loss of the family, the life-changing part, you just told me the early life story of the country's best known post-war social realist. The only difference between Renato Guttuso and Piero Talloni is that nobody talked Guttuso into quitting, did they?"

Waiters show the sense of diplomats, at times. More wine arrived. Was opened. Was poured. Kopak smoked down his cigarette during the pause. When the waiter withdrew, he left two shot glasses of grappa. And while I put together my final thoughts on this matter, Kopak emptied one of these glasses.

"And the reason for that . . ." I said. Thoughts continued to spill in, altering the chemical balance of my presence there, reconfiguring what could be believed about a long period of time up to that precise moment. ". . . is that Guttuso was real. You couldn't have convinced him. Talloni, however, is fiction. Talloni is your

own creation. You could make him stop or start anytime you wanted."

Kopak wiped the corners of his mouth with a handkerchief. Smiled a little, his forehead high and lined with
thought. All at once he looked most robust, I thought.
The darkening under his eyes had cleared. The redness
was gone. His skin looked healthy. His suit was now aris-
tocratically rumpled, not merely dirty. He looked like a
man who had controlled a large untruth and done so skil-
fully. He looked like a man who had owned a great many
things in his day, many interests and properties. Nothing
at all like a guy who had filled a number of Orangina bottles in the middle of the night before, half unconscious in
his Campo di Fiori crash pad.

"Do you mind?" he asked, fingers around the second
shot of grappa.

Not at all.

Kopak swallowed the liquor, throat pulsing once. His
eyes misted and cleared as the alcohol hit.

"Where in Canada did you say you were from?"
Kopak asked. "Not Saskatchewan by chance?"

THE IRISH PUB ON Piazzo Campo de' Fiori was still empty
when we arrived.

"Why do I get the feeling we're still off the record?"
Capri had asked me when Kopak and I came out of the
restaurant earlier. There had just been a strange scene
inside during which I tried to pay for our meal and was

ignored by both the waiter and Kopak. We eventually left without paying and were now standing blinking in the hard grey late afternoon light. It was still raining, but Capri had been sitting out there at one of the terrace tables under the awning. Smoking.

I told her to take the evening off. She looked back at me, running her own assessment of the situation. Turned and left without a word.

Kopak and I were now sitting at the very back of the pub. A dark corner with a high shelf for the pint glasses. He had ordered us two each and came back with two packs of Marlboros for good measure. He shifted himself up onto his high stool with a sigh of relief. At last. Guinness.

"I think we're covered," I said, looking at our table of supplies.

"I can't tell you what a relief this is," Kopak told me, clinking my glass.

It was for me too, unpredictably. I must acknowledge the relief in being recognized. When he mentioned Saskatchewan and I nodded, he said my name without hesitation. "Shane Donald."

At which point I told Kopak that if Piero Talloni was himself a work of art, I was interested in the artist behind the creation. "But not this David Collins character," I said. "I'd want to talk to Dennis Kopak."

He didn't say anything right away, naturally. Didn't officially fold. But when I started to talk about Malevich, we both saw the cards turn over. My hand was unbeatable.

"God," Kopak said, amazed to find the memory, as if he had grown accustomed to losing them. "I do remember that. I remember the crazy painting you had up there."

"You remember accusing me of plagiarism?"

"No, no," Kopak protested. "I recall being dumb-founded."

"You said I was talking to myself. Self-absorbed. Something about that fight I had been in. The accident. I don't even remember all that you said, but you made me blink."

I had rediscovered a little of the righteous indigna-tion I had planned to feel at this point. But again Kopak diverted me.

"It seems to me that I would have welcomed the idea of friendship," he said, shrugging. "I'm not saying this would have been healthy for you at the time, but that's what I had been imagining."

I turned away from him. Lit a cigarette. Kopak was animated. Gesticulating.

"You poked that kid's eye out," he said, sounding as if this memory pleased him more than any single one so far. "Yes, of course. I thought it was the most frightening artistic event I'd ever heard of. You left him half able to look on the object you both desired. You took your half."

"Oh, bullshit," I said. But I'd be lying if I didn't admit to being just faintly pleased.

It wasn't really an interview after that. So few words had been required to unlock the story. Sitting in the dark of the pub, I didn't need to prime the pump with questions. All I had to do was listen. No notes. No recording.

"Why don't you hear this out and then decide what kind of story you want to write," Kopak suggested.

He had gone into computer sciences, as I had gathered. Moved to Silicon Valley. He had good early jobs working for Xerox and then for Microsoft, where he was junior coder working on the first Office suite. "The point here being that I was developing a scroll bar. It was possible to become quite a rich person without ever seeing the entire thing that you were working on."

He left eventually to set up his own firm, leaving stock options and shaking heads behind him.

"Raifort Management Systems," I said. "NewStart."

Kopak nodded.

"Which did what?"

In a nutshell, NewStart was a piece of planning software that helped companies faced with critical decisions about change. "You could call these corporate capsize moments, if you like," Kopak said. "Say a company is forced to change the way it does business. Maybe the stock price is tubing. Maybe competitors are storming the gates. Whatever the case, markets have a way of telling you when stasis is not an option."

Here is where the NewStart management and systems guys came in. They would spend three weeks in a place, plugging the computer model with every shred of historical and forecast data about the situation at hand. Financial data. Market stats. Economic numbers. Employee information: who did what for how much and where.

"Well," Kopak went on, "then we run the numbers and NewStart grinds out some scenarios. Maybe the company should consolidate. Maybe they should downsize. Or expand. Or move into new markets. Maybe—and here is where it got interesting—they weren't even in the right *business*. Maybe, based on the assets and the people they had, based on everything that NewStart could understand about all possible options and outcomes, they should be creating new product lines entirely. Forking off down the path of a new future entirely."

"And how the hell did NewStart do all this?"

"Artificial neural networks," Kopak explained. "Don't panic. Neuromorphic systems are just computers designed to mimic the way the mammalian brain is wired together. Densely interconnected processors like neurones are linked up with connections something like synapses. This is your basic neural net. But it's a robust tool for forecasting, for picking out unseen solutions and patterns."

Better still, if you fire data through one of these things for long enough—even buggy data, *noisy* data as the engineers say—the network gets *better*.

"It learns?"

"I'm not making this shit up. But since that kind of disturbs your average Harvard-educated CEO, I used to tell clients to think of it as a gun you point at a problem."

"You kill the problem."

"You blow a hole through it. Then you look through the hole and see what you see."

"But something else is going on during this time," I said. "Or you and I wouldn't be having this conversation. You left all this behind. What I want to know is, were you aching to get back to art? Were you wishing you could swim back up to the spawning grounds—back to high school, back to that ringing dial phone—and start out to sea again?"

"Per favore," Kopak called over to the bar, holding up two fingers. Some time back we'd switched to Harp lager, and these were sliding down with grace, ease and elegance. Each one sharpening the pleasure of the last.

"Say the last part again," Kopak said to me.

I tried. Something about swimming upstream.

"Poetic," he said. "But not really. First, everybody knew you got rich doing this kind of thing. That was a big reason for doing it. You could just look around a room in those days and flag the geeks who were going to have thirty, fifty million dollars. It was the simplest algorithm of all time. Really smart, pretty smart or not smart. Not smart, well tough. If a kid could code and he was pretty smart, he was going to be rich. If he was really smart, well then he could choose to have more money than he could know what to do with it. But beyond that . . ."

Here Kopak turned away from me slightly. It was the first time in his story that he had showed any sign of being concerned about saying what came next.

"I was never an artist," he said finally. "That stuff . . . the phone, all that . . . that wasn't so much Dada as it was punk. There was nothing under it. And the fact that it couldn't possibly be explained, the nobody-on-the-end-of-the-phone thing, to the best of my knowledge, to the best of my abilities to interpret it now, that was the *point* at that time. And it became even more the point to me as the years went by. I liked what I was doing. I was good at it. But there was no part of what we were doing in Palo Alto that I could not explain. I wasn't involved in anything that might, even conceivably, have had an element of mysticism about it. Any connection to madness. Any connection to the heavens."

Kopak drank, then continued. "I didn't need NewStart to tell me that I should be getting the hell out."

Raifort sold controlling interest of NewStart after a few good years. Kopak made a Really Smart amount of money. He kicked around.

"I set up elaborate croquet courses on the lawn of this mansion I bought up Sand Hill Road in Woodside, California. I hosted a lot of parties that didn't seem to have any specific beginning or ending."

"You bought art," I reminded him.

"Yeah. I kept hoping to get ripped off, to tell you the truth. Too bad I installed this NSA standard security system and now, if I leave it off, my insurance is void."

"Doesn't sound like you need the money."

"There is the principle of the thing."

"What's the principle of you not seeming to pay any-where we go," I asked him. "You get enough money and people don't even want to take it any more?"

Oh, he paid, Kopak assured me. He just left credit card imprints everywhere so he wasn't bothered with the procedure. He ate and drank as if Rome were an enor-mous extension of his own property. Bills ran up. He settled with American Express once a year.

"Once a year?"

"You ever hear of the Black Card?"

American Express Black Card. "Mogul card," Kopak said. "I'm not boasting. Comes a point it's just an assload of money."

"Well, show me. Let's see this thing."

"No. See, that's what I'm trying to say. I don't have one of those."

"I don't get it."

"You ever hear of a Red Card?"

Kopak pulled out his wallet and produced this most rare and bashful of high-end charge plates. Blood red. Black letters. Gold rimmed.

"What's one higher than mogul?" I asked him.

Kopak pocketed the card. Shrugged.

"So . . ." I started.

"Eventually, I suppose it just dawned on me that I had *invented* the solution to my own problem. I had the gun in my hand, so to speak, I just had to point it at my own head."

Which he did, although without much hope that it would tell him anything coherent. They designed NewStart to deal with corporations, not humans, after all. The data bits in a human life were articulated using a fundamentally different grammar than what the program had been trained to interpret.

"I essentially hacked my own product. Illegal in every state given the sales agreement I'd signed but I figured it was personal use. What the fuck. NewStart 2.0."

"You're telling me a computer told you to make up some story about an old painter living in Rome?"

"Not quite," Kopak admitted. He'd been travelling around this time, lugging a copy of NewStart with him on his notebook. He spent a few weeks plugging the square pegs of his personal life into the round holes of NewStart's various templates. He uploaded school records from elementary school onward. Medical records. Tax files. Credit reports. In the 400-odd-point form used to put a digital frame around corporate history, Kopak had informed the model with his past hobbies and obsessions, objectives, failures, successes. He'd assigned scores to past accomplishments, graded his satisfaction across twenty-four evaluation criteria and watched the program flash out a sheaf of charts and flow diagrams, his life being sorted and ordered, made to reveal the internal logic of its patterns before his eyes.

During the last forty-eight hours of this process, Kopak remembered, he'd done without sleep. He was staggering around his hotel room in a white terry robe with a head full of caffeine and Benzedrine. There were empty cola cans and cherry-flavoured Buckley's cough syrup bottles lying around. He had a stuffed head, inflamed sinuses, a strep throat and a stomach so raw from sipping away at Stolichnaya that his room-service breakfast had come up that morning in a single geyser. He hardly made it to the sink before there was a mad rush of Tabasco and yolk.

"I'm a little cut now," Kopak said, nodding at our nearly empty pint glasses and the two replacements that the bartender had already delivered. "But at that particular point in time, I was a *real* mess."

NewStart 2.0 began pumping out scenarios at about seven o'clock that morning and wrapped up thirty minutes later, just as CNN Headline News was starting to repeat itself.

"Gulf War," Kopak said. "I remember a guy in a gas mask in Tel Aviv waiting for the Scuds to land and start the Third World War. I was thinking, I just got my fucking answers here. Maybe you guys over there could get your shit together."

Some of the scenarios were gibberish. Others were eerily wrong. As if the system were spitting out foil answers to highlight how right the right one could be.

"There was one scenario sheet telling me I should go back to Microsoft. Strategies for how to get rehired. What kind of money I should ask for. I was thinking the program must have learned about humour while I was puking."

And then, the right one. "One new-product scenario.

One, out of a dozen scenarios telling me I should tear everything down and start again. One idea that pointed out that I was some number of light years away from my core competencies."

Kopak laughed hoarsely at the terminology. "A new product. A new life work. A new thing that I should be creating."

"Painting," I said, quite suddenly excited for him. And there was something like Pegasus hooves kicking through me too at that moment. I was thinking about Malevich again, and all of the others. Pollock. Curnoe. Borduas. Riopelle. How well I had once known these names. How much they had once told the world about me. "One enormous painting."

"No," Kopak said. He stopped laughing and looked hard at me, a long penetrating, drunken, indecipherable stare.

I couldn't guess. I had nothing. My expression must have been pleading, because he didn't leave me hanging for more than a second or two.

"Not a painting. Artists," he said. "Maybe it was a syntax error in the language modules, I don't know, but the scenario said I should be in the business of creating artists."

Rain was turning the glass around us into a liquid prism. We were in a cab. The windshield wipers were hardly clearing the windscreen enough for the driver to see. Me not remembering the precise sequence of steps that had composed the transition. We had been there. We were now here. At some point someone had bought a bottle of Scotch, and I had just handed this back to Kopak. The burning in my throat confirmed that I had just taken a prodigious glug.

We were spinning through the city. Nobody was out. The streets were rivers. We were leaving a plume of spray on either side of us as we charged east out Plebiscito and Battisti. Piazza Venezia yawned to our right, the great white rain-soiled marble mountain of Il Vittoriano climbing into the angry sky beyond the square.

"Why Rome?" I asked him.

Because he had been in Rome when he finally answered the question. He'd been in a suite at the Grand. He'd been living naked on their floors. Eating nothing but crab bisque by the end of it. Sipping, shivering. Copies of his new-product scenario pasted to the walls.

"But why had you come to Rome?" We were past the piazza now, hard left into Via Pilotta, another hard right and we were across the street from my Tuscan restaurant. I was trying to shake a ripple of dizziness that was making concentric circles in my head.

Kopak drank from the bottle. Wiped his mouth. "You know?" he said. "I can't remember why the hell I was here. But I was. In this city. And I knew that the story I was going to tell, the shape I was going to make on the earth with that story, the creation in total, it had to start immediately."

We were on a tour. Visiting the thirteen nodes of that creation. Around the legs of Pegasus, down the slope of his neck. The places where he had posed as Talloni's son had been the easiest, Kopak said. You spend a few hundred thousand lire on sausage over six months, then tell the butcher your father wants them to have one of his paintings. They'll keep any secret you ask them to keep. The one in the antique store he just wrapped up in heavy wax paper and left in the store room when nobody was looking.

He changed his name too. "I did it a lot around that time." It just happened to be the fake ID he was using at the Grand.

"What about the fire? And the old man? Who the hell did I talk to?"

Kopak laughed. Enrico. An old cabinetmaker who lived around the corner from his studio on Via Giulia. "He made me a chest of drawers. We shared an interest in *frizzante*."

They lit the fire together in the alley. Enrico had about twelve lines of dialogue. Sometimes he jumbled them up, but it always worked.

"The ring of the cash register. My business is not to turn the paint into lire," Kopak recited. "I wrote all that."

"But the paintings?" I said, feeling stupidly emotional at this point. "They're beautiful. You could actually paint if you wanted to."

All done by a professional counterfeiter who lived in Switzerland. Kopak wouldn't say more. "Not a tough assignment. I gave him half a dozen photographs of Guttuso's work and told him to get them wrong."

We circled the city through the driving rain. Up past the scooter shop, through Piazza Colonna past the NetPoint. All the way west down Via Coronari. Down south again past the florist shop. By the time we were in Via del Teatro di Marcello, riding back towards my hotel, there hadn't been any conversation for quite some time.

"So that's your story," he said, finally. He seemed remarkably sober to me, just then. I had been staring out the window, through the rain, and I'd just seen the horseman at the top of the steps to the Capitolini slide out of himself. One horseman. Then two. My vision blurring, doubling with fatigue and alcohol. I blinked him back to a single horseman just as he slipped from view behind the trees and buildings.

"Do you still have a copy?" I asked.

Kopak looked over to make sure he understood what I meant.

"NewStart 2.0," I said. "Must be a pretty smart piece of software by now. Must be able to say some fairly learned things about the future."

Kopak was still looking at me. His expression was plain. It said, Are you sure?

I was sure.

The next spring, Freightling started an alternative sports magazine called *Eiger* and asked me to be the executive editor. I didn't bother trotting out the obvious point that there were many more qualified figures in the world of sports journalism. I knew how little Freightling would be discouraged. He had done his research, identified the market segment. All that remained for me to do was go out and build the thing that had been requested, and this was something that I had steadily earned a reputation for doing.

Mia left *Phrate* to work for an advertising agency. We bought a house near the university and formalized what had been the living arrangement for many months by that point. We bought a dog, a black Labrador retriever we named Rauschenberg.

In the fall, *Phrate* was nominated for several magazine awards, including one for "Thirteen Points in the Eternal City: The Unusual Masterwork of Conceptual Artist Piero Talloni." We didn't win, but even an honourable mention meant that I spent an evening talking about the story.

"I quite liked the ending," a woman said to me at the reception. "Is it a sad story to you? How much effort he went to to make 'Thirteen Points?' The fact that it won't remain? That it will erode?"

I didn't think it was a sad story precisely. "I guess he built what he had to build," I told her. "And it'll last as long as it lasts. Talloni doesn't seem any more or less unhappy for having done it."

"But why did he go into hiding just as he became famous? Did he think that as 'Thirteen Points' disappears, he himself had to disappear?"

"Perhaps that's it," I said to her. "You could be quite right about that."

I never told Mia or anyone else anything more than what appeared in the pages of the magazine. Seven thousand words about the construction of a city-scaled conceptual work, with a map and Capri's pictures of the paintings. It looked enormous on the page. The size and seriousness and devotion required. Literally a lifetime of preparation, I wrote. A moment of exposure. And then Talloni was gone again.

Only Capri even knew to raise an eyebrow, and we only spoke again once, by phone. So I had no idea if she actually raised one or not.

"I'm cleaning out files today," she said, on the phone, inflection neutral. "You don't want a picture of Talloni's Philistine business agent, by any chance?"

"Why, do you have one?"

She did, in fact. A remarkable coincidence. Capri was up shooting her pictures of the Holy Father and who should she run into? "Your blasphemous drunk, Mr. Collins."

He was on his way for a guided tour of the Vatican Museum but he insisted on taking Capri to a café for a glass of wine.

"He is still wearing this name tag from the tour," Capri said, deeply unimpressed. "Only it says Dennis. In big red letters. I said to him, can you take that off? I'm not your tour guide and besides your name isn't Dennis. But, as you know, he is a difficult man. No no, he says. I am going to buy you a glass of wine and you will take my picture. Send it to your writer friend."

The photo arrived by courier a few days later. Capri sent the negative too, as if to make a point about having fulfilled her obligations on the assignment.

Kopak was leaning, on his way to drunk already. He was wearing a black suit and a white French-cuffed shirt. There was a half-empty carafe of white in front of him. Across the table there was a coffee cup where Capri must

have been sitting before rising irritably to take the shot.
Kopak is angled a little away from the camera, his shoulder
pressed against the mirrored wall of the café.

I took a few minutes to find it, looking, looking. I knew
something was there, some message to be revealed. And it
was probably a microsecond before I caught myself looking
and shook myself free of the impulse that I did get it.

Face half turned, a few tables away behind Kopak.
He had a black watch cap and an AS Roma scarf. He
was smiling, his roughened cabinetmaker's hands around a
tumbler of something that was no doubt fizzy and sweet.
The stuff of headaches and inspiration.

And in the foreground, Kopak leaned against the
mirror and laughed. The red letters of his name tag pressing up against their own reflection to form a palin-
drome: *Dennis sinneD.*

I laughed out loud in my office, leaning back in my
chair. A joke, of course. And typically convoluted in its
conception and delivery.

THE WOMAN AT THE RECEPTION had been right about
the erosion. Even before the article went to press, the
paintings were being sold. Two at Christie's for quite a
lot. A few more at good prices. Another one for less. I followed this in the art press for a while and then, abruptly,
stopped paying attention.

I had my souvenir. The photo, yes. But also a sealed
white envelope with what I guessed were several sheets of

paper folded within. It was embossed Raifort Management Systems on the return address corner, initialled DK on the flap. On the front, in a scrawl—this had all been done quite late at night and the whisky, incredibly enough, did not end up being our final drink—Kopak had written the words *The Future.*

The old Shane Donald would have torn that envelope open. At any given moment of my very certain childhood. During my travelling years. During the muggy, musty early days of my relationship with Mia. Every moment I was in Rome, with Capri, running around the city trying to make sense of it all, trying to tease meaning out of what I thought of as a prank or a life work or the product of underutilized genius, depending on my mood. Even up at Kopak's mansion in the Roman hills that final night. Hovering over the computer at the enormous mahogany table in the pointlessly long dining room. Listening to Kopak's Dell workstation grinding the data. Hearing the smooth hum of the fan as the scenarios were computed. That was the old Shane Donald for each and every one of those moments. And whatever NewStart had to tell me about the future, whatever strategic advice it wanted to give on the topic of how I might play my own cards, well, I wanted to hear.

Kopak licked the flap and pressed it shut firmly. He scrawled his initials across the seal. He flipped the envelope over and scribbled those two final words, smirking the whole while. He knew this was not a statement of fact. There was no future in the envelope. A NewStart scenario was not a blueprint or even a suggestion of a future. Instead it was something that lived precariously in the middle of a high-speed intersection of speculation, destiny, the enabling but risky power of technology and, yes, maybe a little of what Capri called blasphemy too.

I carried the envelope home with me in the inside pocket of my suit. I felt it crinkle and bend as I hugged Mia at the airport. I felt it again the next morning, riding with me to work in the taxi. I caught a glimpse of it in my top drawer from time to time during the week I spent writing the piece.

The final few paragraphs of my article about Piero Talloni read:

> *Pegasus, unfortunately, will not remain. He lost a hoof last Tuesday. At Christie's, next month, we can expect the two remaining stars of his noble head to go. But even before I left Rome, I could feel it eroding. Last afternoon in the city I tracked down Talloni at his studio. He was bleary-eyed and stubbled. Seventy-something, still drinking hard and ageing before my eyes.*
>
> *We went for coffee at Haiti Sud. He was short, of course, so I sprang for his doppio. Did it bother him that after a lifetime of work nothing could remain where it had been so carefully placed?*
>
> *He answered me with a quote from Kasimir Malevich, the Russian painter who founded Suprematism and whom, not incidentally, Talloni knew well as a young man.*

*"I have emerged into white. Beside me, comrade pilots, swim in this infinity. Swim! The free white sea, infinity, lies before you!"*

That might have been the end of the old Shane Donald, right there. As I tapped in the last exclamation point. The quote mark. Fired it off to the printer.

Maybe the new Shane Donald was first seen waiting for the draft of the article to slide out of the laser printer. The pages covered in words about Piero Talloni. All that infinite white space between, dedicated to Dennis Kopak.

# ACKNOWLEDGMENTS

The eight stories here appeared previously in other publications: "Smoke's Fortune" in *Grain;* "The Resurrection Plant" in *Canadian Fiction Magazine* and *Coming Attractions* '00; "Francisco's Watch" in *The Fiddlehead* and *Coming Attractions;* "Pope's Own" in *Event* and *The Journey Prize Anthology* 2000; "Prayers to Buxtehude" in *Descant* and *Best Canadian Stories* '00; "Doves of Townsend" in *The Malahat Review* and *The Journey Prize Anthology* 2000; "The Boar's Head Easter" in *Carousel* #13; and "Silent Cruise" in *Descant, Islands West* and *The Journey Prize Anthology* 2000.

## ACKNOWLEDGMENTS

I would like to acknowledge the support of quite a few people over the many years these stories were written. Thank you, Jane, as always. Thanks Ursula K. Le Guin, who wrote encouraging words in the margin of my very first story. Thanks to the members of the long-ago Hopkins Society writers group: Lenore Rowntree, Ross Crockford, Michael Drew Jackson and the founder of the Hopkins Society Vancouver chapter himself, Robert Duncan. Thanks to my editor, Diane Martin. Thanks also Susan Roxborough at Vintage Canada and Deirdre Molina at Knopf Canada for your help with the book. Thanks Louise Dennys and everyone else at Random House of Canada, and Chris Carduff and the staff at Counterpoint, for continuing encouragement.

Finally, I acknowledge the inspiration of watching the last race of the real Silent Cruise, although everything outside the track rails in that story is the purest fiction.

Timothy Taylor was born in Venezuela in 1963 but has lived most of his life in Canada. He is the author of the best-selling novel *Stanley Park* (Counterpoint 2002), which was a finalist for the Giller Prize, the Rogers Writers' Trust Award, the British Columbia Book Prize and the City of Vancouver Book Award. Since 1992 his short stories have appeared in Canada's leading literary magazines, and many have been anthologized in such annual collections as *Coming Attractions* and *Best Canadian Stories*. In 2000 he became the only writer to have three stories chosen for a single edition of *The Journey Prize Anthology*, including that year's prizewinner, "Doves of Townsend." Mr. Taylor lives in Vancouver, where he is at work on a second novel.

Printed in the United States
by Baker & Taylor Publisher Services